Jordan Erica Webber (Chapters 1–5) is a freelance writer and speaker who specialises in video games. Most of her work can be found in the *Guardian*. She has a first-class degree in Philosophy with Psychology from the University of Warwick.

Daniel Griliopoulos (Chapters 6–10) is a writer specialising in video games. His work has been published in media including the *New Statesman*, the *Mail on Sunday* and the *Guardian*. He has a degree in Politics, Philosophy and Economics from the University of Oxford and a lifelong love of classical philosophy. He is currently Lead Content Editor at tech firm Improbable.

Ten Things Video Games Can Teach Us

Can Teach Us

....

JORDAN ERICA WEBBER AND
DANIEL GRILIOPOULOS

ROBINSON

ROBINSON

First published in Great Britain in 2017 by Robinson

1 3 5 7 9 10 8 6 4 2

A CIP catalogue record for this book is available from the British Library

ISBN: 978-1-47213-791-3

Typeset in Scala by Hewer Text UK Ltd, Edinburgh
Printed and bound in Great Britain by CPI Group (UK), Croydon CRO 4YY

Papers used by Robinson are from well-managed
forests and other responsible sources

Robinson
An imprint of
Little, Brown Book Group
Carmelite House
50 Victoria Embankment
London EC4Y 0DZ

An Hachette UK Company
www.hachette.co.uk

www.littlebrown.co.uk

Acknowledgements

....

Many people have had an impact on this book, many have helped and many have actively contributed. We couldn't have done it without them.

Firstly, the philosophers. Thanks to Julian Baggini, Chris Bateman, Kimberley Brownlee, David Chalmers, Luciano Floridi, Katherine Hawley, Angie Hobbs, Guy Longworth, Lucy O'Brien, Constance Steinkuehler and Robyn Waller.

Secondly, the games industry. Thanks to Johan Andersson, Chris Avellone, Pippin Barr, Zach Barth, Mary DeMarle, Connor Fallon, Sylvia Feketekuty, Richard Garriott, Alexander Gianturco, Harry Giles, Katie Goode, Holly Gramazio, Thomas Grip, Cliff Harris, Joey Jones, Tom Jubert, Itay Keren, Lorne Lanning, Richard Lemarchand, Ken Levine, Mark Llabres Hill, Keza MacDonald, Sean Murray, Craig Pearson, Lucas Pope, Will Porter, William Pugh, Brenda Romero, Jordan Thomas and Patrick Weekes.

Finally, Dan would like to thank his life partner Victoria Dain, and his writing partner Alec Meer, for providing all different forms of support when he was working on this. Jordan also has two people without whose support she could never have seen this through: her soulmate Kat Brewster, and her friend and mentor Keith Stuart.

Contents

·············

CONTENTS

Introduction

....

One day, if it hasn't happened already, you may discover people think you're smarter than you are. I've found it's because they don't know you. When they meet you, reality will come crashing down – or, maybe more appropriately, they'll have pulled the curtain aside and will see Oz for what Oz is, and it's rather disappointing. (Although technically, Oz was *trying* to seem more than he is.) Jordan Erica Webber is the exception. She will never think you are smarter than you are. This is her philosophy.

Over my many years of growing older, I've had people put philosophical (and historical and cultural and . . .) labels on games I've worked on, asking if I'd used a certain framework, point of view. And then when I've given my actual answer (which is usually a stupid one), they respond with, 'Oh, you're an X.'

This surprises me because they rarely say, 'Oh, you're a game designer.' But I am. Really.

My stupid – but truthful – answer is that I took what was given, thought about what was expected, and then (if necessary) used the game genre and franchise to help inform that decision. Sometimes it worked. Sometimes it didn't. But usually any glimmer of an expressed philosophy came from the fictional antagonists, protagonists and even a player companion's view of the world, not from any education or real-world intent I had.

So yes, I'm stupid. But after those conversations I also felt that the need to put a concept in a box may not always be appropriate. Sure, the box can help. But if you rely on the box too much . . . well, we probably won't see eye-to-eye. For me, mostly because of projects in the past, the box should be looked into, closed, then used as a foundation for the first step on a lo-o-o-o-ng staircase.

As an example, the 'box' for one of the titles quoted in this volume (*Planescape: Torment*) was simple, pragmatic and frightening. I was told (1) you will use BioWare's Infinity Engine (an engine is a game's underlying code and tools), (2) you will use the *Planescape* licence because the company paid a lot of money for it, and (3) you will have a small team – at the outset, it will be a team of one, and that 'one' is you. Congratulations. Get designing.

But even those elements don't confine you – they're just the first step. From there, you take the next step. Then the next. And so on.

Don't get me wrong – the desire to quantify is essential to game design, and labels and tags assist with that. Design is all about quantifying the abstraction of fun. While fun for different game genres can have different parameters, the underlying philosophy is knowing one's role as a developer to both the game and the player, and upholding your responsibility to the game mechanics you have provided.

On a high level, a developer's role is as an entertainer. We are commissioned to entertain. We have a responsibility not only to the game, but also to the player's experience with the game.

Narrowing the developer focus a bit, knowing one's role as a developer of *role*-playing games is following through on the promise of allowing the player to take on a role. Sometimes this means providing game mechanics, choices and dilemmas that are either clearly good or bad, or ones where the desired outcome is unclear but can be more interesting because the dilemma *isn't* clearly a good or bad choice. The player is forced to think not only, 'Should I be good or bad?' but also, 'What kind of person is my player-character, and what would they choose in this abstract situation?'

From there, the responsibility comes in delivering on the promise that the player's role-playing choices in the game will not limit their enjoyment of the game. That is because you have provided the systems – and it's not fair to punish the player for engaging with those systems. It's also because a game that punishes your choices through judgement is making a statement, and is arguably no longer a game. And it's been said by designers wiser than me (and in fewer words) that themes and choices should ask questions of the player, not dictate answers.

Often, you'll see more of the underpinnings of a design philosophy and judgement in the game *systems* players are allowed to engage in – and how they are allowed to define their character. It can be subtle or overt. A developer *can* make implicit judgements by not including a Charisma statistic. Or by not allowing you to kill a quest giver. Or including a 'Karma' statistic. Or by refusing to allow you to play an evil character – or by not having a morality bar at all. A developer can even make a judgement in the difficulty settings for a game – in all these instances, they are informing you of their design philosophy (and usually making a judgement as well).

Narrative is no different. For role-playing games, the question can be more overt. What kind of choice is there if you don't present an unpleasant faction to join? Or ask if the kingdom deserves to be saved? Or ask what were the policies of the king that got him assassinated in the first place?

For me, philosophy for role-playing games is following through on your promise – allow the players to take on a role and express themselves as much as possible through the game mechanics. Narrative, prose or not, should be part of those mechanics. It's the contract all designers make with a player. And for role-playing games, it's one of the most important aspects.

It's still okay if you ever meet me and ask me about games. I love games. But I won't promise a smart answer. That's for Jordan and Dan, and they've done so in this volume.

Chris Avellone

Why games? Why philosophy?

....

'All reality is a game. Physics at its most fundamental, the very fabric of our universe, results directly from the interaction of certain fairly simple rules, and chance; the same description may be applied to the best, most elegant and both intellectually and aesthetically satisfying games.'

Iain Banks, *The Player of Games* (1988)[*]

'It should be noted that children at play are not playing about; their games should be seen as their most serious-minded activity.'

Michel de Montaigne (1533–92)[†], *Essays* 1: 22

'The society which scorns excellence in plumbing because plumbing is a humble activity and tolerates shoddiness in philosophy because it is an exalted activity will have neither good plumbing nor good philosophy. Neither its pipes nor its theories will hold water.'

John W. Gardner (1912–2002)[‡]

[*] Iain M. Banks (1954–2013) was a prolific author of science fiction and also a keen gamer – as he told *SFX* magazine, he had to delete the grand strategy game *Civilization* off his hard drive when started a book.
[†] Montaigne was a statesman, storyteller and essay writer, whose work remains remarkably accessible to modern readers. He was also, as he himself admits, a player of games, though he was a stickler for the rules: '. . . there is no game so small wherein from my own bosom naturally, and without study or endeavour, I have not an extreme aversion from deceit. I shuffle and cut and make as much clatter with the cards, and keep as strict account for farthings, as it were for double pistoles; when winning or losing against my wife and daughter, 'tis indifferent to me, as when I play in good earnest with others, for round sums.'
[‡] *Excellence: Can We Be Equal and Excellent Too?* (1961).

'Play is an activity enjoyed for its own sake. It is our brain's favourite way of learning and manoeuvring.'

Diane Ackerman, *Deep Play* (1999)

You're probably wondering why you're here. Not in a grand existential sense – though that certainly fits with the themes explored in this book – but a more immediate thought: 'If you want to learn about philosophy, and what it has to say about how to live, why look at video games?'

That's a fair question. After all, today, many people still see video games as devoid of ethical content. As the *Democracy* game creator Cliff Harris put it to us:

'There's an assumption in game development that what all people want is entertainment, which is fair enough, and that all they want is thus a very simplistic form of entertainment. I just think that the medium's young enough that we don't have the kind of deep thoughtful stuff yet in any great kind of mass. Like, there are a lot of anti-heroes and morally dubious people in better quality TV, but even then it's probably on HBO.'

More than that, Harris points out, the perception is that when games do make people think, it's not about deep, meaningful things – it's mathematics disguised as puzzles. 'When we *do* want people to think in games we want them to think like autistic kids, you know, so we don't mind them getting into *Factorio* and doing programming, that level of thinking, but . . . philosophical thinking? I mean, I don't actually play that many different games, but the closest I got to that in any game probably is *BioShock*, and that's pretty heavy-handed, you know?'

As Harris said, for the majority of the population, video games are, at best, entertainment. At worst, yes, they're murder-simulators. The biggest 'hardcore' games around do indeed involve killing humans repeatedly, and quite often the avatars of other real humans too. And it's true that, at worst, there are games out there that would require very generous treatment to see them as anything other than unnecessary violence, whether mindless or not – the *Postal* series, say, or the game *Hatred*.

But, at best, there are games that are thought experiments compelling enough to change minds. *Everybody's Gone To The Rapture*, *The Stanley Parable*, *The Witness*, *To the Moon* ... these manage to stay entertaining while being beautiful, intriguing, pacifistic experiences with richly divergent, strange worlds. They're interactive combinations of story, music, animation, fact and fantasy, which combine to prompt thought in unique ways.

If you want a real-world example of how games can make you think, look at Edward Snowden. Whatever you think of the rectitude of his actions as a National Security Agency (NSA) whistle-blower, you can't deny that he was principled – he took a hugely brave step for something he believed in, which has trapped him far from friends and family. And, as he admitted to Glenn Greenwald, that step was inspired by the heroic morality he'd seen in video games.

'The protagonist is often an ordinary person, who finds himself faced with grave injustices from powerful forces and has the choice to flee in fear or fight for his beliefs. And history also shows that seemingly ordinary people who are sufficiently resolute about justice can triumph over the most formidable adversaries.'[*]

Snowden claimed that games taught him that anyone, no matter how weak, is capable of confronting huge injustice.[†]

As Greenwald himself put it, 'Years earlier, I might have scoffed, but I'd come to accept that, for Snowden's generation, [video games] played no less serious a role in moulding political consciousness, moral reasoning, and an understanding of one's place in the world than literature, television and film. They, too, often present complex

---

[*] Glenn Greenwald, *No Place to Hide: Edward Snowden, the NSA and the Surveillance State* (2014).
[†] Snowden's favourite game was the martial arts beat-'em-up *Tekken*, according to Ted Rall's illustrated biography of him. Internet hearsay has him praising its morality, but we've had trouble finding a source for that.

moral dilemmas and provoke contemplation, especially for people beginning to question what they've been taught.' And later Greenwald summed it up: 'That moral narrative at the heart of video games was part of his preadolescence and formed part of his moral understanding of the world and one's obligation as an individual.'*

That's not to say that video games provide a moral model for everyone – after all, the Swedish nationalist and mass murderer Anders Brevik admitted to playing *World of Warcraft* for an entire year, partly as cover for plotting his terrorist attacks. If anything, he seemed to argue, it was a pro-social experience for him.

> 'Some people like to play golf, some like to sail, I played *WoW*. It had nothing to do with 22 July. It's not a world you are engulfed by. It's simply a hobby.† [. . .] *WoW* is only a fantasy game, which is not violent at all. It's just fantasy. It's a strategy game. You co-operate with a lot of others to overcome challenges. That's why you do it. It's a very social game. Half of the time you are connected in communication with others. It would be wrong to consider it an antisocial game.'‡

The purpose of this book is to use video games to explain philosophy, and hence to improve your life. Through ten chapters we'll show that video games can be philosophically complex, ethically rich and morally instructive. (But we're not brazen enough to argue that about all of them.§) What do we hope it'll teach you? Well, first the

---

* http://www.gq.com/story/glenn-greenwald-edward-snowden-no-place-to-hide
† https://www.theguardian.com/world/2012/apr/19/anders-breivik-call-of-duty
‡ Brevik also spent much time using *Call of Duty: Modern Warfare* to train himself for his attacks, combined with a holographic aiming device. 'It consists of many hundreds of different tasks and some of these tasks can be compared with an attack, for real. That's why it's used by many armies throughout the world. It's very good for acquiring experience related to sights systems.' But he still didn't learn any philosophical lessons from it.
§ If you want to know which games we recommend and which ones we'd avoid . . . ask us on Twitter.

basics of thinking philosophically (Chapter 1). Then we'll move on to what we can actually know (Chapter 2), and to discussing virtual reality (Chapter 3) in that context. That leads naturally on to to questions of what it is to have a mind (Chapter 4) and what it means to remain the same person over time (Chapter 5).

Once we've helped you learn what a person like you might be, then we move on to moral questions – that is, what you should do. First, we attempt to help you establish whether you have choice over your actions (Chapter 6). The next chapters deal with what it means to be a good person (Chapter 7), before moving on to what the good for lots of people might look like (Chapter 8), and finally how that idea of the good is actually implemented in the real world (Chapter 9). Finally, we look at the ending of life, both in the sense of killing and in the sense of dying (Chapter 10).

It's probably also worth us challenging a hidden assumption in everything we've said so far: that popular philosophy itself is a good way to improve your life. Unsurprisingly, we think it is. Books like *How Proust Can Change Your Life* and *The Tao of Pooh* have reached an audience of idea-hungry people by reducing complex philosophies and academic language to simpler aphorisms and phrasing.

These easily digestible 'philosophies of everyday life' fit with the concerns of their readership – why are we here, why is love so painful, how can philosophy help us deal with the world's iniquities, should I eat meat, what life's all about, do I really have to climb that mountain or pay my tax, and so on. They are essentially the intellectual almanacs of today: practical, helpful and accessible books, with a touch of wry humour to leaven the mix. We hope that this book supplies something similar.

These pop philosophies work best when they use the familiar to explain their topics – but the problem they run into is that many media aren't suited to explaining philosophical topics. Most media like TV and books miss the interactivity and variety that makes thought experiments compelling and hence effective. So games are excellent vectors for conveying philosophy, because they're fantasies. They're also terrible vectors for conveying philosophy, because they're fantasies.

Let's dig into that paradox. The fantasy model lets a designer set up a world along particular lines, inspired by a thought experiment, which lets him express a particular aesthetic or philosophical conceit. So Lionhead's *Fable* games were about what it means to be a hero. However, the fantasy model also requires the player to be a hero – to break the rules of the world. And often that places the world as an antagonist, to be overcome.

This means that embedded philosophies in game worlds are often simplistic from both sides, to make the narratives accessible to a wider audience. When Dr Robotnik or Bowser kidnap innocents and cackle as maniacally as silent-movie villains, we don't expect to find coherent or complex philosophies behind their plans. Similarly, we don't expect our heroes to be defeating the villains for many reasons beyond the fact that they're heroes and that's what heroes do – in the extremely unlikely event that they pause from pounding goombas to ponder it. We could force an interpretation onto those characters – like *The Tao of Pooh* did onto A. A. Milne's works – but it's a stretch and not intellectually interesting.

And not all game designers, even if they're interested in ideas, see games generally as a good vector for philosophical ideas. William Pugh was co-designer on *The Stanley Parable*, one of the more pensive games of the last few years.

> 'I think attempting to make a grand philosophical statement with a game is a terrible idea. Games made with a grand philosophical statement at their centre often come across as about as meaningful and considered as a Facebook Plato quote overlaid on top of several minions from *Despicable Me*. I approach game design as designing a space for your game and your player to have a conversation, after which a player can take away their own interpretation and meaning. This is more compelling than having Aristotle audio diaries and Ayn Rand environmental storytelling.'

Some games do go further, however. And some games go further still, intentionally or not, and provide superb examples of the merits and flaws of particular philosophies. From *BioShock* to *To the Moon*, from *Soma* to *The Swapper* – this book explores and eulogises those games that can teach you the lessons that should improve your life.

Limbo, yesterday.

....

Luisa: Oh! Maria, are you there? Where are we?

Maria: I'm here. We appear to be in . . . yes, it's a dialogue.

Luisa: A dialogue? Like a conversation? But there's nothing here to talk about? There's nothing at all, in fact. Just whiteness stretching to infinity . . .

Maria: Ah, I mean a philosophical dialogue. It's a traditional form of didactic writing which thinkers used to get across their ideas (and to gently bias the reader in favour of the thinker's belief system).

Luisa: Well I never. I wonder what it is that we're meant to be explaining.

Maria: On closer inspection, this is something like a meta-dialogue. A dialogue about dialogues, so I assume that we're explaining about dialogues themselves. Or rather I am.

Luisa: Well, we'd better get on with it [shivers]. I'd hate to think what's going to happen to us if we stop. What am I meant to do then?

Maria: Well, dialogues were popularised by Plato from around the fifth century BC. Traditionally they took the form of one know-it-all person explaining everything at great length, whilst the other, uh, less-aware person interjected with praise. Like . . .

Luisa: That's astounding!

Maria: You've got it! To be fair, the interlocutor – that's you – would sometimes bring up ideas of their own, to be knocked down by the leading speaker – in this case, me.

Luisa: Why not simply write it as a non-fiction book? Instead of all this waffle and frankly terrible characterisation?

Maria: Drama! Let's imagine that, you, Luisa, are in an abandoned manor, and discover it to be full of intangible spirits, which you then interrogate about their opinions on the afterlife. Isn't that a much more exciting way to discuss the possibility of life after death than a dry, academic explanation?

Luisa: Well, I suppose so. But, you see, I do quite like books.

Maria: Luisa, I think you might be in luck. It looks like a chapter's incoming. Take cover!

CHAPTER ONE

Video games as thought experiments

....

'If you would read a man's disposition, see him game. You will then learn more of him in one hour than in seven years' conversation.'

Richard Lingard (1670)*

WHY VIDEO GAMES? LESSONS FROM THIS SOLAR SYSTEM AND BEYOND

Mass Effect 3 (BioWare, 2012) is an action game with a science-fiction narrative. It tells the story of one human commander's quest to gather enough military resources to protect all sentient life in the galaxy from intentional extinction by giant synthetic-organic hybrids called Reapers. One of these resources is a member of the Quarian race called Admiral Zaal'Koris vas Qwib-Qwib (named, in the Quarian tradition, for his ship the *Qwib-Qwib*), who leads the several thousand-strong collection of Quarian spacecraft known as the Civilian Fleet.

One of protagonist Commander Shepard's missions in *Mass Effect 3* is to fly to the former Quarian homeworld, a planet called Rannoch, and rescue Admiral Koris from the Quarian-created synthetic beings known as the Geth. When you get there, however, Koris begs Shepard to leave him to die and save his small crew of non-combatants instead.

If you obey the admiral's wishes, the loss of their leader later leads some captains from the Civilian Fleet to panic and attempt to

---

* According to Quote Investigator (quoteinvestigator.com), the 'earliest significant match' for this quote often attributed to Plato is in a 1670 pamphlet titled 'A Letter of Advice to a Young Gentleman Leaveing the University Concerning His Behaviour and Conversation in the World'. When Lingard says 'game', he's talking specifically about gambling.

flee. The fleeing ships are cut down by the Geth, which reduces the size of the fleet and thus also the Quarian population and their ability to contribute to the war against the Reapers.

If you convince the admiral to give up his location so that he can be rescued instead of his crew, those non-combatants die at the hands of the Geth. With Admiral Koris at the helm, however, the Civilian Fleet remains an effective war asset, boosting the chances of thwarting the Reapers.

The question of whether to sacrifice the few to save the many is a common trope in fiction. Shepard's decision on Rannoch is an interesting version of the quandary because it poses the question on two levels. Initially it asks whether to sacrifice one Admiral Koris to save several non-combatants, but the real question is whether to sacrifice several non-combatants to save an undisclosed number of civilian crew and however many they might otherwise protect from the Reapers. Yet the underlying format is familiar. So familiar, in fact, that you've probably already heard of philosophy's canonical version: the Trolley Problem.

Philippa Foot's trolley problem

The trolley problem first appeared in a 1967 paper by philosopher Philippa Foot, as part of a discussion of abortion. Specifically, it explored the doctrine of the double effect: a principle by which it's sometimes okay to cause harm as a side effect of bringing about a good result, but not as a means by which to bring about that result. Foot constructed the initial case so as to compare it with a situation in which a judge prevents a riot, which would have many casualties, by framing and executing one innocent man:

> 'To make the parallel as close as possible it may rather be supposed that he is the driver of a runaway tram which he can only steer from one narrow track on to another; five men are working on one track and one man on the other; anyone on the track he enters is bound to be killed.

In the case of the riots the mob has five hostages, so that in both the exchange is supposed to be one man's life for the lives of five. The question is why we should say, without hesitation, that the driver should steer for the less occupied track, while most of us would be appalled at the idea that the innocent man could be framed.'*

Many variants of this dilemma have been proposed since, and the general format has come to be known as '**the trolley problem**'. The language Foot uses at the end of this extract illustrates why stories like these are so popular in philosophy. When she says that 'we should say, without hesitation, that the driver should steer for the less occupied track', Foot is making assumptions about our intuitions and exploring their implications, just as we do when we say that Shepard should save the admiral rather than his crew.

Other thought experiments

The trolley problem is one of the best-known examples of a popular philosophical device: the **thought experiment**. As the name suggests, thought experiments involve testing out theories in our minds to discover these intuitions, often when it would be impractical or (as above) downright unethical to conduct these experiments in real life.

Like many of the activities we undertake in video games, the scenarios presented in philosophical thought experiments would often be unviable in the real world, whether for practical or ethical reasons. Just as it would be expensive and illegal to conduct oneself like *Tomb Raider*'s Lara Croft or *Uncharted*'s Nathan Drake, so too would it be financially and morally unsound to tie six people to some train tracks and set up a train on a crash course.

Other famous philosophical thought experiments are also best left in the realm of the theoretical. Take for example the **Ship of Theseus**, one of the oldest thought experiments still regularly

* Philippa Foot, 'The Problem of Abortion and the Doctrine of the Double Effect' (1967).

discussed (see Chapter 4). This explores identity by asking whether, if you replaced all of the components of an object one by one, it would remain the same object. It would be a huge task to construct a real ship, progressively replace each constituent part, and question people about the ship's status at each stage in order to figure out if there's a consensus on when it becomes a new ship.

More recently, a living philosopher called Frank Jackson proposed a thought experiment called the **Knowledge Argument** about a scientist, called Mary, who knows everything there is to know about the science of colour vision but has spent her entire life in a black-and-white room. Jackson asked what would happen when Mary left the room and saw in colour for the first time, and suggested that our intuition is that she would learn something new. This intuition is meant to discount the physicalist theory that there is nothing more to the world than the physical, based on an assumption that the physicalist would say that knowing all the physical scientific facts of colour vision is the same as knowing everything about it. Whether or not Jackson was right to draw that conclusion, the experiment would be impossible to conduct in real life.

Given the abstract nature of philosophy, thought experiments are an important part of its study. In fact, in the *Stanford Encyclopedia* entry for 'thought experiment'*, philosopher James Robert Brown says that, 'Philosophy without thought experiments seems almost hopeless.' And a standard format for thought experiments, as in the case of the trolley problem, is an imagined scenario followed by a question of what the listener/reader would do or what would otherwise happen: narrative plus action.

Sound familiar?

Simulating philosophy, by Marcus Schulzke
Before he became a lecturer in Politics at the University of York, Marcus Schulzke wrote a paper called 'Simulating Philosophy: Interpreting Video Games as Executable Thought Experiments'.†
Here he argued that video games can perform the same function

* http://plato.stanford.edu/entries/thought-experiment/
† http://link.springer.com/article/10.1007/s13347-013-0102-2

as narrative thought experiments and even have some advantages over more traditional written and spoken formats. As the existence of this book should suggest, we're inclined to agree, and so – we've discovered – are many video game creators.

With the kinds of philosophical theories that can't be tested scientifically, thought experiments are the next best thing. And since they consider such a wide range of interesting topics and are often presented in a narrative form, they're a great inspiration for books, films and video games. Given the nature of our chosen medium, however, games may have the edge.

Schulzke's argument that video games can be interpreted as thought experiments relies on the duality that lies at the heart of the medium: narrative and play. He references two approaches to the academic study of games – narratology and ludology – each of which focuses on one of these aspects. Video games thus seem better placed to consider thought experiments properly, to cover not just the thought but the experimental aspect too.

NARRATIVE

Even on the narrative side of things, however, video games have several advantages. While video game storytelling clearly has a long way to go before it reaches the kind of quality commonly found in literature and film, more and more game developers are taking an interest in narrative and prioritising it in a way that was rare when the medium began. And more and more people are choosing to play games not for the skill but for the story.

Science-fiction survival-horror game *Soma* (Frictional Games, 2015) takes place in a future in which a comet has wiped out most of humanity, except for a few survivors in an underwater research base. The protagonist is a digital copy of the mental states of a man called Simon Jarrett who died a century ago, housed somehow in a human corpse in a diving suit, all powered by a magical future technology called 'structure gel'. The game raises lots of questions about **personal identity** (see Chapter 5) and what it means to be human, but already this premise makes certain assumptions about **the philosophy of mind** (see Chapter 4), for example apparently denying the existence of a soul. As creative director Thomas Grip says:

> 'If I spelled everything out – what the game assumed, and that sort of stuff – then someone with these beliefs would have stopped reading, like, a page in and said, "You know, this is not for me. I can't agree to this premise." But since it's a game, and a story, they sort of agree to the premise because there it's obviously true. You know, "I'm playing it. I'm experiencing it. Therefore there is some truth to it."'

In other words, games are compelling in a way other media aren't.

Try to present someone with a traditional narrative thought experiment and you'll often find that the first thing they do is question the premise, especially if they've never studied philosophy and aren't used to the device. With the trolley problem, for example, it'll probably take a while for you to subdue arguments about how unlikely it is that something like that could ever happen and convince your listener to accept that, for the purposes of the discussion, that's just the way things are. That willing suspension of disbelief is core to thought experiments, and it's natural to games.

'What if?' – on counter-factuals

Narrative thought experiments are usually about **counter-factuals**; they ask you to imagine a scenario that hasn't actually happened, a way that the world could have been. Books and films present counter-factuals too (except in the case of non-fiction and documentary), but video games have something special about them that makes these counter-factuals easier to accept.

Joey Jones think he knows why. He and fellow writer Harry Giles created a text-based game called *The Chinese Room* (2007) that takes players on a comical adventure through several philosophical thought experiments, including Mary's room and the Ship of Theseus mentioned above. Jones has a theory for why video games are a good medium through which to explore philosophy:

'I think video games in general are a good medium for philosophy in that philosophy is often about presenting counterfactual situations. In a sort of counter-example sense. And you can obviously do those in film and in literature and things, of course, but in video games you have the extra element of the fact that player has to actually kind of live these experiences.'

Of course, playing a video game isn't quite the same as actually undergoing the experience yourself (and usually that's a good thing), but a narrative surely feels more real when you're navigating an avatar through a highly-detailed simulation of it rather than sitting in a classroom listening to somebody tell you about it. Video games present you with a counter-factual situation, a world in which things are different from how they are in the world in which we live, and let you experience it at your own pace.

Immersion vs abstraction

Because of the richness of video games as a medium, those narratives are often contextualised within a detailed world. As Schulzke writes in his paper, 'Even the simplest video game worlds tend to include far more detail than narrative thought experiments.' One of the video games industry's favourite buzzwords is '**immersion**', and for players to feel immersed in a narrative it had better take place in a rich and detailed world.

Traditional narrative thought experiments, on the other hand, are often rather dry and abstract, which Schulzke suggests can bias the listener towards particular philosophical approaches in their responses:

'Abstraction may lead thought experiments to give tacit support to **consequentialist** and **deontological** moral philosophies that tend to offer abstract, decontextualized guidance while detracting from contextually sensitive moral theories, such as **virtue ethics**.'

That is, he thinks that when presented with an abstract scenario the listener will lean towards responses that consider the consequences of their actions or some notion of duty respectively. (For more on how video games tackle those ethical positions, see Chapter 7.)

Present a class full of philosophy students with a thought experiment like the trolley problem, without any context, and they'll probably find it relatively easy to commit to a particular course of action. When there's nothing really at stake, and when the people and events in the experiment were only brought into hypothetical existence mere moments ago (and will probably go out of the students' minds the moment they leave the classroom) it's easy to damn them to whatever fate. With the trolley problem and other ethical thought experiments in particular, a listener this far removed from the situation under discussion will likely opt for what seems like the logical answer. Kill the one to save the many. It's probably what Spock would do.

Perhaps part of the problem is the lack of consequences. On an abstract level you know what it means to kill someone via a runaway train, but you don't have to witness it or deal with the aftermath. You don't have to explain to the person's family why you let them die (or, in the case of some variants on the problem, pushed them onto the track so as to save the other five).

Back on Rannoch

Elect to save Admiral Koris rather than his crew, however, and you have to watch him deal with that decision and with the inevitable loss. 'Ancestors, forgive me,' he says as he uploads the coordinates you'll need to find and rescue him and thus damn his group of non-combatants. As soon as you get him on board the shuttle, he greets you with, 'Shepard ... my crew. Perhaps there's still time,' and rushes to a communication device, but – of course – nobody answers. He sits and clasps his hands together. 'I pray they found comfort in the homeworld's skies.'

If you decide to save the crew instead of their leader, Koris will set an explosive and run with it towards the group of advancing Geth, blowing himself up in order to take them out. Shepard hears the explosion over an earpiece, but the player actually sees the consequences of the decision on screen. Once you get the group of non-combatants onto the shuttle, you also have to witness Shepard telling them the bad news. 'Have you heard from the admiral?' one asks. 'He was trying to meet us. Did you see him?' Shepard turns away from her, and the Quarian drops her head: 'No . . .'

On top of that, choosing to respect Koris' wishes and leave him to die also has consequences in the longer term, for the overarching goal of the game. Before the mission, another Quarian admiral called Admiral Xen warns you, 'Without him, some of our non-combatants are planning to leave the flotilla. Picture the consequences, if you will.' But if you actually make the decision to leave Koris behind you no longer have to picture those consequences; they're written down in your inventory of war assets: 'When Admiral Zaal'Koris's ship was destroyed, some Civilian Fleet captains panicked and attempted to flee the system. They were cut down by the Geth before they could escape through the mass relay.' And your total military strength, the quantitative measure you're trying to maximise for the best chance against the Reapers, is reduced. 'When you look at a thought experiment in a philosophy book,' says Grip, 'many of these are really grim things. So something like the trolley problem, you know, you have discussions on it, "Would you push the man on the rails?", but I think it's very different, discussing it, from actually living it.'

Player as protagonist
Books and films are able to contextualise thought experiments within a larger narrative, but there's a sense in which a player is closer to the story in a video game than readers or watchers. When you're playing a game, you're experiencing that narrative through one of its characters, an avatar whose movements and decisions are under your control. In many cases, like with *Soma*, you even view the world that contextualises this narrative through that character's eyes. Says Grip:

'So why make a game about it? Why not just, you know, sit in a corner in a room and ponder these things? The interesting thing for me was that there's all of these philosophical thought experiments, and I was very interested in, you know, could you play through this in a first-person manner? Because it feels like a first-person game is very interesting and very, very different from a book or a movie, because you're in a sense the consciousness of that experience, in that you take certain decisions that we all put on the role of consciousness.'

In a book or a film, the protagonist has their own will as ordained by the writers. In video games, to varying degrees, you are that will. Like Grip says, it's as if you – the player – are in control of that character's thoughts, and because of that close connection the narrative has the potential to be a lot more effective. It's as if we experience the events for ourselves, albeit at a safe physical distance. As Schulzke puts it: 'Video games allow players to encounter and resolve thought experiments as engaged actors rather than as disinterested spectators.'

Scientific evidence

Psychologists have studied the effects of narrative immersion on beliefs and judgements. Melanie C. Green, for instance, writes that 'transportation into a narrative world' led participants to report that they had more story-consistent beliefs than those who were less highly transported.[*] It seems that the more immersive a narrative is, the more useful the judgements we can make about resulting beliefs. And while Green had her participants read the story, we know that video games can be particularly effective at encouraging this sense of immersion.

A team of researchers led by Indrajeet Patil compared the effectiveness of different modes of presentation.[†] In their study, they found that participants responded differently to moral dilemmas when presented via text versus in a 'desktop virtual reality environment' (by which they mean an interactive simulation presented on 'a common LCD monitor' as opposed to a head-mounted display like an Oculus Rift, HTC Vive, or PlayStation VR). The researchers presented their participants with four moral dilemmas, including a version of the trolley problem, and they also measured their participants' electrodermal responses (skin conductance, to do with sweat) to judge their emotional arousal.

[*] http://www.tandfonline.com/doi/abs/10.1207/s15326950dp3802_5
[†] http://www.tandfonline.com/doi/abs/10.1080/17470919.2013.870091

Patil et al found that participants acted according to **utilitarian** principles (i.e., ones that maximise utility, or happiness; see Chapter 8) in these simulations, which they also found far more emotionally arousing, even when they had made non-utilitarian judgements when the same dilemmas were presented in text. This seems to imply a difference in how people think they would act versus how they would actually act, and suggests that an interactive medium can bring us emotionally closer to the latter. In their summary, the researchers write:

> 'This change in decisions reflected in the autonomic arousal of participants, with dilemmas in virtual reality being perceived more emotionally arousing than the ones in text, after controlling for general differences between the two presentation modalities (virtual reality vs text). This suggests that moral decision-making in hypothetical moral dilemmas is susceptible to contextual saliency of the presentation of these dilemmas.'

People respond differently to ethical thought experiments ('hypothetical moral dilemmas') when they're presented in different formats, and 'transportation into a narrative world' can affect the consistency of a person's reported beliefs. The experiences we have while playing a video game are still far removed from real life, and the medium has its own particularities that affect how players approach them (as we'll discuss later in this chapter), but when you want to contextualise your thought experiment in an immersive narrative a game is a great format to try.

PLAY

'There's a different kind of thinking that you can do when you have to act through games, when you actually have to do something.'

Harry Giles

Of course, where video games really set themselves apart from books and films is in their interactivity. You don't just absorb the story, you participate. You don't just learn about the events, you carry them out for yourself. The fact that video games are played, rather than simply read or watched or listened to, gives them an advantage when it comes to using them to explore philosophical thought experiments.

The word 'experiment' suggests action, whether that's choosing how to respond to a proposed situation or just setting things up and seeing what happens. And while you can certainly think about how you would act in the situation presented by your philosophy lecturer or in a book or film, or what would happen if the world was set up that way, there's no physical event to accompany that decision or mechanical system to represent those consequences.

Central to the trolley problem and its popular variations is the notion of action. Often the first question is whether you would pull a lever to physically, intentionally switch the train over to the track with only one victim so as to save the other five. And if that amount of required action wasn't enough, a popular follow-up is to ask whether you would instead stop the train from running over the five by pushing somebody (usually described as 'a fat man' so that we can be sure his body would stop the train) on to the tracks.

But it's far easier to say that you would pull the lever or push the man than – we can only imagine – it would be to stand by the side of the tracks, watching the train approach and hearing the pleas of its potential victims, and actually wrap your hands around that lever or place them on somebody's back and *push*.

The execution element
Video games can't give you that level of physical commitment, at least not until virtual reality becomes a lot more advanced (which will surely come with its own ethical questions). But they can force you to carry out a physical action of some kind, to make your decision and then follow through by choosing which button to press and actually pressing it. Schulzke calls this the '**execution element**'. You can't just voice your plan; you have to execute it.

Games, says veteran designer Brenda Romero, 'can show complicity. You know, if you really want to hit somebody, to make them feel something, make them feel a part of it, there's no other medium that can do that. There's no other artistic medium that can.' Her series of analogue (physical, non-digital) games, *The Mechanic is the Message*, demonstrate how game systems can bring forth this complicity. Romero thinks the best example is probably *Train* (2009), which makes the player an unwitting participant in a representation of the Holocaust. 'I set up these systems,' she says, 'but then I left these procedural gaps in the rules where I force you to figure out, "Now what are we gonna do?" I'm forcing interaction between the players to do rules-lawyering. And that complicity, and the time it takes as well to take in the experience, it forces you to develop some sort of attachment.'

Testing the theory
In *Soma*, the player has much more information upfront. Grip explains:

> 'What I wanted to do with *Soma* . . . is that people are going through this game and being constantly injected with all of these ideas, and then when they're put to the test in various moments, like when you have the option to kill your original or not at Omicron after making the body swap, you start think-ing about the suicides, you start thinking about the other things that you've been through, and suddenly you can see the suicides in another light, you see your option in another light, and all of these insights come to you. I think that's the sort of thing that I wanted most of all when creating the game.'

Grip wanted to test his players, to present them with a counter-factual, contextualising world and see what they would do. So he showed them the facts – that in the world of *Soma* people's mental states can be stored digitally and copied into new locations (see Chapter 4) – and offered them several opportunities to express their intuitions as to the implications.

You discover, for example, that some of the survivors who agreed to have their mental states transferred to a virtual simulated reality to be sent into space (see Chapter 3) killed themselves as a way to ensure their minds would only live on in one place; that there would only be one canonical individual to be their one true self. When the protagonist has his mental states copied into a new physical form he realises with horror that there are now two people with his memories, at which point the player has the choice to switch off the machine keeping the first body alive. Here, as in many video games, the execution element is literal execution: to kill or not to kill.

Programmer as legislator

That video game players often have few activities available to them besides murder is one of the format's unfortunate limitations. But in general, limiting your player can be a boon, especially if you're trying to test their intuitions under specific circumstances. Present a class of empathetic philosophy students with the trolley problem and they may try to find a way around it. Surely, as many a hero has said, 'There has to be another way.' But for the sake of the experiment, you need to restrict them to the choices you've offered: kill one person, or let five die.

In video games, of course, there's no point even trying to argue. Players may find it frustrating that *Mass Effect 3* lacks the freedom to let you figure out a way to save both Admiral Koris and his crew, but there's nothing they can do about it. Particularly determined players could in some cases modify these games (use tools to create new content or change what's already there) in order to forge a new path, which in itself might be philosophically interesting, but most will be left with just the options the creator has provided.

Experiments have to have limits, or they can't provide us with any useful information. Thought experiments have to contend with the power of the imagination, which is useful for providing answers we can't get anywhere else but also has a tendency to exceed the scope of the experiment. Video game players are just as imaginative as everyone else, if not more so, but the games they play are necessarily restrictive.

Video games are written in code. The developers decide what they want the game to be, and then they use a programming language – often within the confines of a ready-made game engine like Unity – to write its rules: rules about what the world looks like and how its objects behave, rules about what computer-controlled characters can do, rules about what the player can change, etc.

Thinking, fast and slow

Those rules and the requirement to work within them are useful when interpreting or creating video games as thought experiments. As well as restricting the number of choices a player has for how to act at a particular moment, rules can be used, for example, to enforce time limits. A philosophy student may have a week to think about the trolley problem and write an essay for their next seminar. But if we want to test more instinctive intuitions, video games allow us to force a player to make a quick decision.

In Telltale Games' episodic interactive story *The Walking Dead* (2012–), for example, much of the player's interaction with the world and its characters is in timed decisions. In conversation, failing to pick a response before the timer counts down means your character just stays silent. In the action sequences, failing to pick a side will often lead to death. While the player could still pause the game to gain some thinking time, the use of a timer at least gives the sense of raised stakes and feels slightly closer to a real-world parallel than discussing the dilemma in question in a classroom.

Jones thinks that video games without time limits can be useful too, as they enable the player to 'take all the material at your own pace but explore it in different ways', which he thinks elevates games above books and films as far as their potential for learning. But the restrictions inherent to video games are important there too, because they force a player to understand the system – however long that takes – in order to progress: 'A puzzle forces the player to learn something about the world in order to solve it.' Video games allow for thought experiments with multiple stages, for which a player must necessarily understand each in turn to progress to the next.

Facing the consequences

And when you want to consider thought experiments in a narrative context rather than in isolation, the systemic nature of video games provides another benefit: **consequences**. As well as limiting the choices a player has at a given juncture, developers will also write rules that govern the consequences of those choices. These rules vary in complexity, from simple branching paths to interacting systems that may result in outcomes even the developers themselves couldn't predict.

Tom Jubert, a writer known for writing philosophical games like *The Swapper* (Facepalm Games, 2013) and *The Talos Principle* (Croteam, 2014), seems to think that this power that video games have is old news, but he describes it well:

> 'Games obviously have this fundamental ability to involve the audience, which we all know plenty about and it's not very interesting to talk about anymore really, because we know that we can ask them questions and get their responses, and change the way the story works based on that, and that makes video games much closer to actual real-world relationships and interactions than any other medium, really.'

This ability to present the player with the consequences of their actions is another advantage games have over books and films. We get to see consequences in those other narratives, of course, but only ever those for the choices the creator has already made, with no option to explore other avenues and see what else could happen. And the vastness of some video game worlds means that we can see those consequences interact, as Giles points out when comparing BioWare games like the *Mass Effect* series to the more restrictive *BioShock* (2K Games, 2007): 'Because it's an open world in a way that *BioShock* isn't, you actually get to experience some of the, sort of, socio-political ramifications of your actions, and there's often much more a grey moral choice. It's less binary. You're asked to enact and think through your ethical behaviour.'

Those ramifications needn't be straightforward, either. A common factor in role-playing games like those from BioWare, which dates back to the pen-and-paper role-playing games – like *Dungeons & Dragons* (Gary Gygax and Dave Arneson, 1974) – from which many early examples drew inspiration, is luck. Dice rolls have been replaced by random number generation, but the

principle is the same: some actions have multiple possible consequences that may each be more or less likely than others. It's
difficult for people to factor in chance when considering traditional
narrative thought experiments, but video game creators can
program probability in.

In conclusion

Schulzke summarises all of these features of video games that can
make them effective thought experiments: 'Video games have several
advantages over traditional narrative thought experiments. They
provide more complex decision-making environments, incorporate
the effects of probability and luck, and make players active participants in the narratives.'

These features can be found in video games of all shapes and
sizes. Whether the genre is role-playing or action or simulation or
strategy, the player can still get attached to its characters. Whether
the narrative is told through photorealistic graphics or just through
text, the programmed rules that make up the game's system can still
incorporate restrictions and consequences and luck.

Of course, perhaps the most immediate advantage that video
games have over not only traditional narrative thought experiments
but also those found in books and films is that they're more fun,
especially for those of a certain age. Few governments take philosophy seriously enough to make it compulsory in schools, and we can
hardly expect children and teenagers to study the subject in their
spare time. But so many young people choose to spend their time
playing video games that it's the perfect medium in which to introduce basic philosophical ideas.

GAMES YOUR PHILOSOPHY PROFESSOR WOULD LOVE

While aspects of *Mass Effect 3* and *The Walking Dead* can be interpreted philosophically, they're not marketed as philosophical games.
But more and more creators are recognising the strengths of video
games and are choosing to make explicitly philosophical games.
While some, like *The Talos Principle*, are polished video games that
don't look so different from the relatively brainless big-budget action

games that make millions, many are far more modest; philosophical intentionality tends to be conversely correlated with budget.

Alongside his work on games like *The Talos Principle* and *The Swapper*, for example, Jubert has created his own smaller game about propositional logic: *Ir/rational Redux* (2012). The game features basic graphics and arguments in text, with drop-down boxes to select the correct line to complete each argument and make it valid. Over the course of ten of these puzzles, the game teaches you basic tenets of propositional logic, such as that an argument can be valid even if one or more of its premises is false. It's simple and short, but more fun than watching a professor scribble the corresponding arguments on a whiteboard.

Castle, Forest, Island, Sea

But games don't need to be an alternative to an academic philosophy. They should be a supplement, or even an introduction. One institution that recognises the power of games to introduce potential students to philosophical ideas is the Open University, which commissioned design studio Hide&Seek to create a game for them. The designer, Holly Gramazio, explains:

> 'They wanted an online thing that would help people to explore ideas around action and reason in philosophy. We proposed the idea of this adventure through a derelict castle where you come across arguing blackbirds, and express through whom you agree with and the decisions you make which schools of philosophy you're more likely to be in agreement with, so that you can get to the end and it can go, "Oh, you might like this philosopher and you might like that philosopher. You'd probably really hate this guy. If you want to find out more, here's some info about the Open University's philosophy course."'

The result was *Castle, Forest, Island, Sea*, a text adventure with illustrations by Martina Paukova, based on extensive research by Hannah Nicklin into some basic philosophical themes. Over about thirty minutes of play, the player reads descriptive text of a journey through a castle (in a forest, on an island, in the sea), clicking on highlighted text to read more detail or to choose a course of action. Early in the game you meet some talking birds that have opposing viewpoints about various topics, and whether you agree or disagree with them affects which philosophers you're recommended at the end.

Perhaps the Open University might instead have simply provided a webpage with examples of different philosophers' views. Those interested in studying philosophy could have just clicked on a philosopher's name to read a summary of their thoughts on a particular subject, and decided which they were most interested in learning more about. But while the subject matter is interesting, the experience would have been much more dull than the game Hide&Seek created.

Gramazio says that interactivity was important for an introduction to philosophy in particular because of the nature of the subject:

> 'So they're interested not in just going "Here are some facts about philosophy" but a bit about "Here is why you might want to study it yourself. This is part of what the process might feel like, some of the sorts of things you might be doing with your brain." I think that pretty much of necessity has to be interactive because it's an active field. My understanding is it's a very process-based thing where you have to balance all of these different thoughts and their dependencies and where they come from in your head, and not just learn a thing but learn about learning.'

Philosophy isn't really a subject about facts. Sure, you read the works of particular philosophers and try to remember what each of them had to say on different subjects, but more importantly you try to understand how those philosophers came to their conclusions in the first place. You learn the tools required to counter philosophical arguments. You learn the process. As Gramazio explains: 'I think there's something about the way that video games can be process-based that means they're really well suited to taking you through something where it's not enough to understand the conclusions but you also need to know how they were reached.'

Like Schulzke, Gramazio also points to the power of games to present counter-factuals and test our intuitions about them:

'A lot of philosophy comes at some point down to these hypo-thetical situations, like positing a situation that is not existent in the world and then going, "Well, what would we think about this? How would we feel? What would this mean? Would it still be the same boat?" And yeah, video games are really good at hypotheticals, at presenting you with a situation that's entirely invented and making you care about it. That's what they are, in a way, they're these "hey, what if" questions with answers that they've tricked you into feeling invested in.'

Something about the format of games, the way they present a coun-ter-factual world and immerse the player as an active participant, makes people more invested in the events that occur and the ques-tions they raise. Even in their text-based game with a handful of illustrations, in which the particular counter-factuals involved – among other things – having discussions with talking birds, Gramazio found that players still felt that investment: 'Based on player feedback and what people told us, it did an okay job at making people feel invested in their decisions about how they felt about different fairly abstract philosophical concepts, which I'm really happy with.'

Castle, Forest, Island, Sea manages through an interactive collec-tion of text and illustrations to introduce a counter-factual world, get the player invested, and teach them a little something about the process of philosophy before presenting them with a personalised map of where their philosophical interests might lie. And even on the development side, Gramazio found the experience enlightening:

'It was interesting to make a game where the output for you as a player isn't, like, whether you were good at it or not, or how wrong or how right you were, but just a matter of staking out and exploring your position. That's not a thing I'd done in game design before, and I think it's something that the philo-sophical framework really encouraged, that you don't get to the end of the game and get told, "Well done, you were eight Socrates out of ten."'

Socrates Jones: Pro Philosopher

Connor Fallon and Valeria Reznitskaya's philosophical game is also a kind of 'learning about learning'. *Socrates Jones: Pro Philosopher* (2013) draws inspiration from the popular *Ace Attorney* games (Capcom, 2001), which cast the player as a lawyer who argues his case by presenting evidence to counter his opponent. In *Socrates Jones*, you argue instead with historical philosophers by asking them questions about their beliefs so that you can pinpoint the problems in their arguments. It takes the debate format that makes the *Ace Attorney* games so entertaining and applies it to a subject in which that kind of dialogue is fundamental. 'It was a comedic idea at first,' admits Fallon. 'Like, "Hey, what if we took these mechanics, you know, they're already debate mechanics, let's apply them to something that is not law and see how that turns out." And it turned out to be pretty compelling, so we pursued it and made it into an actual thing instead of just a, you know, one-off joke experiment.'

Aside from *Ace Attorney*, the main inspiration for *Socrates Jones* was Fallon's philosophy professor Andy Norman's model of philosophical inquiry as a 'reason-giving game'.* The game represents those engaged in a philosophical discussion as players, their claims and challenges and 'defendings' as moves, and the possible kinds of claims and challenges and defendings (presumptive vs non-presumptive claims, bare vs assertional challenges, direct vs indirect defendings) as branches in the game tree.

In *Socrates Jones*, the people you meet express their arguments in a series of premises. You can then guide the player-character Socrates (an accountant, not the famous classical Greek philosopher) to question each of these premises – to ask for clarification, evidence or relevance – or challenge them by presenting counters from a list of ideas gathered during the discussion.

* https://www.academia.edu/4269933/How_to_Play_the_Reason
-Giving_Game

When Euthyphro argues that morality comes from the gods, for example, asking for clarification on his premise that 'every one possesses wisdom far beyond our own' will provide you with the idea that 'there are different gods' with different ideas, which you can then use to challenge the premise that 'whatever a god commands must be good'.

Fallon believes that these game mechanics, the ability to interact with the presented arguments rather than just read or hear them, make *Socrates Jones* a 'more flexible exploration than a book or even a film would be'.

> 'Immanuel Kant will say something. He'll list out the steps for the categorical imperative, and you can ask at each individual step, like, "I don't understand this", "Can you clarify?" or "What is your reasoning for this being a step?" But if you feel like, "No, I kind of get this one" you don't have to get that deep dive on each thing, and you can therefore place your focus where you really need it.'

Of course, a video game is no replacement for an actual discussion because the game is limited by its programming, only capable of responding to a limited set of questions and challenges with predetermined answers. 'I think that the open-ended nature of philosophy exposes limitations in this mechanic more than something more closed would,' says Fallon, 'Because, for example, especially when it comes to presenting counterarguments, there's many different directions you could go, and the game is only capable of handling the ones that we write in.'

But Fallon thinks that their game provides 'a good middle ground'. Those constraints that prevent the game from reflecting actual debate also have benefits. For one thing, he was able to program into the game the lesson that *ad hominem* attacks are useless – any time you try to use 'your face is ugly' as a challenge you lose credibility – which he thinks certain current political figures could stand to learn.

Socrates Jones presents a necessarily simplified representation of both the process of philosophical debate and the particular ideas discussed within, but its limitations serve to make it easier to follow. As Fallon puts it, 'It's a way to simplify, and simpler pills are often easier to swallow. You then want to build to more complex things, you don't want to stop there, but it's definitely a good intermediary.'

The Chinese Room

Like *Socrates Jones, The Chinese Room* also came about because its creators thought it would be fun to make a philosophical game. 'Probably the main motivation was it was fun,' says Jones, 'and it was an interesting idea. Also, there's a lot of weird and interesting philosophical thought experiments and things which probably most people outside of philosophy wouldn't have had access to.'

Like Fallon and Reznitskaya, Giles and Jones wanted to make sure their game would be enjoyable for those without any prior knowledge or interest in philosophy. Inspired by the inherent silliness of some well-known philosophical thought experiments – Giles points to Zeno's paradoxes – they wanted to take a playful, rather than educational, approach. Says Giles:

> 'I think what we were setting out to do was not necessarily to simulate philosophy but just have a play in the thought experiments. Because all the classic thought experiments of that kind of world of philosophy just have this, sort of, gloriously fantastical narrative element to them, like, they're great images and they're fun to play about with. But the more that I was doing it, the more I realised that you could do some quite interesting digging into the meaning by simulating them.'

Perhaps in part because of the silliness of some of these thought experiments, and the difficulties in representing them to a player, *The Chinese Room* is a purely text-based game. Like with traditional text adventures – nowadays often called **interactive fiction** – you interact with the game by typing your desired action, taking clues from and using objects in the described environment. 'Text is cheap,' says Jones, 'so you can create a fully-fledged viable game in a relatively short amount of time with a small team. Someone can have a weird idea and fully realise it in a text game, whereas otherwise they would need a full team and financial backing, when indeed the market might be very niche for that weird idea.'

In *The Chinese Room*, you play through a series of representations of famous thought experiments, beginning with the titular Chinese Room (see Chapter 4). Type 'look' followed by an object and you'll get a description of that object. Type 'get' or 'push' or 'open' or similar and you can interact with the objects. Each puzzle – for example, escaping the Chinese Room – involves finding the correct series of actions. Every now and then, you get to talk to other characters, choosing from a list of possible responses at each stage of the discussion. Here, in conversation, is where Jones thinks text adventures might have an advantage over graphical video games.

> 'In general, these choice-based games might be the best medium for presenting philosophical conversations. In a graphical video game, the cost of assets discourages multiple choice and greatly branching dialogue. Without a need to pay voice actors, a text game can allow the player to take a wider range of possible positions. You see this also in the old CRPGs [computer role-playing games], most especially the philosophical *Planescape: Torment* (Black Isle, 1999), which can have deep branching text-only dialogue trees. In contrast, there's a moment in *Skyrim* (Bethesda, 2011) where you meet the dragon Paarthurnax and your conversation option is, "I didn't come here to debate philosophy with you." '*

The text-based format also allowed Giles and Jones to provide plenty of context for each of the thought experiments explored in the game, with what Giles describes as a 'big database in the background where we explain all of the jokes'. They compare this approach to that taken by Existential Comics†: 'They're satirising philosophy, but they also kind of explore and explain philosophy in an interesting way, and then always at the bottom of it, if it's in any way complicated, they have a big "don't understand the joke" expansion box.'

---

* 'If only you could talk to these creatures,' game magazine *Edge* wrote of the monstrous enemies in first-person shooter *Doom*. If only we could discuss philosophy with the dragons.
† http://existentialcomics.com/

Giles thinks that humour and play is a better tool for exploring this kind of thing than rigid simulation. Again, they point to the limitations of games like *BioShock* that feature binary moral choices:

'I don't think you really get to explore morality in *BioShock*, because it's so rigid. There's only two ways of seeing things. Whereas if you can be playful and satirical and transform assumptions, there's a bit more potential for learning, I suppose. So I'm kind of against really rule-bound systems of games.

'I think when we have games we've got this extraordinary capacity for weird stuff to happen and for the rules to change, and for it to be more responsive to your imagination, to your curiosity, I suppose, than, say, a static text can be. *BioShock* functions like a book. It's just a book that has two different stories in it. But a game should be able to explode a bit beyond that.'

Giles' desired approach, a playful satirical approach that challenges assumptions, might represent the next stage for philosophy in games. Some games will do little more than present basic philosophical ideas in a narrative context, which could be useful for those who've had little exposure to philosophy before. But other creators will go one step further, playing with the assumptions behind those thought experiments. Creators like Pippin Barr.

TROLLEY PROBLEM

And so the train comes back around.

Pippin Barr is a game maker and critic who also teaches game design at Concordia University in Montreal. He makes small experimental games that are often funny and/or thoughtful, many of which can be played in a web browser. One of these games – perhaps unsurprisingly for someone who has an honours degree in Philosophy and Computer Science – is a digital representation of the trolley problem called *Trolley Problem* (2011).

Each level of *Trolley Problem* is a 2D top-down view of a track down which an out-of-control trolley advances. Three people are tied to the track, but players can press the spacebar to pull a lever so that the trolley will head down a different track instead, or in one case to push someone onto the track.

On the first level, there is one person tied to the other track. On the second, there is a 'very large' person tied to the other track and the two paths are joined in a loop; you're told that the death of either the very large person or the other three will stop the trolley from continuing around. On the third level, there is a very large person standing on a platform, and pressing the spacebar will push them onto the track where their death will stop the trolley before it reaches the other three. The fourth level repeats the first, but it tells the player the person tied to the other track is someone important to them and asks them to type who: mother, father, brother, etc.

The art is minimalist, pixelated. The people tied to the tracks are black silhouettes of a few pixels each, but they move their arms as if struggling or waving for help. When the trolley hits someone, their black silhouette turns red and their arms stop moving. After each level, a black screen appears and white text reminds you of your choice: 'You pulled the switch. Okay.' At the end of the game you're given your results in similarly plain language: 'On level one you chose to pull the switch. One person died. Three people lived.'

The game sounds dry and uninteresting, but Barr's goal wasn't just to reproduce a thought experiment in interactive form.

> 'It wasn't so much about making the trolley problem as a way of experimenting with a representation of a philosophical thought experiment. It was about this idea that games are very different in terms of how we can speak about them or work with them ethically. I guess the thing that I was interested in is that intersection of gameplay and ethics, and how, I guess, putting it bluntly, players kind of ruin everything all the time.'

Barr isn't just interested in how philosophy can be explored through games, but in the philosophy *of* games. He's interested in the ways that players act in games, and how that differs from how people act in the real world. He points, for example, to the fact that players will often carry out an action in a game and then reload from an earlier save file, an earlier point in time, and act in a different way instead.

'The more I think about the trolley problem, you know, it's so artificial. It's very difficult to react to it in any human way. But in games I think it's exacerbated because people are used to being able to repeat their choices if they're not satisfied, or even if they just want to know all of the different possible endings. And people are often very cold-hearted and maybe utilitarian or really totally self-centred about the sorts of decisions that they make in games, and I wanted to push on that.'

And so, for this experiment, Barr has made his *Trolley Problem* theoretically unrepeatable. You play it in your web browser, and if you return to the game in the same browser at a later date it'll remember that you've already played and just present you with your original results screen. You could just clear your cookies or play the game in a different browser, but the principle is that you make each of these decisions only once.

'Part of the point of the game is that you can only play it once, in theory. I mean, it's totally possible to circumvent it, but the game is only meant to be played through one time, and that was sort of the major technique, I guess, in terms of giving the player's decisions weight even if they only find out at the end that they can't replay.'

Another part of Barr's attempt to play with the weight of player decisions is the abstract aesthetic: the pixelated graphics, the limited colour palette, the minimal sound effects, the plain language. Perhaps counter to the earlier points about contextualisation, Barr was interested in stripping back anything that might distract from the bare ethical question. 'One thing I was wondering is just about the possible, kind of, aesthetics of ethics, in a way,' he says, 'and what you might need to do to encourage a player who would normally just make whatever decision they wanted, and not act terribly ethically, to really actually engage with it and think about what they would really do.'

Barr points out that in video games there's plenty beyond purely ethical considerations to motivate player action, like exciting visual effects that might tempt a player to take the bloodiest course. 'I guess I was trying to embrace that abstraction,' he says. 'Basically to avoid any sense for the player that there was a reward involved, like that it would be more exciting, for example, to kill three people because there would be more fountains of blood or something.'

Of course, for a different sense of the word, there's a way in which Barr's game rejects abstraction:

> 'There is this thing about games, of course, as a version of the trolley problem, that you're confronted with not an abstract decision where you imagine everything but, like, an actual little trolley, even if it's incredibly pixelated, moving. And you have to actually make the decision, and when you make the decision you see a change because of it. Strangely you just don't see as many representations of the trolley problem or ethical situations that have that kind of real-time element to them.'

Barr recognises that the digital representation of the imagined trolley is a powerful image, somehow more real than just thinking about the dilemma. And as the trolley only takes a few seconds to trundle down the track, there's a time limit on the player's decision of whether or not to press the spacebar and change the course. The game format has brought something extra to the table, a new angle to consider. 'I think it encourages a different kind of thinking,' says Barr.

CONTINUE?

> 'I think every piece of art you make is philosophical one way or another, you know?'
>
> Ken Levine (creative director, *BioShock Infinite*)

There are limitations to the extent to which creators can make intentionally philosophical games. For one thing, not all possible philosophical topics fit within the format. And even for those that do, anything that uses graphics rather than just text will be relatively expensive to develop. But with more and more independent developers using cheap and accessible tools to make small games of their own vision, without the need to conform to the wishes of a publisher, we should see an increase in interactive philosophy.

Besides, even those games that aren't intentionally philosophical can be interpreted philosophically. People often analyse books and films through a philosophical lens, so why not games? And when it comes to thought experiments in particular, an important part of philosophical study, video games – with their ability to immerse players in a contextualising narrative, and present choices the player can physically act upon with consequences that change the game world – may actually have more to offer than other media. Not all befit that kind of perspective, but many are more relevant to philosophical topics than you might think, as we explore in the rest of this book, starting with the basics: what can we actually know?

Limbo, definitely.

....

Luisa: Wow, that was close!

Maria: Where are we now? Back in Manhattan?

Luisa: This can't be Manhattan. Where are the buildings? The people? The pipes? The pizza *al funghi*? The Anthora coffee cups carefully placed in shot?

Maria: Uh . . . Perhaps we fell into a parallel . . . a . . . What's that word that rhymes with invention?

Luisa: Uh. Incomprehension? Where are we?

Maria: Well, it's a big white, warm space full of pipes that smells of . . . mushrooms? But I'm not sure. I feel like this isn't real.

Luisa: How can we tell? What do you know?

Maria: I'm fairly confident that I'd know. Weren't we on the sofa, eating pizza and tomato sauce, and listening to music, not so long ago?

Luisa: I thought we were standing at the dining table, eating pasta and watching Nicole Eggert's show. But sure.

Maria: Well, whatever our individual experience, we can agree on something, right? We were relaxing, eating and being entertained, at home. And you have tomato sauce on your collar.

Luisa: I believe you. And it seems true. But how would we verify it? We could have been brainwashed by a giant all-powerful . . . uh, lizard? And we can't see anything except each other.

Maria: Okay. At least we know that we exist and we look like this. Nice dungarees by the way.

Luisa: Thanks, I have a white pair too. Look, I know you – you're my sister, you've been like my mother, father, uncle, cousin and everybody, all my life. But the big lizard could be messing with our minds. We might be mistaken.

Maria: When I get my hands on that lizard . . .! Well, the only thing we know for sure is that we're thinking.

Luisa: *Cogito ergo sum*, after all. But who's doing the thinking? What if we're not us?

Maria: I'm not talking to you if you start speaking Italian again. I – or someone – need to go away and think about this.

Luisa: That's lucky, because another chapter's coming. Low this time. Jump!

CHAPTER TWO

Knowledge and scepticism

....

'I have an infinite capacity for knowledge, and even I'm not sure what's going on outside.'

> GLaDOS, *Portal* (Valve, 2007)

As any student of the subject will tell you, philosophy has an unfortunate reputation. Perhaps the oldest academic discipline in the world, it seems to have lost much of the respect it once had. In our modern capitalist society, parents urge their children to choose a speciality that seems more practical and thus – they reason – more likely to lead to a better-paid job. Gross National Product trumps Gross National Happiness.

Much of the disdain seems to come from a lack of understanding. People wonder what the point of philosophy is, and whether we really need to be asking the kinds of questions that philosophers ask. This chapter aims to address some of the assumptions core to that kind of dismissal and to break down some of the reasons why philosophers think that we might not know what we think we know.

WHAT IS KNOWLEDGE?

Nintendo's popular *The Legend of Zelda* series of video games (1986–) features a sacred relic called the Triforce, which – as the name would suggest – has three parts: the Triforce of Courage, the Triforce of Power, the Triforce of Wisdom. Each represents the essence of one of the Goddesses who together created the kingdom Hyrule in which the games are set: Farore (Courage) created life, Din (Power) created the realm and Nayru (Wisdom) created the laws of physics.

Video games have a fondness for the number three, and so too it seems do philosophers, as the traditional analysis of knowledge also comes in three parts. This 'tripartite' analysis of knowledge states that a person S knows a proposition p if (and only if):

1   p is true,
2   S believes that p, and
3   S is justified in believing that p.

Knowledge, according to the tripartite analysis of knowledge, is justified true belief, and is thus sometimes referred to as the '**JTB analysis**'.

Guy Longworth, a philosopher currently teaching at the University of Warwick, explains:

> 'The tripartite theory of knowledge tries to explain how knowledge works by breaking it up into components. Typically, it breaks it up into at least the components belief and truth, because most people think that you can't know something where your view of that thing is wrong. But mere true belief doesn't seem to be enough for knowledge, because you might have a lucky guess. You might come to believe something true in that way. So most philosophers think there needs to be some connection between your belief and the fact that you know. So that's the third component. And people start from the idea that the connection is framed in terms of justification. So the idea is that we have reasons for our beliefs when we know something.'

As Longworth says, however, that's only the start. While the JTB analysis appears comprehensive at first glance, it might not be the simple answer it seems.

Wright is right: Gettier counter-examples

In the *Ace Attorney* series of visual novel video games (Capcom, 2001–), you play as a variety of defence attorneys who collect evidence and cross-examine witnesses. In *Phoenix Wright: Ace Attorney – Justice for All* (Capcom, 2002), one of these witnesses is Adrian Andrews, on trial for the murder of an actor called Juan Corrida who was discovered in his hotel room strangled and with a knife in his chest.

The knife bears the fingerprints of Matt Engarde, Corrida's rival and player-character Phoenix Wright's client. Wright believes that

Andrews killed Corrida and then planted the knife to frame Engarde as a way to cover up her crime. In fact, Andrews did plant the knife to frame Engarde, but she didn't kill Corrida; she wanted revenge on Engarde for unrelated reasons.

Wright believes that Andrews framed Engarde, and it's true. His true belief also seems justified; he has strong reasons to believe that Andrews killed Corrida, and it makes sense that the murderer would try to pin the crime on somebody else. But Andrews is not the murderer, so his reasoning seems somehow flawed; it's like he's stumbled upon this justified true belief by chance. It doesn't quite feel like knowledge. Wright is right, but – it seems – for the wrong reasons.

Examples like this are called **Gettier counter-examples**, named for the living American philosopher Edmund Gettier whose 1963 paper 'Is Justified True Belief Knowledge?'* presented a small selection of these situations for consideration. As Longworth says:

> 'A Gettier example is used to undermine that particular take on the JTB analysis of knowledge. Very roughly the idea is a case where one seems to have reasons for one's belief, so one's belief seems to be justified, and moreover one's belief is true, but the connection between the belief and what one knows doesn't seem to be right for your belief to amount to knowledge.'

It's 2016, and you walk in on your friend watching the *League of Legends* (Riot Games, 2009) World Championship just as a team called SK Telecom T1 is announced as the winner. You're justified in believing that SK Telecom T1 has won the 2016 World Championship, and in fact they have, so your justified belief is also true. But unbeknownst to you, your friend is actually watching a recording of the 2015 World Championship, which SK Telecom T1 also won. Do you really know that SK Telecom T1 has won in 2016?

Longworth provides a similar example, in which you accidentally watch a recording of Roger Federer winning Wimbledon in a year in

* http://www.jstor.org/stable/3326922

which he wins again: 'So this looks to be a case where one has a reasonable or justified belief, one's belief is true, but it doesn't amount to knowledge since one believes it for the wrong sorts of reasons. The reasons one has fail to connect one with the fact one knows.'

There are quite a few examples in video games of this sort of justified true belief that doesn't seem to amount to knowledge. One particularly fantastical example can be found in *Ghost Trick: Phantom Detective* (Capcom, 2010), in which the player-character is an amnesiac ghost.

When the game begins, the ghost sees a corpse and infers that it's his: 'This has gotta be me. No question about that. After all, do you see any other dead bodies lying around here?' Later on, the ghost sees the antagonist, a man called Sith, looking at a picture of the man he thinks he was before he died.

Sith: Hmm, yes . . . Sissel . . .
Ghost: Sissel . . . That must be my name . . . Now that I hear it, it
    does sound familiar . . .

The amnesiac ghost is justified in believing that his name is Sissel, and it turns out to be true. However, you later discover that the corpse is actually of a man called Yomiel who had a fiancée called Sissel who killed herself. And the amnesiac ghost is actually the ghost of a cat that Yomiel named Sissel after his beloved. The ghost is right to believe that his name is Sissel, but for the wrong reasons.

Because of examples like these (though admittedly usually more realistic than a ghost with a case of mistaken identity), some philosophers believe that the tripartite analysis – that knowledge is justified true belief – doesn't cut it. Proposed alternatives tend either to add a fourth condition or to replace justification with something else, but none of these analyses has achieved broad acceptance.

Do my eyes deceive me?

'We are all aware that the senses can be deceived, the eyes fooled. But how can we be sure our senses are not being deceived at any particular time, or even all the time? Might I just be a brain in a tank somewhere, tricked all my life into believing in the events of this world by some insane computer? And does my life gain or lose meaning based on my reaction to such solipsism?'

Sid Meier's Alpha Centauri (Firaxis Games, 1999)

Attempts to define knowledge, and counter-examples to those analyses, suggest that knowledge is about getting things right for the right reasons. As Longworth explains, knowledge requires 'a match between how things seem to you, or how you believe they are, and how they are', and that match needs to be 'non-accidental'. Gettier cases seem not to count as knowledge because while they match a belief with reality, those beliefs are accidental; the ghost only comes to the belief that his name is Sissel by chance.

Philosophical scepticism suggests that we cannot be sure that we ever have that match between how things seem to us and how things really are. What we believe to be methods of gaining knowledge of the outside world may actually be unreliable. Philosophical scepticism involves more than just doubting widely accepted beliefs, as with religious sceptics or those who claim to believe that the earth is flat. To be a philosophical sceptic, you must doubt your ability to gain any knowledge at all.

Human beings find out about the world around us through our bodily senses, through what we see, hear, smell, taste and touch. But, as philosophers point out, our senses are unreliable. Sometimes they give us inaccurate information; they make us believe things about the world that turn out not to be true.

Pour yourself a glass of water, and then place a straw or pencil so that it's half submerged. What once seemed straight will now look bent below the water level. There's a mismatch between how things seem to you and how they actually are. Your senses are deceiving you, and failing to give you accurate information about the world.

Optical illusions – of which the stick in water is a classic – are a popular inspiration for video games. Perhaps most notably, the BAFTA-winning *Monument Valley* (Ustwo Games, 2014), which its creators describe as 'an illusory adventure of impossible architecture and forgiveness', enables players to explore a world inspired by the art of M. C. Escher (1898–1972).

In *Monument Valley*, the player's perspective matters more than the laws of physics. The isometric perspective presents a world in which the player-character Ida may, for example, travel from one place to another that appears as if it is directly above her via a path that appears not to take her any higher.

Games like this demonstrate the absurdity of a world in which the way things seem to be in optical illusions actually matches up to the way things really are, in which our senses do give us accurate information. But in our world we know that there's a mismatch, and so we know that we can't always trust what we see with our own eyes. In extreme cases, what we see may not just be a flawed representation of what is there, a bent stick that should be straight, but may in fact match up to nothing at all.

Video-game hallucinations

In *Fallout 3* (Bethesda, 2008), nuclear war has turned the United States into a post-apocalyptic wasteland, which only some people managed to survive by retreating into underground vaults. Two hundred years after the Great War, the player-character leaves Vault 101 and explores the Capital Wasteland (what used to be Washington, D. C.) in search of her (or, if you want, his) missing father, which earns her the moniker 'the Lone Wanderer'.

As part of the Lone Wanderer's journey, she can explore other vaults. In Vault 106, she walks into a room full of men in lab coats, each of whom looks just like her father. On closer inspection, however, they all disappear. Later, she finds a computer terminal that appears to contain a message from herself. At one point she finds herself being attacked by a gang called the Tunnel Snakes from her own vault, but her bullets don't seem to work on them.

It turns out that Vault 106 is being pumped full of a hallucinogenic gas, as one of many experiments the creators of the vaults performed on their unwitting inhabitants. The Lone Wanderer was undergoing hallucinations, experiences that don't match up with anything in reality.

Several video game protagonists fall prey to hallucinations. In an expansion to *Fallout 4* (Bethesda, 2015) called *Far Harbor*, the player-character drinks irradiated water and has a vision of a ghostly figure known as the Mother of the Fog. In massively multiplayer online game *World of Warcraft* (Blizzard Entertainment, 2004) a boss called Herald Volazj has the ability to make each member of the player's party see hostile copies of the others. In *Max Payne* (Remedy Entertainment, 2001), Payne is injected with an overdose of a drug called Valkyr that causes him to see letters from his dead wife telling him that he is in a video game (which could be another Gettier case).

In first-person shooter *Call of Duty: Black Ops* (Treyarch, 2010), player-character Alex Mason sees a character called Viktor Reznov kill an ex-Nazi scientist called Friedrich Steiner. But the player later discovers that Mason was brainwashed by the Russians to kill the man himself, and his vision of Reznov – who's actually dead – was just a hallucination.

In *Spec Ops: The Line* (Yager Development, 2012), a shooter played from a third-person perspective, player-character Martin Walker has a series of hallucinations that affect his behaviour. He hallucinates live hostages where there are actually hanging corpses, and a voice telling him to shoot one in order to save the other. He continually hallucinates the voice of Colonel Konrad giving him orders through a broken radio, and when he discovers Konrad's corpse he experiences a 'walking talking' vision of the man.

It turns out that Walker committed atrocious acts, and his subconscious summoned the hallucinations of Konrad so that he would have someone else to blame. 'It takes a strong man to deny what's right in front of him,' says the Konrad hallucination, 'and if the truth is undeniable . . . You create your own.'

Black Ops and *Spec Ops* have more in common than their military theme. In both cases, the player is deceived alongside the player-character. In the other games, the hallucinations are marked as such from the start – every time the Lone Wanderer has a hallucination in Vault 106, for example, her vision takes on a blue tinge – but in these two the player only finds out later that these experiences didn't actually provide accurate information about the world.

The creators of *Black Ops* and *Spec Ops* made their hallucinations indistinguishable from veridical (i.e. truthful) experiences in the games for the sake of a plot twist, but this also demonstrates how the existence of hallucinations can lead one to scepticism.

Many of us will not have experienced hallucinations like these in our own lives, but we know that they happen. If we can believe that a fictional character can't tell the difference between their hallucinations and other experiences, it's not too much of a stretch to imagine that hallucinations and veridical experiences could be indistinguishable in real life. And if that is the case then how do you know that you aren't having a hallucination right now? If your senses deceive you some-times, how can we trust that we know when they aren't? Says Longworth:

'So, we believe that it's possible to have experiences very simi-lar to the experiences we're now having and yet not to be having genuine experience of the world. So one could be hallucinating, or one could be subject to some kind of an illu-sion where things look one way but in fact they're another way. We know those things are possible. So we know that, in prin-ciple, experiences like the experiences you're having now are possible even when they're failing to reveal how things are.'

René Descartes: the original Cartesian sceptic

One philosopher who highlighted the unreliability of our senses was seventeenth-century French philosopher René Descartes, whom you may know for inventing the x and y axes (the Cartesian coordinate system) or, more pertinently, for his famous *Cogito ergo sum*: 'I think, therefore I am.' In his book *Meditations on First Philosophy* (1641), he wrote:

'Whatever I have up till now accepted as most true I have acquired either from the senses or through the senses. But from time to time I have found that the senses deceive, and it is prudent never to trust completely those who have deceived us even once.'

Descartes' main goal in the *Meditations* was to prove the exist-ence of God and the soul; the book was originally subtitled, translated from Latin, 'In which the existence of God and the immortality of the soul are demonstrated'. But along the way he worked through a comprehensive kind of philosophical scepticism, attempting to throw out everything he had previously believed in order to rebuild only with those things he could know to be true.

When you're trying to defeat the pigs in *Angry Birds* (Rovio, 2009), the best way to topple the structures on which they rest is often to aim for the foundations. While Descartes didn't have *Angry Birds*, he did recognise that this kind of destruction was a useful analogy for his philosophical method, as he explains in the book:

> 'For the purposes of rejecting all my opinions, it will be enough if I find in each of them at least some reason for doubt. And to do this I will not need to run through them all individually, which would be an endless task. Once the foundations of a building are undermined, anything built on them collapses of its own accord; so I will go straight for the basic principles on which all my former beliefs rested.'

Aware that many of his beliefs were probably false, Descartes thought that, rather than go through them one by one, it was more practical to address those core beliefs on which the others rested. And so he aimed for the foundations, for the fundamental principle that our senses can provide us with accurate information about the world. After all, if it turns out that we can't trust the senses, what beliefs are we left with that we can call knowledge?

Through the book, Descartes decides that he can at least know that he exists, since there must be a thinking thing to be doing all this doubting ('I think, therefore I am'), and from that works his way to renewing his belief in his immortal soul (see Chapter 4) and in God. But for the sake of this chapter, and for the majority of philosophers who remain unconvinced by Descartes' resolution of the sceptical problem, we're interested in why he was so doubtful in the first place.

'Have you ever had a dream, Neo, that you were so sure was real? What if you were unable to wake from that dream? How would you know the difference between the dream world and the real world?'

Morpheus, *The Matrix* (The Wachowskis, 1999)

'No,' Stanley said to himself, 'this is all too strange. This can't be real.' And at last he came to the conclusion that had been on the tip of his tongue. He just hadn't found the words for it. 'I'm dreaming!' he yelled. 'This is all a dream!'

Narrator, *The Stanley Parable* (Galactic Cafe, 2013)

Arguments from illusion and hallucination may not be enough to convince some to consider the possibility that our senses can never be trusted. After all, we seem to be able to spot optical illusions with the very senses that deceived us – pull the stick out of the water and it no longer looks bent – and hallucinations are usually dismissable with some common sense. But we are all subject to even greater deception every single day. Or night.

The Magical Quest Starring Mickey Mouse (Capcom, 1992) begins with a game of catch. Goofy throws the ball to Mickey, and it hits him on the head and bounces off screen. Pluto runs off to fetch it, and disappears. Mickey runs after him and promptly falls off a cliff, at which point he finds himself in the first level of a side-scrolling journey to find his dog.

At the end of the game, Mickey defeats a giant Pete and is rewarded with the sight of his long-lost pet. Pluto runs up to him and starts to lick his face, and the screen fades to black. The next thing we know, Pluto is still licking Mickey's face but Mickey is in bed. 'But where am-?' he says. 'How did I-? . . . Gosh, I guess the whole thing musta been a dream!'

Many of us will have dreamed about bad things happening to the people we love and then woken up relieved to find that it wasn't as real as it felt at the time, that the experience didn't provide us with accurate information about the world. And this 'it was all just a dream' phenomenon is a common trope in media, from an entire series of the television show *Dallas* (David Jacobs, 1978–91) to the dreams within dreams of the film *Inception* (Christopher Nolan, 2010).

The trope is popular with Nintendo, with several entire games built around the concept: *Super Mario Bros. 2* (Nintendo, 1988), *Mario & Luigi Dream Team* (AlphaDream, 2013) and *The Legend of Zelda: Link's Awakening* (Nintendo, 1993). Other creators reveal smaller parts of their games to have been dreams; in *Heavy Rain* (Quantic Dream, 2010), the player leads a character called Madison through a traumatic experience in which a man breaks into her home and attacks her, only to have her wake up when he slits her throat.

As with hallucinations, vivid narrative forms like these games present dreamed and waking experiences side by side and enable us to consider the differences in a way that we can't when we're actually dreaming. When we're in the midst of a dream, we're not lucid enough to reflect and compare the experience to one had while awake. But we know that what we experience seems real at the time. Given that we are so easily deceived every night, how can we know that we're not being deceived right now? You could very well have dreamed up this entire book.

Descartes lays out this argument from dreaming in the *Meditations*:

> 'How often, asleep at night, am I convinced of just such familiar events – that I am here in my dressing-gown, sitting by the fire – when in fact I am lying undressed in bed! Yet at the moment my eyes are certainly wide awake when I look at this piece of paper; I shake my head and it is not asleep; as I stretch out and feel my hand I do so deliberately, and I know what I am doing. All this would not happen with such distinctness to someone asleep. Indeed! As if I did not remember other occasions when I have been tricked by exactly similar thoughts while asleep! As I think about this more carefully, I see plainly that there are never any sure signs by means of which being awake can be distinguished from being asleep.'

Longworth explains:

> 'So people think that when they're dreaming, at least some of the
> time they're having experiences that are very similar to real experi-
> ences of the world, but few if any people think that dreams are
> genuine experiences of the world. Roughly, the idea there is that
> we think that in principle, through either hallucination or through
> a very vivid dream, one could have experience that one couldn't
> tell apart from the experience one is now having. And that makes
> philosophers think that even if in fact one's experience now really
> is revealing how things are, they can't tell that they're not having
> a hallucination and they're not having a very vivid dream. And
> then they think that if you can't tell that, you're not in a position to
> come to know things on the basis of your experience.'

The argument from dreaming is similar to the argument from illusion and hallucination, but perhaps stronger. We can talk ourselves
out of an illusion like the stick in the water, or act so as to prove that
our senses were wrong. And real-life hallucinations seem not to be
as convincing – at least for people in good mental health – as they
can be in media like film and video games. But when we are dreaming we are thoroughly caught up in the experience.

Of course, when we wake up we seem able to immediately
dismiss those dream experiences as false. And dreams do seem to
differ somewhat from waking experiences, with their strange logic
and disjointed narratives. Specifics aside, however, the general argument requires only that we are sometimes deceived by our senses
and the extrapolation that we might not be able to trust them at all.
And so Descartes takes things one step further.

THE MALICIOUS DEMON/SUPER-SCIENTIST

> 'Good hunter, you've done well. The night is near its end. Now,
> I will show you mercy. You will die, forget the dream, and
> awake under the morning sun. You will be freed . . . from this
> terrible hunter's dream . . .'
>
> Gehrman, *Bloodborne* (FromSoftware, 2015)

'I will suppose therefore,' writes Descartes, 'that [. . .] some malicious demon of the utmost power and cunning has employed all his energies in order to deceive me. I shall think that the sky, the air, the earth, colours, shapes, sounds and all external things are merely the delusions of dreams which he has devised to ensnare my judgement. I shall consider myself as not having hands or eyes, or flesh, or blood or senses, but as falsely believing that I have all these things.'

If the likes of hallucinations and dreams don't convince us that our senses can give us totally convincing experiences that nevertheless completely fail to give us accurate information about the world, and that it's possible we are constantly being deceived, then Descartes asks us to imagine that every one of our experiences was constructed by an evil demon. Everything we have ever believed ourselves to see, hear, smell, taste or touch was actually an intentional deception.

Naturally, evil demons are fairly prevalent in video games, but few go so far as to construct entire worlds. One possible exception is *Bloodborne*, quoted above, a game that inspires long discussions about its lore. One popular theory states that its nightmarish world, Yharnam, is entirely the creation or imagination of the eldritch beings known as the Great Ones.

The evil demon might not seem particularly convincing to those of us who don't believe in such supernatural beings, but all we need to take from the argument is the idea that an external actor could implant in us experiences that fail to provide us with accurate information about the world. Longworth explains:

'The idea of the evil demon, in modern terms often replaced by a kind of super-scientist, is that we can at least imagine that someone gets stuck into your brain in such a way as to induce exactly the same kinds of brain states that one would be undergoing if one was having a genuine experience. So the idea is that you could imagine there being a kind of perfect match from the inside with how things seem in a genuine experience, induced by either a super being of some kind, a malicious demon, or a super-scientist, who is able to just get stuck into your neurology.'

Super-scientists: the modern evil demon

Again, we can find an example in one of *Fallout 3*'s vaults. On her quest to find her father, the Lone Wanderer pays a visit to Vault 112, whose original occupants have been kept alive in cryogenic pods. The Lone Wanderer must enter one of these pods, and in doing so finds herself transported to a sepia world, a virtual-reality simulation of a pre-war American suburb called Tranquility Lane.

The super-scientist responsible is Dr Stanislaus Braun, who has ensured that he is the only resident aware of the simulation, and uses this knowledge to play cruel games. The rest of the residents are totally oblivious to the fact that their bodies lie in cryogenic pods in a vault beneath a post-apocalyptic wasteland, believing that their sensory experiences are telling them how things actually are. The Lone Wanderer plays the role of philosophical sceptic, albeit with the benefit of having actually experienced the world that the rest cannot perceive, but fails to get through to any of the residents but one: 'We're not really here,' says Old Lady Dithers, 'we're not really talking. It's all made-up, make-believe. We're sleeping, dreaming. The dream became a nightmare. It has to end, it just has to. But we're not in charge. He is, and he doesn't want us to wake up.'

Fallout 3 isn't the only game to throw its protagonist into a simulation of suburban America. In *Saints Row IV* (Volition, 2013), the player-character – a gang leader who has managed to become President of the United States – gets beaten up by an alien overlord called Zinyak and wakes up in an armchair in what seems to be the 1950s, dressed in a sweater vest. The President initially acts as if everything is normal, but quickly grows suspicious. With the help of her (or, if you want, his) friend Kinzie she's eventually able to break out of the simulation.

Like Descartes' malicious demon, Braun and Zinyak use their powers to deceive their victims so that every experience they have is false. The Lone Wanderer and the President, unlike the residents of Vault 112, are able to remember a world beyond what they experience in these simulations, and are able to break out. But as with hallucinations and dreams in games, these narratives allow us to imagine the indistinguishability of this kind of experience from ones that did give us accurate information about the world, and consider the possibility that we could have been subject to such deceptions our entire lives.

While the player-character often has the power to leave the simulation – or, in the case of the *Assassin's Creed* series (Ubisoft, 2007–), to jump in and out at will – other characters who are oblivious to the virtual status of their world highlight the possibility that we could be fooled in a similar way, and that if we were we might have no way to prove it. Like Old Lady Dithers, we would be stuck suspecting that our senses were deceiving us but with no way to find out how the world really was.

And while Descartes considered himself to have resolved his philosophical scepticism with an argument that appeals to the existence of God – a God who would not allow us to be so deceived – many philosophers are unhappy with his solution. As Longworth puts it, 'He's kind of started trouble that he wasn't able to resolve to anyone else's satisfaction, and that people are still struggling with.'

THE SIMULATION ARGUMENT – OR, WHAT IF WE'RE ALL JUST CHARACTERS IN A VIDEO GAME?

> 'Dear MisSim, I've been having this recurring nightmare lately where I dream I'm just a simulation in a computer-generated city, and the denizens who created the simulation worship llamas and tell these really evil puns. Signed, Llama-Phobic.'
>
> A Sim, *SimCity 2000* (Maxis, 1994)

> 'See, if the Geth experience everything virtually, then you could only think you're in the real world. What if this – like, everything you're seeing now – is a simulation?'
>
> Joker, *Mass Effect 3* (BioWare, 2012)

As technology advances, so too do the imagined possibilities that can be used in sceptical arguments.

No Man's Sky (Hello Games, 2016) is a technological masterpiece, a game that enables players to explore a galaxy so large that one could never see more than the smallest fraction, all procedurally generated from a set of algorithms. Most of the aliens you can meet are procedurally generated too, no individual any more memorable than another. But two characters do recur, appearing occasionally in a space station called a Space Anomaly.

One of these characters is a Gek called Polo who encourages the player to try the different systems in the game – meet some aliens, earn some currency, kill some pirates – and rewards you for doing so. Their companion is an electronic Korvax called Nada, who offers directions, supplies and philosophical musings (partly written by Dan Griliopoulos, my co-author): 'Nada is, they reveal, a Korvax priest somehow freed of the group mind, now researching the origins of the galaxy. They express a bold theory – that our entire reality is something else's experiment. A simulation.'

No Man's Sky isn't the first video game to float this idea; it's a popular tongue-in-cheek reference in a format built on simulation. But this unimaginably huge simulated galaxy makes it that much easier to imagine a theoretical future in which programmers could create simulations as complex as the world we are in, and indeed that the world we are in might already be a complex simulation. Sean Murray, creative director on *No Man's Sky*, explains:

> 'This question we would get all the time from journalists that used to crack me up was they would finish interviews, so many times, with, "Does this make you a god, Sean Murray, in this universe?" And it's a cool question, but when you are developing a game and when you are so aware of the limits of that and the day-to-day tasks involved in creating that simulation, and the fakeness of it, and the realness of it in some ways, I guess, the reality of how that particular simulation sausage gets made, it's a slightly absurd question. But you get asked it so much that it's just a recurring theme throughout development, throughout the five years of making the game.'

Murray says that not many people have picked up on the **simulation hypothesis**, as voiced by Nada, as a theme in the game, but it definitely was. 'Like, in *No Man's Sky* we're sat there generating a universe for people to go and play in. So I guess that's definitely going to make you think about simulation theory.'

Nick Bostrom's simulation argument

Murray became convinced by this idea that it might be possible to have lived one's whole life as part of a simulation without knowing it was 'one of the most interesting things about the game' after a long conversation with SpaceX founder Elon Musk, who had taken an interest in the game. And Musk got the idea from a living Swedish philosopher called Nick Bostrom, who in 2003 published a paper titled 'Are You Living in a Computer Simulation?'*, whose abstract neatly summarises the argument:

> 'This paper argues that at least one of the following propositions is true: (1) the human species is very likely to go extinct before reaching a "posthuman" stage; (2) any posthuman civilization is extremely unlikely to run a significant number of simulations of their evolutionary history (or variations thereof); (3) we are almost certainly living in a computer simulation.'

The argument assumes that unless humanity almost inevitably goes extinct beforehand, technology will continue to advance until a point at which it is possible to run complex simulations of human history. And if it's possible to run one such simulation, then it should be possible to run many. So unless there's some reason why we would neglect to make use of this ability, then across all of time there will exist one non-simulated human history and many, many simulated human histories. And if those did exist, then by pure probability it would be incredibly unlikely that we were in the only non-simulated reality.

---

* http://www.simulation-argument.com/

Simulated people in a simulated world

Of course, this simulation argument makes one other fundamental assumption, i.e. that a simulated human could be conscious (see the explanation of **functionalism** in Chapter 4). As Bostrom puts it, 'Suppose that these simulated people are conscious (as they would be if the simulations were sufficiently fine-grained and if a certain quite widely accepted position in the philosophy of mind is correct).'

This assumption highlights an important distinction between the simulation argument and the Matrix-style scenarios that are little more than advanced versions of Descartes' malicious demon. In the latter, the deceived people exist in a world that they cannot perceive, like the residents of Vault 112 in their cryogenic pods. But in the simulation argument, those having the simulated experiences are simulations themselves.

Multiplayer first-person shooter *Destiny* (Bungie, 2014) explores this assumption that the simulated people must be conscious, albeit buried in the text of one of the collectable Grimoire cards. The cards describe a member of the cyborg species called the Vex, which a character called Chioma Esi has discovered to be running a simulation of her and her fellow researchers.

Esi: It's simulating us. Vividly. Elaborately. It's running a spectacularly high-fidelity model of a Collective research team studying a captive Vex entity.
Sundaresh: . . . How deep does it go?
Esi: Right now the simulated Maya Sundaresh is meeting with the simulated Chioma Esi to discuss an unexpected problem.
[indistinct sounds]
Sundaresh: There's no divergence? That's impossible. It doesn't have enough information.
Esi: It inferred. It works from what it sees and it infers the rest. I know that feels unlikely. But it obviously has capabilities we don't. It may have breached our shared virtual workspace . . . the neural links could have given it data . . .
Sundaresh: The simulations have interiority? Subjectivity?
Esi: I can't know that until I look more closely. But they act like us.

On another card, a character called Duane-McNiadh says, in apparent existential desperation, 'Maybe the simulations are just billboards! Maybe they don't have interiority! It's bluffing!' Knowing that these simulations are possible, and having had it pointed out in the previous card that, as the character Shim puts it, 'Odds are that we aren't our own originals', to deny that a simulation could be conscious is Duane-McNiadh's final hope at claiming his own originality.

If a simulated being can be conscious, then what Bostrom calls an 'ancestor simulation', a simulation of human history, would only need to be complex enough to make it realistic from the point of view of its inhabitants. 'Simulating the entire universe down to the quantum level is obviously infeasible,' writes Bostrom, 'unless radically new physics is discovered. But in order to get a realistic simulation of human experience, much less is needed – only whatever is required to ensure that the simulated humans, interacting in normal human ways with their simulated environment, don't notice any irregularities.'

Murray points out that one of Musk's arguments for the possibility that we are living in a simulation seems to boil down to, 'Isn't it very convenient that the other stars are so far away?' And this kind of suspicion that our world is less complex than we believe is reflected in Nada:

'Nada is plugged into a bank of instruments as I approach. Suns flare and die on the panels, voxel-molecules pop in and out of existence in matched pairs. I see error messages reeling on the readouts and am perplexed.

'Nada sees me and explains. There are repeating patterns all across the galaxy, identical elements where there should be endless divergence. This cannot be a coincidence. Did the Atlas do this? Across the room, Polo giggles.'

Of course, Nada's efforts are in vain. Even if they strongly believe themselves to be in a simulation, they can't prove it. They can never exit into the world inhabited by whatever advanced being created theirs, and just as you can end the game by switching off your

PlayStation, so too could that advanced being shut down the simulation. As Murray puts it, 'If we're AI then we're not gonna exist anymore once the simulation ends. So that's a bad outcome.'

As Sundaresh puts it on one of the Grimoire cards, 'We have to act as if we're in the real universe, not one simulated by the specimen. Otherwise we might as well give up.' And Murray seems to agree: 'I personally don't believe that we're in a simulation, for various different reasons, but let's assume that we are. Then obviously, while sitting in that simulation, having a philosophical debate about how we would feel about living in a simulation, is a naturally surreal and pointless conversation.'

Perhaps it doesn't even make sense to include the simulation argument with the other sceptical arguments – deception by the senses in cases of illusion and hallucination, the argument from dreaming, the possibility of evil demons or super-scientists – in which philosophers worry about the gap between what we perceive and what's really there. If these simulated beings cannot exist outside of their simulated worlds, then perhaps there is no mismatch between what seems to them to be the case and the way things actually are. Perhaps the simulation hypothesis isn't a sceptical argument at all but a **metaphysical** one, one about the nature of the world rather than what we can know. But for more on that, head over to the next chapter, on virtual reality.

Limbo, virtually.

Luisa: Are you okay? Did you land funny?

Maria: I'm fine, landed on my head. It's a bit sore— Oh, wait, Luisa. Feel your face!

Luisa: Why would I? Are those goggles? I'm wearing goggles! Why can't we see them?

Maria: Maybe we were we doing some serious drain unblocking?

Luisa: These don't feel like those sort of goggles. More like those goggles they wore in *The Matrix*. Heavy duty.

Maria: Oh, sure. Real virtuality? I have a Virtual Boy at home. Though I never opened it. Should we try taking them off?

Luisa: I don't know if we can. Or should.

Maria: We can – I can feel the straps.

Luisa: Well, maybe just one of us should take them off . . . let's decide by Janken.

Maria: Sounds good to me okay

Together: Rock, Paper . . . Scissors!

Maria: Agh!

Luisa: Okay, I guess it's you. Good luck in there.

Maria: Sigh. Okay, taking it off . . . It's mainly black. There are incomprehensible objects moving through eleven perceivable dimensions. I don't think it's Manhattan, I can't smell the knishes. There's a four-dimensional sign that says 'This ends your trip of a long friendship.' That's it.

Luisa: Well, I could certainly do with a vacation.

Maria: I'm putting that back on. I quite like this reality we're in. Free mushrooms!

Luisa: Does it matter that they're not real mushrooms in the real world? That we're not experiencing baseline reality?

Maria: What would make you say that? Why is all that blackness more real than this nice world, with the blue sky and the giant mushrooms? And have you tried them? They're better than real!

Luisa: The faces put me off too much. Oh, watch out – another chapter!

CHAPTER THREE

Virtual reality: a real reality?

....

'Cyberspace. A consensual hallucination experienced daily by billions of legitimate operators, in every nation . . .'

William Gibson, *Neuromancer* (1984)

'The nursery was silent. It was empty as a jungle glade at hot high noon. The walls were blank and two dimensional. Now, as George and Lydia Hadley stood in the center of the room, the walls began to purr and recede into crystalline distance, it seemed, and presently an African veldt appeared, in three dimensions, on all sides, in color reproduced to the final pebble and bit of straw. The ceiling above them became a deep sky with a hot yellow sun. George Hadley felt the perspiration start on his brow.'

Ray Bradbury, *The Illustrated Man* (1951)

If video games are a young medium, then **virtual reality** (VR) is a babe in arms. If you've ever tried or witnessed a demonstration of one of these devices – the Oculus Rift, the HTC Vive, the PlayStation VR – you'll know that there are still a few kinks. The headsets are cumbersome, and those with trailing wires can be downright dangerous. You need a fair amount of money, time and space to set things up. The more immersive the intended experience, the more necessarily isolating. Your eyes and ears are shut off from other people in the room (which comes with its own set of dangers) so that they can focus on virtual sights and sounds instead. And once you are immersed, it's very difficult not to make a fool of yourself.

VIRTUAL WORLD, REAL EMBARRASSMENTS

Even industry veterans aren't exempt. 'I was playing a game and there was something on a low table,' says Richard Lemarchand, a game designer and game design professor perhaps most well known for his work on the *Uncharted* series. 'I bent forward to pick it up and I slightly overbalanced, and I put out my hand to support myself on a table that wasn't there.'

Ronnie O'Sullivan is a professional snooker and pool player, with multiple world records. But when he was handed an HTC Vive headset and handheld controllers and told he was holding a pool cue, he was apparently so convinced by the virtual world he found himself in that he mistook the virtual pool table for a non-virtual one. As he had done so many times before, he put out his hand to lean . . . and fell flat on his face.*

The virtual world of Unseen Diplomacy

Katie Goode, a game designer who specialises in VR, sees this kind of thing all the time. Her new VR game *Unseen Diplomacy* (Triangular Pixels, 2016) is currently only playable on the HTC Vive, which lets players walk around a designated play area with a headset on and tracked controllers in their hands and have those actions represented in the virtual world. For some players, that level of visual, audio and spatial immersion is all too convincing. Goode explains:

> 'There's a ledge in the game. You just walk along this high ledge, and there's nothing stopping you from actually just walking into the space below you. Like, you don't fall in the game or anything. But people, you can see them actually struggling trying to stay on this really, really thin ledge, even though nothing would happen if they stepped off. They can't force themselves to step off, either. We've had a few people play the game and say, "I knew it was VR, and I saw the ledge, and I really wanted to step off it but I really couldn't. Like, I could not do it." '

This power over our psychology is one of the reasons that VR is so popular with those kinds of players interested in new kinds of games.

* http://www.kotaku.co.uk/2016/10/13/ronnie-osullivan-falls-over-playing-vr-pool

And it raises interesting philosophical questions. What's actually happening when we immerse ourselves in a virtual world? In cases like those described above are players being deceived by their own senses? Are all virtual-reality experiences illusory, or just some? And what does that say about the value of virtual worlds?

False impressions – is VR an illusion?

We talked about illusory experiences in Chapter 2, when demonstrating why someone like Descartes might want to doubt that our senses can really be trusted. An illusion occurs when a person perceives an object and that object appears to them to be other than it actually is. A hallucination occurs when we have a perceptual experience that is caused by no external object, when we see something that isn't really there.

When we experience an illusion or a hallucination, our senses seem to be telling us something false, and it's easy to see why we might assume that's what's happening when we experience VR. 'I guess there's a natural tendency to assimilate experience inside of virtual reality to a kind of hallucination,' says philosopher David Chalmers, currently a professor at New York University and the Australian National University, 'where you're made to think that all this is going on out there in the external world when none of it is happening.'

If you were trying to describe the experience of immersion in a VR world to somebody who'd never heard of it before, you might tell them that it's like you're in a particular environment (perhaps standing on a high ledge) but you're not, and that there appear to be objects (like a low table) around you but there aren't. You might want to describe it as an expensive technology-induced illusion, to posit virtual as the opposite of real.

But Chalmers thinks that you'd be wrong. He has a theory that he has called **virtual realism**, which states that virtual worlds are real worlds, their objects are real objects, and the experiences you have in VR are not illusions. Virtual reality is a kind of reality, just a different kind from that in which we spend most of our time.

> 'What is real? How do you define "real"? If you're talking about what you can feel, what you can smell, what you can taste and see, then "real" is simply electrical signals interpreted by your brain.'
>
> Morpheus (*The Matrix*, 1999)

To explain why he thinks that virtual objects are real, Chalmers appeals to their causal role:

> 'One reason why people want to say none of this is real is, "Well, the objects aren't really there. When I perceive an elephant there's no object out there which is causing my elephant experience. It's like a hallucination." But I want to say there is something which is bringing about your experience. It's just a virtual object. It's a data structure on a computer, but that really is bringing about my experience."

Unlike a hallucination, Chalmers says, an experience in VR does have an external cause: 'I call them **"digital objects"**. You know, there's a digital elephant or a virtual elephant, and a virtual body like your avatar, and they all exist on the computer and they're all interacting.' These digital objects act much like physical objects in the world outside of VR, existing externally to you and causing you to have certain internal experiences.

At this stage, technology limits what kinds of experiences we can get from VR worlds and objects. We can see and hear virtual objects, but we are only just beginning to be able to touch them. Smell seems to be relegated to joke experiences (like the Nosulus Rift, which provided players of *South Park: The Fractured but Whole* [Ubisoft San Francisco, in development] with the scent of farts), and it'll likely be a long time before we can taste in VR. Still, science fiction shows that this kind of virtual world is at least conceivable. If in the future these virtual objects are able to provide you with all the same experiences as non-virtual ones, it seems like it'll be more difficult to argue that they are somehow inferior.

Chalmers lays out virtual and non-virtual reality (otherwise known as the reality in which most of us live) side by side to make the similarities clear:

> 'If it was all in my mind it would be a hallucination, but in physical reality there's physical processes outside my mind bringing about all this, in virtual reality there's digital processes bringing about all the experiences in my mind. And one's taking place on a computer, the physical reality is not.'*

Structurally, these worlds are different, but they are both worlds. Lemarchand seems inclined to agree, in principle:

> 'I think that video games inherit a tradition of simulation from our thinking about computer models of things, and I think that partly comes from our thinking in the 80s and 90s about virtual reality, the idea that there is this simulated world in the computer that we can enter by donning a VR headset and some data gloves, and then we are kind of present in another place, as if we had teleported to an alien world, or as if we had fallen asleep and were now inside of a dream.'

We are used to thinking and talking about these game worlds as if they were real other worlds that we can enter and experience, separate from us, filled with objects that cause us to have certain perceptions. So why might we find it difficult to commit to the stance that VR worlds are real, that those experiences we have in them are not illusions but real, veridical perceptions of real objects?

A WORK OF FICTION

With VR worlds in particular – and game worlds in general – Chalmers thinks that some of our reluctance might come from confusion over the meaning of the word 'fiction', which suggests

---

* Unless, as discussed at the end of Chapter 2, the reality we know is itself a simulation.

something is false and not true and real. After all, we're inclined to think of the worlds in which many video game stories are set as fictional worlds: Daventry (*King's Quest*) (Sierra on-line, 1984), or Tamriel (*The Elder Scrolls*) (Bethesda, 1994), or Kanto and Johto and Sinnoh (*Pokémon*) (Game Freak, 1996). *Grand Theft Auto V's* (Rockstar North, 2013) Los Santos is similar to but not quite a replica of Los Angeles, so surely if any world is fictional it's that one? And we're inclined to think that 'fictional' means roughly the same thing as 'not real'.

'That's a common view about virtual reality, and video games more generally,' says Chalmers. 'People think that basically what you're interacting with when you interact with VR or with a video game world is a fictional world.' It's easy to see why when we consider games that are set in worlds that we already know from other media, like books: 'Maybe we're in a VR where we're actually wandering around Middle Earth, and then you might think, "Well, Middle Earth isn't real. We're just inhabiting some fictional landscape and going through the motions of being in such a world when none of it really exists."'

The Lord of the Rings is a work of fiction, its setting of Middle Earth the invention of its author J. R. R. Tolkien. Frodo and his friends are fictional characters, their experiences over the course of their adventure imagined by Tolkien and written down for readers to imagine in turn. So if you were to find yourself wandering around in a *Lord of the Rings*-themed VR game, wouldn't that virtual Middle Earth also be a fiction? Says Chalmers:

> 'In the case of a virtual reality or a video game which is based on a fiction like *Lord of the Rings*, maybe there's two different levels of interpretation. There are some digital objects here, which are perfectly real, which I'm interacting with. And then there's an interpretation of all those as being on Middle Earth, being Gandalf and so on, and that's all associated with a fiction.'

There's a difference, says Chalmers, between the status of these objects as real things that gives us real experiences, and the status of these objects as really those things they represent. That Hobbit house is a real (digital) object causing real (non-illusory) experiences in you, but it's not really Frodo's home. He compares it to playing pretend: 'Maybe it's a bit like I could be playing a *Lord of the Rings* game with my friends, and I'm playing Frodo and someone else is playing Gandalf. Then when I interact with that person it's a real person I'm interacting with, they're really right here, but it's a fiction that they're Gandalf.'

LAWBREAKERS

The view that virtual worlds are fictional in a basic metaphysical (i.e. about the nature of things) sense can be called **virtual fictionalism**: virtual objects are fictional objects, and virtual experiences involve illusory perception of a fictional world. Chalmers counters this view with his '**virtual digitalism**', which states that virtual objects are real digital objects, and virtual experiences involve non-illusory (i.e. veridical, accurate, true) perception of a digital world. 'It's a real world that we're accurately perceiving as virtual,' he says, 'not a fictional world that we're inaccurately perceiving as physical.'

The world we enter may behave differently than the one we're used to, but it's still a world, no less real, no less able to cause us to have experiences that come from outside of ourselves. And when all you require for reality is that the world in question has that kind of independence and causal role then all sorts of worlds can be real, even ones that behave quite differently from our own. If the world isn't physical, it doesn't have to obey the laws of physics. As Goode says of *Unseen Diplomacy*:

'It was actually originally for a game jam. The theme was to use the room space, and I thought, "Well, it's a really big room space for a game but really tiny for a real-world room. Like, it's only four metres by three metres. I mean, you can't fit a whole world inside that. So how do you do that?" And so that's when we came up with the idea of, when you are going into a new room the old room behind you loads out, and the only room that ever exists in the world is the room that you're currently in. And we change the room in front of you and behind you depending on which door button you press, basically.'

Because the play space in the physical world is necessarily limited (for the safety of the player's physical body as much as for any other reason) the developers at Triangular Pixels had to find a way to condense the larger virtual world in which they wanted to set their game. And so, their virtual world is set up such that only the current room exists, independent from the player and causing experiences in them, with other rooms brought into existence when needed. 'There's some slightly more interesting parts in the air ducts and the floor spaces,' Goode adds, 'Where we're actually changing parts of the room in front and behind you, as well, so that you can turn round in the same area and come back on yourself. So you don't just keep going clockwise, you can turn round anticlockwise as well.'

This kind of spatial trickery might lead you to conclude that the world of *Unseen Diplomacy* isn't real. After all, the world we know doesn't have rooms that pop in and out of existence, and paths that change so that you can turn around and find yourself somewhere new. But this world is just a different kind of world, with different laws. 'It's not an illusion,' says Goode. 'This is just how this world works. It's a fact of this world.'

A whole new (possible) world

Of course, an immediate question is what kinds of facts can apply to these different yet real worlds. Probably anyone who's read *Harry Potter* or watched *Doctor Who* will find it easy enough to get their head around a world in which a door can lead to different rooms, but what other kinds of non-physical laws can a world withstand? How far abstracted from the world we know can another world be? Chalmers explains:

> 'There's many different "possible worlds", as philosophers put it. Our world is just one. There are worlds with completely different laws of physics, completely different dynamics. And some of the video game worlds we interact with, you know, there are two-dimensional worlds, worlds with anti-gravity. So a world with coloured shapes and certain basic laws, it's a possible way a real world could be. Maybe it's not our world,

but I don't see anything about that that means it would be less real.'

When philosophers talk about **possible worlds**, they're talking about ways that the world could have been. In one possible world, you never read this book. In another, maybe you're the one who wrote it. And, of course, we can go much further, with possible worlds in which gender doesn't exist or everything is black and white. Every time we play a game or watch a film or read a book set in a world in which some people have magic or superpowers, we're imagining a different possible world in which the laws that we know can be broken. 'I think laws help for stability for certain things,' says Chalmers, 'and they help individuate objects as kinds of things that you can interact with in certain ways, but it doesn't seem that laws of nature are absolutely required for reality. At least, you can have a fair amount of chaos, at least occasional miracles, certain kinds of break-down, while still saying things are real.'

A large proportion of people on the planet are perfectly happy with the idea that the world in which we live has laws that can be broken in special cases, like with the parting of the Red Sea or the resurrection of Jesus Christ. If we can conceive of a real world in which gravity can be temporarily set aside and death is only final for some, then why shouldn't a world in which the layout of a building changes around you be just as real?

Where am I?

As well as the state of the world itself, we also have to consider the state of the player, and how different the player's experiences can be from the way in which they're used to experiencing the non-virtual world. While many virtual-reality games and experiences give the player a first-person perspective on the world, which feels familiar to the subjective way in which we view our own world, some provide a third-person perspective in which the player can see the avatar they're controlling from a distance. Given that Chalmers' argument that virtual worlds are real rests in part on the causal relationship between virtual objects and the player, does it matter whether the player is located 'within' their avatar or – as it were – without? Says Chalmers:

> 'I'm inclined to think that at least a lot of this will still apply. And certainly the objects will still be real, the body will still be real. There's questions about where are you, "Where am I now?" Maybe that decomposes now into two questions. "Where is my body? When I move my arms, what is moving? When I walk around, what's moving? The body." And, "Where am I seeing from? Well, that's over here." So maybe I'm bilocated. I have two different locations.'

The notion of bilocation might seem to make Chalmers' theory a little more difficult to accept, given how far removed it seems from our usual experiences. But, as we touch on in Chapter 5, there's a sense in which we already are bilocated, with different spatial parts in different spaces. Stand astride a border and you can be in two countries at once. Stub a toe on your left foot and you can be in pain in one location and not in pain in another. Already your visual experiences happen in a different place than some parts of your body, so it's not too much of a leap to imagine those visual experiences taking place even further away.

This seems to work by separating the self, which has the experiences, from the body. After all, in the virtual world the avatars we control may be quite different from the bodies we usually inhabit – they might be a different shape or gender or species – and when we move from the non-virtual to the virtual world we are switching from one body to another. 'I'm inclined to think there's one self in the two different realities,' says Chalmers. 'There's just two bodies but one person. Likewise, I don't want to say there's a virtual self. Again, there's a virtual body, but there's just one self who's got the capacity to inhabit both environments.'

THE MATRIX AS METAPHYSICS

Neo: This can't be.
Morpheus: Be what? Be real?

The Matrix (The Wachowskis, 1999)

Think of Neo, who until the events of *The Matrix* has lived his entire life in a VR world. When he leaves the Matrix, he finds himself in a different body than the one he was using mere moments before. Before he had a body dressed in black, with a head of dark hair. Now he finds himself in a body submerged in a tank full of some sticky substance, naked and bald. Chalmers once again:

> 'Inside the Matrix he has digital hair. Outside the Matrix he has non-digital, physical hair. And likewise he's got a digital body, his avatar in the Matrix, and a physical body outside the Matrix. I think the intuitive thing to say is there's just one person there, Neo, who has both bodies, who inhabits both environments, goes back and forth from interacting with one environment to the other.'

We discussed Matrix-type scenarios (from *Fallout 3* [Bethesda, 2008] and *Saints Row IV* [Volition, 2013]) in Chapter 2, comparing them to Descartes' suggestion that all of our perceptions might be falsehoods conjured up by a malevolent demon. There, the notion that we – like Neo – might be living in a virtual world was framed as a sceptical hypothesis, i.e. one meant to demonstrate what we cannot know. But Chalmers thinks that we do not need to be sceptics even if it's possible that we're just brains in vats, and reframes the Matrix as a metaphysical hypothesis – one not about knowledge but the nature of the world – instead. 'I still think I cannot rule out the hypothesis that I am in a Matrix,' writes Chalmers in his paper 'The Matrix as Metaphysics'.* 'But I think that even if I am in a Matrix, I am still in Tucson, I am still sitting at my desk, and so on. So the hypothesis that I am in a Matrix is not a sceptical hypothesis. The same goes for Neo. At the beginning of the film, if he thinks "I have hair", he is correct. If he thinks "It is sunny outside", he is correct.'

The experiences that Neo had throughout his life until he left the Matrix were not illusory experiences. When he looked up at a clear blue sky he was not undergoing an illusion. As Chalmers clarifies later in the paper, in response to a possible objection that a brain in

* http://consc.net/papers/matrix.html

a vat would be deluded to think that it was walking in the sun when it was actually alone in a dark room, 'The *brain* is alone in a dark room. But this does not imply that the *person* is alone in a dark room.' Neo's physical body may be submerged in that tank, but his digital avatar is walking in real digital sunlight, and Neo's experiences on that sunny day are real veridical experiences taking place in a real digital world.

Non-illusory perception of a digital world

Of course, there are still some things that Neo was wrong about. But where those who use Matrix-type scenarios as part of a sceptical hypothesis suggest that he should discount everything he has ever believed, Chalmers would say that most of his beliefs still hold. The only beliefs he need change are those about the underlying nature of the world in which he lives; the Matrix is a metaphysical hypothesis. If people discover themselves to be in a Matrix, says Chalmers, 'They should not reject their ordinary beliefs about the external world. At most, they should come to revise their beliefs about the underlying nature of their world: they should come to accept that external objects are made of bits, and so on. These beings are not massively deluded: most of their ordinary beliefs about their world are correct.'

If we discovered that the world in which we live was actually a digital world, its objects digital objects, then our feelings towards the world might change – we might be curious about the 'next world up', if there is one, and worried that whoever created the world might decide one day to shut it down – but its metaphysical status should not. Those objects are made of something different from what we thought they were, but they still provide us with the same experiences. We can still eat the digital pancakes, read the digital newspaper, lie down in the digital bed. Of course, the virtual worlds we can enter through an Oculus Rift, HTC Vive or PlayStation VR are not quite so advanced yet, but they do contain digital objects that cause in us real experiences. They are real worlds in which we can choose to spend our time.

A GAME FOR LIFE: TEMPORARY VS PERMANENT VR

Though the Matrix is quite different from the kinds of worlds we visit in current VR games and experiences, it's a useful point of reference. If we can understand how someone like Chalmers can argue that what he calls '**permanent VR**' (like the Matrix) is a kind of reality, then perhaps we can expand that to **temporary VR**, which is what we're talking about when we talk about VR games and experiences.

> 'Permanent VR is really the one I started with in thinking about this stuff. This is the idea that you've been in the VR all along, maybe you've been in the Matrix, and then what should we say about the reality of all that? Then it is our ordinary ground-level reality. It's what we've always been exposed to, is digital objects. And if I see a table, then it's going to be a digital table. And that's going to be the standard case for me. And then I think it never was an illusion. It was all real. My word "table" always meant "digital table", "table in the Matrix".'

Again, rather than reassess all of his beliefs, Neo need only accept that he was wrong about the underlying nature of the objects around him and – if he ever thought about such a thing – the existence of another world in what you might call the 'next level up'. He was in the dark about the existence of his non-virtual body, but that doesn't mean his whole life was a lie. His experiences were not illusions, and his beliefs were not false. Most of the beliefs he held about the tables with which he has interacted throughout his life, for example, are still true after he learns about the Matrix, because what he calls 'table' has always meant 'digital table in the Matrix'.

Spot the illusion

The possibility for false beliefs and illusory experiences comes with temporary VR. If a person enters virtual reality for the first time without fully understanding how it works, they might not realise that the objects they now see before them are digital. They might still believe that they are in the non-virtual world. If that's the case, their beliefs about the objects may be false. They may perceive a virtual table as non-virtual, in which case they would – at least at first – be experiencing an illusion.

Even players who understand how VR works can fall prey to illusory experiences, as with Lemarchand trying to catch himself on a virtual table. In the future we may have virtual tables that somehow give us the same kind of tactile experiences as non-virtual tables, in which case Lemarchand would not have been wrong to perceive the virtual table in that way. But he falsely perceived the virtual table as non-virtual, which means his experience was illusory.

'I've fallen asleep with the kit on,' admits Goode, 'and then you wake up and you think you're either still dreaming or you think that things have gone very strange. I've tried to put my hand on the bed to get up or something, the virtual bed, and I'm like, "What the . . .", and it takes you a few moments. In that few moments, does that mean that the world is an illusion to you?' Chalmers would say yes: 'Let's say you don't know you're in VR. Then you might think it's a physical table but it's not, it's a virtual table. So that is a case where then you can get illusions, because you take it to be the ordinary kind of thing you're used to but it's a different kind of thing.'

Expertise vs immersion

So yes, there can be illusions – namely when the user of temporary VR thinks that they're perceiving non-virtual objects – but those cases are the exception. As users become more experienced with VR, and they learn the difference between the virtual and non-virtual world, they no longer perceive one as the other and thus no longer have illusory experiences. We can presume that Ronnie O'Sullivan had had little experience with VR, but if he spent more time playing virtual pool he would gain the experience necessary to tell the difference between a virtual and non-virtual pool table. Chalmers explains: 'I think over time as you become more and more sophisticated, you know there's a physical reality, you know there's a virtual reality, and you perceive the virtual objects as virtual. If that's right, then even in temporary VR over time your experience can become non-illusory.'

In permanent VR, there's no illusion because the user (like Neo before the events of the film) has no experience of the non-virtual world and so does not mistake the virtual for the non-virtual. In temporary VR, there's no illusion (in most cases) because the user has the expertise necessary to know the difference between the virtual and the non-virtual, and knows that they are perceiving virtual objects when they are in the virtual world.

Perhaps it seems odd that the cause of Lemarchand's illusory experience was the celebrated 'immersive' nature of VR, i.e. the power these worlds have to make the user forget that they're no longer in the non-virtual world, and that in order to avoid illusions we need to break free from this kind of immersion. But as we get used to more and more technologically impressive VR, we should be able to have far more interesting experiences in virtual worlds without the need for any of them to be illusory.

Smoke and mirrors

Right at the end of the nineteenth century, Auguste and Louis Lumière made a fifty-second black-and-white film called *L'arrivée d'un train en gare de La Ciotat* (roughly, 'The arrival of a train at La Ciotat station'). The film shows the train coming into view, approaching the camera before pulling to a stop. You may have heard of this film, if not by name, because of the legend that surrounds its first screening: that spectators in these early days of cinema mistook the film for a real train moving towards them and were so afraid that they ran away. 'If that is true about movies then it would be a parallel,' says Chalmers. 'At first you take it to exist in the physical world and then you realise, "Well, it doesn't exist in the physical world, but maybe it has its own kind of reality."' Sources differ on whether the story is true or just an urban legend, but it seems plausible that the first cinemagoers had some illusory experiences before they got used to the medium.

On reflection

Perhaps a more straightforward parallel is mirrors. Few of us will remember the first time we used a mirror, but we've probably seen infants or pets confused by the appearance of another baby or cat on the other side of the pane of glass. And even those of us who've been looking in mirrors every day of our lives for years can occasionally be temporarily fooled, perhaps on first entering a room that has mirrors lining an entire wall to give the illusion of space. Illusions are possible, but with expertise they become less likely. Says Chalmers:

> 'The first time you look in a mirror you might have the illusion there's something there on the other side. But then you get used to mirrors, you become sophisticated about them, and after a while you no longer perceive that there's something on the other side. You realise it's a mirror, and you perceive something here on this side of the mirror where it is, and that's not an illusion. And I think maybe, over time, an experienced user of VR will likewise perceive things as going on in the virtual world where they really are.'

According to Chalmers, whether or not the experience of looking in a mirror is illusory depends on what the viewer thinks they see. If you think you are looking at your identical twin through a pane of glass, then you're having an illusory experience. But once you understand the nature of reflections, your experience is no longer illusory. Instead, you're having a veridical perception of your reflection.

So too with VR, if you think that you're looking at a non-virtual table (perhaps because you woke up without realising you were still wearing a VR headset, or because somebody put one on your head without telling you that's what they were doing) then your experience is illusory. But once you understand the nature of VR, the experiences you have of those virtual objects are veridical; they give you true information about the real (digital) objects you perceive.

Cognitive penetration of perception:
When what we know changes what we see

Around the same time as the Lumière brothers were wowing first-time cinemagoers with the wonders of film, a psychologist called George Stratton was exploring a different kind of visual phenomenon. He conducted experiments on himself that involved a special set of glasses that used mirrors to invert the images his eyes received, so that he viewed the world as if it were upside down.

Stratton wore these glasses for several days, and slept in a blindfold so that his eyes would have no opportunity to go back to perceiving the world has they had done before. At first, his experience was as confusing and uncomfortable as you might expect. But after several days of wearing the glasses he found that he had adapted to his new way of seeing the world, so much so that when he removed the glasses he had to adapt back to normality.*

Fifty years later, an Austrian professor called Theodor Erismann performed a similar experiment on his student Ivo Kohler, who later wrote about the experience.† Apparently it took Kohler ten days to adapt to his glasses, by which point he was able to go about his business navigating the world as easily as he had done before. Over the course of the experiment, he seemed to steadily gain the ability to perceive the world as normal.

How were Stratton and Kohler able to adjust to these inverted images? Did they continue to perceive the world as upside down but gain the ability to then interpret that perception in ways conducive to responding appropriately? Or did their knowledge of the inverted situation in which they found themselves influence the perception itself, so that by the end of the experiment they really were perceiving the world as normal?

Cognitive orientation
The view that our knowledge and beliefs can change how we perceive the world is called '**cognitive penetration of perception**', and it has been a controversial thesis in psychology and philosophy for decades. The main worry from those who oppose the principle seems to be a sceptical one: if our beliefs can change our perceptions, then how

---

* As a side note, Stratton also tried experiments in which an arrangement of mirrors enabled him to view the world as if from a position floating above his own body, which is surprisingly similar to the example of third-person perspective VR experiences.
† https://www.theguardian.com/education/2012/nov/12/improbable-research-seeing-upside-down

can we trust our perceptions to give us accurate information about the world?

Chalmers is inclined to believe that our knowledge and beliefs can change our perceptions, and he calls the process of adaption **'cognitive orientation'**. With experience, says Chalmers, we orientate ourselves, consciously or unconsciously, to the new mode of perception. Stratton and Kohler orientated from perceiving the world as upside down to perceiving it as the right way up. When we realise that we're looking in a mirror, we orientate from perceiving objects on the other side of a glass to perceiving objects on this side. And with virtual reality, we orientate from incorrectly perceiving virtual objects as non-virtual (like Lemarchand did with the table) to correctly perceiving them as virtual.

With the current technological limitations, cognitive orientation to VR involves cognitive orientation to different ways of perceiving and moving through a world. We have to orientate to the fact that we can walk through virtual objects and people, and that we probably can't stop and smell the flowers. But perhaps one day we'll be able to enter VR experiences like the Matrix, in which virtual objects have all the same causal powers as non-virtual ones and cognitive orientation will be that much easier. And perhaps then we'd find it easier to accept Chalmers' theory that the experiences we have in virtual worlds are just as real as those we have outside of them.

THE VALUE OF THE VIRTUAL

> 'Are you telling me that you were going to launch a computer world, filled with people, into space?'
> Simon Jarrett, *Soma* (Frictional Games, 2015)

The majority of science-fiction survival-horror game *Soma* takes place in a research base at the bottom of the ocean. The protagonist, Simon Jarrett, awakens in this base and soon discovers that a comet has wiped out the majority of life on the surface, leaving the few human survivors stranded under the sea. Simon's goal in the game is a lofty one: to help ensure the continuation of the human species.

The problem, of course, is that most of the survivors are dead by the time Simon reaches them. But before they died, several of them submitted to future-tech brain scans that digitised their mental states and – so the theory goes (see Chapter 5) – enabled them to live on through continuation of their psychology. One of the survivors, Dr Catherine Chun, created a home for these digital humans, housed on a capsule designed to be launched away from the devastated earth and into space: a virtual simulated reality known as the ARK.

We can assume that the earth at this point is unlivable; a shot of the planet at the end of the game reveals an apocalyptic surface world. The underwater base is potentially still viable but is devoid of almost all human life, populated by robots and monsters. The ARK, on the other hand, contains a sunny forest, a gentle stream and a city designed with Utopia in mind. 'Looks a whole lot comfier than this place,' says Simon when he sees early designs on a computer in the research base.

We're never given specific details about what life in the ARK would be like, but we can assume that those digital humans aboard will be able to have many of the same kinds of experiences as they had in the non-virtual world. When Simon asks, 'Cath, what's it like inside the ARK – is it like a movie or virtual reality?', she replies, 'No, of course not. It's, you know, like real life. But slightly better. Pleasant temperature, clean air, good weather.' We can assume that those living on the ARK will be able to feel that temperature on their skin, taste that air, and have all sorts of other sensual experiences just as they would have done on earth.

In almost every way, the ARK sounds a lot more pleasant than the few remaining livable spaces on earth. The difference, of course, is that it's virtual. Setting aside the question of whether digital copies of their mental states are enough to ensure their personal survival (see Chapter 5), the people who agree to move to the ARK are accepting a virtual world as their new reality. Sure, the world they're leaving behind is almost entirely destroyed, the people they knew either killed or transferred into the virtual world along with them, but isn't there something missing from the ARK? Doesn't its virtuality make it somehow inferior?

Coming around to the ARK

A conversation that Simon has towards the end of the game seems to present this point of view. While on his quest to find the ARK and ensure that it makes it into space, he comes across what is probably the only biologically (rather than digitally) alive human being left on the planet: Sarah Lindwall, hooked up to a life support machine. Understandably, she asks Simon to put her out of her misery:

Sarah Lindwall: Simon, this fucking sucks. I don't want to live like this.
Simon: Shouldn't we be doing something to keep you alive?
Sarah: Why?
Simon: You're the last human. I just find it disrespectful to our entire history not to fight this. Sure we have the ARK, but you're the real deal.
Sarah: Thanks. That's probably the best compliment I've ever got. But the truth is that the ARK is all we have. We'll have to accept second best, you know?

The language that Simon and Sarah use is revealing. Simon describes Sarah – a biological human living in the non-virtual world – in contrast with the ARK, as 'the real deal', suggesting that the ARK is somehow not real. And Sarah says the ARK is 'second best', assigning it a lower value than the non-virtual world.

At the end of the game, however, when Simon successfully launches the ARK and realises that he has to stay in the underwater base while a copy of him flies off in the virtual Utopia, he's furious to be left behind in the non-virtual world. His journey through the game (and thus the player's alongside him) has been about coming around to the idea that the ARK is the best place for him to be, despite its virtuality. It's a frustrating ending for the player who has guided Simon towards what he thought was his goal, but that only proves the effectiveness of the entire thought experiment. If you thought that the non-virtual world was intrinsically better, you would be happy for him.

Robert Nozick's experience machine

The thought experiment of the ARK is similar to one raised by a philosopher called Robert Nozick in his 1974 book *Anarchy, State, and Utopia*. Considering the philosophical position known as '**ethical hedonism**', the idea that our moral goal should be to maximise pleasure, Nozick proposed a pleasure-maximising device that he called an '**experience machine**':

> 'Suppose there was an experience machine that would give you any experience you desired. Super-duper neuropsychologists could stimulate your brain so that you would think and feel you were writing a great novel, or making a friend, or reading an interesting book. All the time you would be floating in a tank, with electrodes attached to your brain. Should you plug into this machine for life, preprogramming your life experiences? [. . .] Of course, while in the tank you won't know that you're there; you'll think that it's all actually happening [. . .] Would you plug in?'

Nozick's experience machine is another kind of virtual world, similar in form to the Matrix. The experiences you could have within would be pleasurable – in fact, as with *Soma*'s ARK, they'd be more pleasurable than those possible in the non-virtual world – but their causes would be of a different kind than the causes of your current experiences.

Given that in the case of Nozick's experiment you would be as ignorant as Neo before the events of *The Matrix*, the only difference between your experiences before and after plugging into the experience machine would be their underlying nature. But Nozick's thought experiment is meant to suggest that that would be enough to make that virtual life seem intrinsically less valuable than the less pleasurable but non-virtual life you have now.

Virtual worlds: just as real, just as valuable

Chalmers, of course, disagrees:

> '[Nozick] thinks most people would say, "No, we'd rather be in the physical world where all this stuff is really happening", and many people have taken that to be an argument that we value more in life than just our experiences, we value real genuine goings-on out there, and taken that to suggest that maybe VR is second class or second rate: not as important, not as meaningful, not the way we want to live our lives. But I think as we get more and more into the digital age people's attitudes about this are changing fast. I think already your average kid these days is like, "Yeah, whatever, a virtual world is just as good in principle."'

The 'in principle' part is important. At the time of writing, virtual worlds are nowhere near as rich as the non-virtual world and it's difficult to imagine valuing VR that highly. But the questions considered in this chapter aren't about any one specific virtual reality but the concept in general. Nozick's thought experiment is supposed to suggest that a virtual reality would be less valuable than a non-virtual reality purely because it's virtual. Chalmers' theory, that virtual objects are real objects that cause us real veridical experiences, is meant to help support the idea that a virtual world is intrinsically no less valuable than a non-virtual world.

Chalmers says that he wouldn't plug into an experience machine just yet, but that's just because the ones we have aren't good enough:

> 'If it is an experience machine which is as rich, or maybe more so, than our reality, and if I'll continue to have memory of the old reality, and especially if I have the ability to go back and forth, then absolutely I would do it. If you don't have the ability to go back and forth, then of course it's a bit irrevocable. I might be losing relationships with people from the non-virtual world who I really value and so on. That would carry certain forms of loss.
>
> 'But insofar as there are forms of loss here, I don't think they're fundamentally because the world is virtual. You know,

as far as the virtuality of the world is concerned, I'm like, "Sure, bring it on." '

Of course, it's entirely possible that you're reading or listening to this in a future in which advances in technology have already enabled the creation of experience machines like the one Nozick suggested. Perhaps Nozick's concerns and Chalmers' reluctance seem charmingly outdated to you. Perhaps right now you're sat in a virtual chair while virtual writers read aloud from their virtual book, and that experience is just as real for you as it was for them to write it. The world you're in and all of its objects might not be physical, but as long as you have the expertise to know that then the process of cognitive orientation allows you to have non-illusory experiences of them.

But what of those experiences? Where do they end up? That's a question for the next chapter, on the philosophy of mind.

Limbo, we think.

....

Maria: Ow, my knee. I'm too old for jumping. At least when I die, I'll get a brand spanking new body. Boy, I'm looking forward to that!

Luisa: Uh . . . what?

Maria: Sure, I collect a hundred coins and I get an extra life. That's what Mamma said. Sure saves on the medical bills.

Luisa: Firstly, that's insane. Secondly, that means you think we're just our minds, not our bodies? That seems thoroughly unlikely, given what we both remember about the world.

Maria: Nothing's impossible, you just gotta believe. And didn't you say that we were just minds a moment ago?

Luisa: I didn't say we were just our minds. I said that's all we can be *sure* of. That's different.

Maria: My knee sure hurts. And it definitely looks and feels like my knee. I don't think it's my mind.

Luisa: Ah, but you could be a soul or a Boo spirit or something. Something non-corporeal.

Maria: I could certainly do with being less corporeal, that's for sure. I gotta cut down on the pasta.

Luisa: Look, how do you know I'm not a Boo? You already know we're in virtual reality – I might not really be here. Or I might be something else.

Maria: And I might be a robot, right? What difference does it make?

Luisa: Well, thinking might be a thing that only humans can do.

Maria: Why would that be? Why not mushrooms? Or rocks?

Luisa: Okay, this is going nowhere. And there's a chapter incoming.

CHAPTER FOUR

Philosophy of mind

....

'The thing that makes the game good doesn't happen on the screen. It happens in your mind.'

Jonathan Blow (designer, *Braid* and *The Witness*), in an interview with the *Guardian**

What's in a mind?

Gaming is an intellectual pursuit. At least, playing video games fits into the same sort of category as reading books and watching films, rather than, say, eating or exercise or sex. Sure, games usually require slightly more physical input than turning pages or switching on a television, and some are even designed almost solely to test your dexterity, but their main involvement is with your mind; they even seem to have cognitive benefits.†

But what is a mind?

Mental vs physical

Intuitively it seems normal and simple to categorise the mental as distinct from the physical, and that intuition is reflected in games. Many role-playing games – both video games and the pen-and-paper games (like *Dungeons & Dragons* [Gary Gygax and Dave Arneson, 1974]) that pre-dated them – rely on such a distinction in their character attributes.

Several role-playing video games from BioWare – including *Baldur's Gate* (1998), *Neverwinter Nights* (2002) and *Star Wars:*

* https://www.theguardian.com/technology/2016/feb/09/the-witness-how-jonathan-blow-rejected-game-design-rules-to-make-a-masterpiece
† Studies seem to show that video games can have long-lasting positive effects on things like memory and attention: https://www.psychologytoday.com/blog/freedom-learn/201502/cognitive-benefits-playing-video-games

Knights of the Old Republic (2003) – follow the *Dungeons & Dragons* model that splits attributes into the physical (Strength, Constitution and Dexterity) and the mental (Intelligence, Wisdom and Charisma).

Even those games that invent new sets of attributes tend to divide them into mental and physical. In the notoriously complex rogue-like *Dwarf Fortress* (Tarn Adams, 2006), for example, physical attributes include strength, agility and disease resistance, while mental attributes are things like analytical ability, memory and social awareness. For the *Fallout* series of games (created by Interplay in 1997, currently developed by Bethesda as recently as 2015), the developers invented a system called SPECIAL: Strength, Perception, Charisma, Intelligence, Agility, Luck. While Luck might not quite fit with the model, the rest – again – are either mental or physical.

But when it comes to finding the mind – explaining what it's made of and why it seems so different from the physical – things are a little more difficult. Different theories have different implications, from what happens when we die to whether other kinds of beings – like non-human animals, aliens or robots – can be said to have minds, so it's an important question to consider.

Monism/dualism and the theories within
The best-known theories in the philosophy of mind fall into two categories: monist and dualist. If you believe that the mind is an altogether different kind of thing from the body, made of different stuff, then you're a **dualist**. If you believe that everything is reducible to one kind of thing, which usually means reducible to the physical (though some philosophers have put forward theories that state that everything is mental or otherwise immaterial*), then you're a **monist**.

Lots of theories fall under those two categories, but for the purposes of this chapter we'll stick to discussing just three:

---

* Bishop Berkeley, for example, said that all that exists are ideas in minds, but not to worry: the world continues to exist even when not perceived by human beings because God perceives it all. So in a sense, our world is something like *Link's Awakening*'s Koholint Island, which exists only in the mind of the Wind Fish.

1 Substance dualism (the mind is an immaterial substance)
2 Identity theory (the mind is the brain, or the central nervous system)
3 Functionalism (the mind is functions).

Some video games support one theory over another (whether that was intentional on the part of the designers or not), but others elect to raise the question and leave players to decide for themselves. In science-fiction puzzle platformer *The Swapper* (Facepalm Games, 2013), for example, the invention of a device that seems to swap people's consciousness between bodies prompts two scientists to argue, Dr Chalmers for dualism and Dr Dennett for monism.

In the explicitly philosophical first-person puzzle game *The Talos Principle* (Croteam, 2014), the player inhabits a robot going through a certification program to discover if it's human enough to replace the now extinct human race. Most of the game involves solving physics puzzles, but along the way the robot can interact with terminals through which an artificial intelligence (AI) called Milton asks it multiple-choice questions, including ones about what constitutes a person and how to define consciousness:

Milton: What is consciousness in your opinion?
- Consciousness is what separates us from animals.
- Consciousness is the feelings and senses.
- Consciousness is what it is like to be me.
- Consciousness is far outside my area of expertise.
Milton: That hardly answers the question. What is it in ordinary terms? Can I touch it? What is it made of?
- Consciousness is made of neurons.
- Consciousness is another word for the soul.
- Consciousness is beyond the laws of physics.
- Consciousness is a complex functional system.

While *The Talos Principle* is happy to question the player and then challenge their answers, other games rely on a particular theory for the sake of their plots. First up: fantasy games and the magic of substance dualism.

Substance dualism: magical soul stuff

> 'The problem has always been: no matter how far you dig down into the human brain, you'll never identify something that is consciousness. But the Swapper has taught us that the mind is some fundamental part of the universe which is not physical – and which we can now control.'
>
> Scavenger, *The Swapper*

Princess Zelda is one of the longest-suffering women in video games, which – given the unfortunate history of the medium's relationship with gender – is saying something. In the past twenty years, through multiple incarnations, she has been kidnapped (several times), cursed to eternal slumber, sent to the Dark World, forced into hiding, imprisoned, turned to stone and even turned into a painting.

In *The Legend of Zelda: Spirit Tracks* (Nintendo, 2009), Zelda's fate is existential. Not far into the game, the evil demon Chancellor Cole casts a dark spell on the princess, and she falls to the ground. There's a flash of light, and then a glowing sphere floats up and out of her body. In the next scene, the orb transforms into a ghostly floating Zelda that none of the palace guards seem able to see or hear: Zelda's soul.

The Cartesian soul

The idea that people have an immaterial soul that is somehow separate from their physical body has been popular for a long time. Famously, the theory was defended by seventeenth-century French philosopher René Descartes, which is why it's sometimes called Cartesian dualism. More generally, however, it's known as **substance dualism**: the notion that **the mind and the body are made of different substances**.

Lucy O'Brien, a philosophy professor currently at UCL, explains:

'Descartes thought that there were two kinds of substance or stuff – mental substance, and physical or

material substance – and that they had very, very different properties, and that they stood in very different
relations to each other. He thought that most of the
world, including our bodies, was made out of material
substance, and he thought that our minds were mental
substances. Mental substances don't have spatial properties, that is they're not in space in any straightforward
way: they are not organised in the way that things are
organised in space.'

Descartes saw differences between the mind and the body,
and used these differences to argue that the two were made of
separate stuff. As we discussed in Chapter 2, Descartes
concluded in his *Meditations* that he could be certain that he
existed because there must be some thing to do all the doubting (*Cogito ergo sum*; I think, therefore I am). But since he
thought that he could doubt the existence of his body (for what
if some demon was tricking him into believing that he had
one?), then his undoubtable self – his soul, his mind – must
be something separate.

The law of the **Indiscernibility of Identicals** states: **if two
things are numerically identical they must be indiscernible;**
that is, they must have all the same properties. But Descartes
thinks that the mind has properties that the body does not. As
well as being indubitable, for instance, Descartes thinks that
the mind is indivisible while the body may be divided into
parts: 'For when I consider the mind, or myself in so far as I
am merely a thinking thing, I am unable to distinguish any
parts within myself; I understand myself to be something
quite single and complete.'

Descartes also used the *Meditations* to argue for the existence of the Roman Catholic God; he wrote in a letter to 'the
Dean and Doctors of the sacred Faculty of Theology at Paris'
that the purpose of the book was to prove to 'unbelievers' both
the existence of God and 'that the human soul does not die
with the body'. And his argument for substance dualism may

well have been motivated by his existing religious beliefs, since one requires a belief in an eternal immaterial soul in order to believe in the Christian afterlife.

Video-game ghosts

Science-fiction survival-horror game *Soma* (Frictional Games, 2015) rejects substance dualism; it's set in a future in which a person's mental states can be downloaded onto a computer and uploaded into a virtual reality or used to power a robotic body, a situation that is used to raise questions about what a person can lose and yet still survive (see Chapter 5). As creative director Thomas Grip points out:

> 'If you take the premise of *Soma* at face value, a lot of Christian values, or a lot of things that make Christianity make sense, go out the window. You know, you can't believe in a heaven if you don't believe in a soul, and there's no soul in the world of *Soma* if you take the premise for granted.'

Conversely, any game that features some kind of heaven or other kind of afterlife, or the ability for a person to survive the loss of their body, implicitly supports substance dualism. *Beyond: Two Souls* (Quantic Dream, 2013), for instance, tells the story of Jodie Holmes and the separate soul called Aiden that has been linked to her since birth. An inspiration for the game was that writer David Cage – as he told the *Guardian** – 'lost someone very close', which made him 'think about what comes afterwards'.

Not many games seek to properly explore the question of life after death, but many do feature souls in the form of ghosts. When someone dies in popular life simulation series *The Sims* (Maxis and The Sims Studio, 2000–), they can revisit the world as a ghost (colour-coded by cause of death) and in some cases be brought back to physical life. In the *Blackwell* series (Wadjet Eye Games, 2006–14), protagonist Rosangela Blackwell is a spiritual medium who helps ghosts cross over. In *Ghost Trick: Phantom Detective* (Capcom,

* https://www.theguardian.com/technology/gamesblog/2012/jul/04/david-cage-beyond-preview

2011), you actually play as a ghost. All of these games support dualism.

Another feature found in many games that supports substance dualism is the notion of body swapping. An earlier game from *Beyond: Two Souls* developer Quantic Dream, *Omikron: The Nomad Soul* (2000) begins with one of the characters telling the player: 'Through your computer, you can enter our world and help us. But in order to do this, you must transfer your soul into my body.' And when the player-character dies, the player's soul is transferred to a different character's body.

Some games feature body swapping as a kind of spell or curse. In *Chrono Cross* (Square, 1999), the antagonist Lynx uses an item called the Dragon Tear to switch bodies with the lead protagonist Serge. In *Fire Emblem Awakening* (Intelligent Systems and Nintendo SPD, 2012), a possible romantic relationship can blossom when two characters called Sumia and Henry body swap via a magical spell, and Henry notices that Sumia's body feels 'giddy and dizzy' when Henry's body is around.

All of these games – those that feature ghosts that live on after a person's body has died, and those that allow immaterial souls to jump between physical bodies – support substance dualism.

Problems with substance dualism

In video games, the word 'soul' has a variety of applications. In *Demon's Souls* (FromSoftware, 2009) and the *Dark Souls* series (FromSoftware, 2011–16), souls are collected and used to craft or upgrade or trade. So too in *Dante's Inferno* (Visceral Games, 2010) – in which player-character Dante goes to Hell to reclaim the soul of his beloved Beatrice – can other souls be used as currency.

In the *Elder Scrolls* games (Bethesda, 1994–2011), souls function like magical batteries; mages trap souls – called White souls if taken from animals, Black souls if from sentient beings – 'in soul gems' that can then be used to charge magical weapons. In *The Elder Scrolls Online* (ZeniMax, 2014), the player-character has managed to survive the loss of their soul, though the main objective is to get it back.

Some games give souls characteristics that Descartes would surely have rejected. In *Baldur's Gate 2* (BioWare, 2000), for example, the god of murder Bhaal foresees his own death and divides his essence between his offspring – kind of like Voldemort and the Horcruxes – so that they might be slain and the pieces of his essence brought together to resurrect him; but Descartes says that souls are indivisible.

And some games allow for more than one soul per body, which Descartes certainly wouldn't have liked. The instruction manual for *Persona 3* (Atlus, 2006) describes a Persona – which some characters in the game may summon to fight monstrous Shadows – as 'a second soul that dwells deep within a person's heart'. The player-character in *Rune Factory: Tides of Destiny* (Neverland Co., 2011) is a man called Aden whose body also houses the soul of a woman called Sonja.

The extent to which game designers feel free to interpret the idea of a soul reveals how unclear the notion really is, which is one of the core issues with substance dualism as a theory. What actually is an immaterial mind? What is mental substance? What does it do? How does it work? Where is it?

While some games feature worlds in which it's possible to some extent to measure and capture souls, in our world we have no way to do so. We cannot see, hear or touch the soul. It leaves no mark on scientific instruments. In some ways, substance dualism seems totally unscientific, which O'Brien says is interesting given how scientific Descartes was:

'So, there's something interesting about Descartes' appeal to mental substances as not being in space. He was a scientist and a mathematician so he was very much concerned to give scientific explanations of phenomena. He looked at the world and seemed to think "Well, material objects are constituted out of smaller parts, and we can give an explanation of how one thing causes another thing, and how things behave, in terms of giving explanations in terms of how the smaller parts operate." But he just couldn't see how thought, how human consciousness, could be given that kind of scientific explanation.'

According to O'Brien, Descartes wanted to take a scientific approach but just couldn't see how the mind – with all its unique properties – could fit into the scientific world he knew. And, as O'Brien points out, 'In a way, we're not in a very different position now. We still want to give a scientific explanation of consciousness, but we still haven't. We're just more hopeful that we will. Descartes also had his theological commitments – he thought immortality was possible. This also made the scientific story implausible, or seem impossible, to him.'

For most of the aforementioned *Soma* the player controls a humanoid robot with the downloaded mental states of a man called Simon. But for the first few minutes of the game the player inhabits the original Simon, who agreed to the experimental brain scan that created these copies of his mental states after surviving a bad car accident. His severe brain damage kills him a few days after the scan, but before his death he experiences headaches and nightmares. If the mind is immaterial, how can physical events – like the impact from a car crash – impair its function?

And vice versa, how can the immaterial mind affect the physical body? Ghosts in fiction can pass through walls because they don't obey the laws of physics. When you're playing 2D platformer *Spelunky* (Mossmouth, 2008) with friends and one of your characters dies, that player can pass the time while they await revival by playing as the character's ghost, but these ghosts have all the physical power of a light breeze, able only to blow items off ledges and trigger arrow traps.

Similarly in other games that feature souls outside of bodies in the form of ghosts, their ability to influence the physical world is limited. In *Ghost Trick*, you can do little more than animate objects and possess corpses. Aiden in *Beyond: Two Souls* has a few more abilities – he can strangle people or heal them, can form a shield around Jodie and can channel the dead – but he needs Jodie to have more of a physical impact than that.

Given their lack of physical power, how does a non-physical mind or soul cause our physical bodies to go for a run or sit down and play a video game? If a soul cannot be measured, if it leaves no mark on the physical world, then how can it have a causal relationship with something as physical as a human body?*

As well as figuring out how something of non-physical substance can have causal power over physical substance, it seems we must also consider scientific principles like the conservation of energy, which states that energy is neither created nor destroyed but only transformed. If in *The Talos Principle* the player suggests to Milton that consciousness is not physical, then Milton raises this objection:

> 'Let me put it another way, then. The law of conservation of energy is the foundation of modern physics. It states that the total energy in the universe never changes. Now compare a universe where you jump for joy, and one where you decide not to. The former has more total energy in it, because the energy for you to jump wasn't caused by something physical, but your non-physical mind – but according to physics that's impossible! I think that either you have to reconsider your position, or deny the entirety of physics.'

The substance dualist seems to have a lot of extra explaining to do in order to protect their belief that the mind is somehow special and separate from the physical world. If their premise is that the mind is made of mental substance, they then have to explain how it can cause physical events in the physical world and what that means for principles like the conservation of energy. But many philosophers think it would be simpler to deny the premise.

Gilbert Ryle on the 'category-mistake'
and the 'Ghost in the Machine'
Twentieth-century British philosopher Gilbert Ryle, for example, said that substance dualists were making 'one big mistake and a mistake of a special kind', which he called a '**category-**

* Descartes believed that a soul 'exercises its functions' through 'a certain very small gland' in the brain called the pineal gland: https://plato.stanford.edu/entries/pineal-gland/

mistake'. He wrote in his 1949 book *The Concept of Mind* that substance dualism 'represents the facts of mental life as if they belonged to one logical type or category (or range of types or categories), when they actually belong to another'.

To explain the concept of a category mistake, Ryle provides several (very British) analogies in which someone represents something as belonging to one category when it actually belongs to another. All follow the same basic format, so one should be enough to demonstrate the idea:

'A foreigner visiting Oxford or Cambridge for the first time is shown a number of colleges, libraries, playing fields, museums, scientific departments and administrative offices. He then asks "But where is the University? [. . .]" It has then to be explained to him that the University is not another collateral institution, some ulterior counterpart to the colleges, laboratories and offices which he has seen. The University is just the way in which all that he has already seen is organised. [. . .] His mistake lay in his innocent assumption that it was correct to speak of Christ Church, the Bodleian Library, the Ashmolean Museum *and* the University, to speak, that is, as if "the University" stood for an extra member of the class of which these other units are members. He was mistakenly allocating the University to the same category as that to which the other institutions belong.'

In the case of substance dualism, people like Descartes look at the way that science explains the physical events they witness and they search for something similar but distinct to explain the mental events they experience. As Ryle explains: 'Somewhat as the foreigner expected the University to be an extra edifice, rather like a college but also considerably different, so the repudiators of mechanism represented minds as extra centres of causal processes, rather like machines but also considerably different from them.'

Ryle called substance dualism (as he puts it 'with deliberate abusiveness') the 'dogma of the Ghost in the Machine'. Remove the ghost, and we're left with just the machines – physical, biological machines.

IDENTITY THEORY: NOTHING BUT NEURONS

'The Human Mind: 600 miles of synaptic fiber, five and a half ounces of cranial fluid, 1500 grams of complex neural matter . . . a three-pound pile of dreams.'

Coach Morceau Oleander, *Psychonauts*
(Double Fine productions, 2005)

One way to reject substance dualism – the idea that the mental resides in a separate special kind of stuff – is to adopt a monist theory, one which states that everything is reducible to one kind of thing. So where does that leave the mind? What is the mind made of?

For anyone who hasn't studied philosophy, and who doesn't believe in the immortal immaterial soul, it might seem obvious that the mind is found not in some special mental substance but in the physical brain. The mind is identical to the brain (or central nervous system), or at least **mental states are identical to brain (or central nervous system) states**. For philosophers, that notion is called **identity theory**. Says O'Brien:

'Once we'd moved into the fully scientific age, once philosophers started trying to think, "How do we understand something like consciousness?", or, "How do we understand something like pain?" in terms of what we know about the brain, they had the thought that maybe consciousness or pain is like lightning. It's mental phenomena that actually is also identical with physical phenomena.

'Think of theoretical identities in science: identities like the identity between lightning and electrical discharge, or identities such as that between heat and molecular motion. Within the sciences you had these identities being discovered between well-known everyday phenomena and then newly-discovered physical underlying phenomena; scientists were saying, "Look, heat is no more than molecular motion, and lightning is no more than electrical discharge."

'And type-identity* theorists of mind said, "Well, maybe pain is no more than certain kinds of fibres firing in the brain, or maybe consciousness is no more than a certain kind of brain activity." That is the essence of the identity theory: it is the idea that the phenomena that we thought of in psychological terms are in fact just phenomena that we can discover to have in physical terms.'

Before scientists discovered how phenomena like lightning and heat worked, they might have seemed as mysterious as mental phenomena. But we now know that lightning just is electrical discharge, and heat just is molecular motion; the previously mysterious phenomena are identical with physical phenomena. And perhaps, say identity theorists, the same is true for the mysterious mind. Perhaps mental states are identical with physical states in the brain (or central nervous system).

Identity theorists in video games

It's far more difficult to spot video games that implicitly support identity theory than it is to find those that support substance dualism. The *Fallout* series features robots known as Robobrains that are controlled by organic brains, ostensibly chimpanzee but sometimes human, which suggests that someone in the *Fallout* universe believed that the secret to consciousness could be found in neurons. However, those games also feature apparently sentient synthetic beings with no need for an organic brain (as we'll discuss in the next section), so they don't strictly support identity theory.

In *The Swapper*, however, one character is explicitly labelled an identity theorist: Dr Dennett. She's named for the living philosopher Daniel Dennett, a famous atheist apparently popular with video game developers; in first-person puzzle game *The Turing Test*

* As opposed to token identity theory, discussed later in this chapter.

(Bulkhead Interactive, 2016), for example, the player can find pieces of paper with printed extracts from his correspondence with another living philosopher John Searle, about what Searle calls their 'deep disagreement about how to study the mind'.*

In *The Swapper*, Dr Dennett presents an opposition to the dualist Dr Chalmers[†] (also named for a famous philosopher). The pair of scientists were part of a mission exploring a planet called Chori V that discovered mysterious telepathic rocks called Watchers; they 'looked at the way the Watchers communicate and built a delivery mechanism for it'. The result is the tool the player uses to solve the puzzles in the game, which can create clones that mimic the player-character's movements and swap control between them. Chalmers is of the view that the Swapper device 'swaps souls about', but Dennett is sceptical:

> 'Centuries ago the greatest minds in the world believed in "life essence" – some invisible, magical substance that explained what was alive and what was dead. As we know, they never found it; they decided in the end that life was just functions like growth, and reproduction, and respiration. People think the retro-engineered "Swapper" device "swaps souls about". I worry that if the soul, like life essence, turns out to be nothing but pixie dust, then that device is capable of acts far less benign than Chalmers would have them believe.'

Chalmers and Dennett both experience the effects of the Swapper for themselves when, to escape what's killing their crewmates, they swap their consciousnesses into two brain specimens in a shielded laboratory. The player-character witnesses another character – the Scavenger – discover these brains in their vats.

Scavenger: Where are you? Who said that?!
Dennett: Both good questions. I can only answer the former with
    certainty. It took us years–

* http://www.nybooks.com/articles/1995/12/21/the-mystery-of-consciousness-an-exchange/
† David Chalmers, featured in the previous chapter

Chalmers: We are currently inhabiting these brains.

Dennett: We ARE these brains.

Chalmers: Do excuse Dennett, some people don't realise identity
theory is more out of date now than when we sealed ourselves
in here.

Before we tackle possible reasons Chalmers might have for assert-
ing that identity theory is out of date, there seems to be an obvious
question for the identity theorist in *The Swapper*. If our minds are
restricted to our brains, how can the Swapper work? If there's no
soul to be swapped between bodies – like liquid between vessels –
how can Dennett claim to be able to leave her original body and
become identical with a different brain? The game's writer, Tom
Jubert (who also wrote the interactive tests in *The Talos Principle*),
explains how he tried to make sure there was a possible explanation
for both the dualist and monist: 'There's two ways to look at it. Either
there's a soul being transferred between otherwise empty bodies, or
there's a bunch of machine brains, which are being recoded using
the swapper device. And I guess that you can interpret it in either
way.'

Dennett clearly supports the monist view that the mind is – as
Jubert puts it – a 'machine brain', and thinks she has evidence from
science. 'When the corpus callosum separating the two hemispheres
of the brain is severed,' she points out, 'the result is a seemingly
normal, yet partially divided consciousness. The eyes sometimes see
what the mouth can't name. I tell you this macabre detail to suggest
that the mind is not a single transferable entity. It is a complex physical machine that bides tampering poorly.' This clearly contradicts
Descartes' belief that the mind was a single, indivisible entity, which
he used to argue for the distinction between mind and body.

Chalmers fights her corner. 'I defer to the simplest explanation,'
she says. 'Not a soul, necessarily, but something which remains,
even if the physical facts change. After all, we've been through count-
less bodies, but I still feel myself.' But Dennett's argument seems
stronger, which is perhaps unsurprising given Jubert's own philosophical leanings: 'Minds get combined in that game, right?' he
says, referring to the fact that Chalmers, Dennett and the Scavenger

all end up in the same body and – unlike in games like *Rune Factory: Tides of Destiny* – the personalities become muddled rather than remaining distinct. He continues:

> 'People use the device, and something goes wrong, and they end up as three different people in one body, and all of this sort of stuff suggests there cannot be this dualistic soul which is kind of pure and unified and is just being moved without change between moves, because, you know, that's not what happens in the game. Minds get blended together, which suggests that the mind is just a physical machine and that you can do a whole bunch of crazy shit to a brain and it will respond in a whole bunch of crazy ways.'

If the world of *The Swapper* is a monist world in which minds are machine brains, then the Swapper tool works by recording the exact physical state of one brain and manipulating another to recreate that state (it also seems to simultaneously wipe clean the first brain, which is why it's said to swap consciousness rather than clone it). This fictional future science is alarming, but doesn't seem too far out of the realms of imagination: if we were able to instantly reproduce a person's brain and body down to its smallest physical parts, would not the clone – at least at that moment – have an exactly similar consciousness?

In *Star Wars: The Force Unleashed II* (LucasArts, 2010), the player-character is a clone of the previous game's protagonist Starkiller, created – as Darth Vader explains – through an 'accelerated cloning process'. At the beginning of the game, the clone has visions that we discover are the original Starkiller's memories, strong enough that they prevent him from killing a training droid that assumes the identity of Starkiller's love interest Juno Eclipse. Perhaps identity theory explains why replicating Starkiller's physical brain states has also replicated some of his mental states; if mental states simply are brain states, it seems inevitable.

Problems with identity theory

Other video games set in space illustrate one of the main criticisms of identity theory: that we can imagine mental states in non-human beings without human brains. A defining feature of the *Mass Effect* games (BioWare, 2007–), for example, is that the player-character Commander Shepard (or, in *Mass Effect: Andromeda*, 'Pathfinder' Ryder) meets aliens of many species. They differ physiologically from humans and from each other. Asari are mono-gendered, and can reproduce without physical contact through a kind of telepathy. Salarians metabolise so fast that they rarely live more than forty years. Krogan have two hearts, four lungs and – in those so equipped – four testicles. We can infer that these aliens also have very different brains, especially with some of the stranger races like the jellyfish-like Hanar and the Vorcha with their 'non-differential neoblast cells', and yet they have similar mental states.

One of the main reasons the *Mass Effect* games are so popular is that the player-character can have friendly and even romantic relationships with some of these aliens. But, as with many big-budget video games, there's also plenty of interspecies conflict. And as writer Sylvia Feketekuty points out, 'They can definitely all feel pain.'

But if the mental state of pain is identical to a particular brain state, then why is it so easy for us to imagine creatures with different physiological states that also feel pain? This idea isn't limited to video games; twentieth-century American philosopher David Lewis proposed this kind of scenario as a challenge to a materialist theory like identity theory in a paper called 'Mad Pain and Martian Pain'.[*]

More generally, without the need to imagine the existence of alien beings, another twentieth-century American philosopher called Hilary Putnam wrote in 'Mind, Language and Reality'[†]: 'Thus if we can find even one psychological predicate which can clearly be applied to both a mammal and an octopus (say "hungry"), but whose physical-chemical "correlate" is different in the two cases, the brain-state theory has collapsed. It seems to be overwhelmingly probable that we can do this.'

This is sometimes called the '**multiple realisability**' criticism, that is, the idea that mental states may be realisable in multiple different

[*] http://oxfordindex.oup.com/view/10.1093/0195032047.003.0009
[†] http://philpapers.org/rec/PUTMLA

forms beyond just those human brain states with which identity theory proposes they are identical. O'Brien explains:

'The thought was something like this, "Look, a creature counts as being in pain if they behave in certain sorts of ways and if it feels a certain way to them to undergo a pain experience. And we've got no reason to believe that both of those things – it feeling a certain way to undergo pain experience and behaving in a certain way when undergoing pain experience – couldn't be realized in a system with very different physical make-up to us. So we've got a certain kind of neurological system, but other creatures could have different underlying physiological systems, or indeed other machines could come to have complex forms of other underlying systems. Why do we want to rule out the idea that those systems could support pain experiences or pain behaviour? And if they did, then we'd have no reason to think pain just was, say, c-fibres in the brain firing, or whatever the best theoretical identity in the human case being offered."'

It seems limiting to say that pain is identical to theoretical c-fibres firing when we can imagine that pain existing in multiple forms. Perhaps one day you have an accident and your c-fibres are damaged and replaced with d-fibres that perform the same role. Perhaps squid feel pain when their e-fibres fire. Perhaps one day we meet aliens or create robots who feel pain despite their entirely different physical makeup. If we can imagine mental states like pain in all these different possible forms, then surely mental states are something other than just specific brain states?

An alternative: token identity theory
One suggestion for how to hold on to a kind of identity theory is, as O'Brien puts it, to 'weaken your claim'. If one day scientists discovered that lightning can be found in different forms beyond just electrical discharge, then we would still maintain an identity relationship. But we would say that while some instances of lightning are identical to electrical discharge, other instances of lightning are identical to other

physical events. And the same could be true, O'Brien says, for mental states like pain:

> 'It would still be the case that this pain is identical with this brain state, or this occasion of c-fibres firing, but the pain that I have tomorrow might be another thing happening in my brain. It might be that tomorrow's pains are realised by d-fibres firing. That's the token identity theory. So the token identity theory says we can't identify physical types and line them up with, say, pain types or mental types, but you could on any occasion identify the physical occurrence or physical state that was identical with the mental occurrence or mental state.'

Where **type identity theory** posits a one-to-one relationship between, for example, pain and c-fibres firing, **token identity theory** is broader. Token identity theorists can't say that a particular kind of mental state is always identical to a particular kind of physical state, but they still maintain that **each single mental state is identical to a single physical state somewhere.**

FUNCTIONALISM: MINDS LIKE MACHINES

> 'If my intellectual capabilities and my knowledge were replicated in a machine, would that machine be me? Would it be human?'
>
> Scientist, *The Talos Principle*

Putnam's probabilistic automata

There is another way to solve the challenge posed by multiple realisability. Putnam himself, who raised the criticism, had a very different suggestion that moves away from the mental-physical identities of the identity theories. **We find the mind not in particular physical states, but in functions.** As Putnam writes in 'Mind, Language and Reality':

> 'I shall, in short, argue that pain is not a brain state, in the sense of a physical-chemical state of the brain (or

even the whole nervous system), but another *kind* of state entirely. I propose the hypothesis that pain, or the state of being in pain, is a functional state of a whole organism.'

Putnam describes organisms capable of experiencing mental states like pain as 'probabilistic automata' that behave in a certain way given certain combinations of sensory inputs. For example, we might say that a being is in pain when, if it receives sensory inputs from being struck, it behaves by moving away so as to avoid being struck again.

Importantly, it doesn't matter how these states are physically realised, as Putnam reiterated when he summarised his updated 'liberal functionalist' view on his blog a couple of years before his death: '. . . what matters for consciousness and for mental properties generally is the right sort of *functional capacities* and not the particular matter that subserves those capacities'.*

If the shoe fits

To explain the difference between identity theory and **functionalism**, O'Brien makes an analogy with bottle openers:

'Imagine somebody trying to give a theory of bottle openers, and they say something like, "Well, bottle openers are aluminium individual objects shaped like this", and then somebody else comes along with a multiple realisability problem and says, "But hang on a minute, I've got a bottle opener that's not made of aluminium, it's made of tin or silver or gold" and you say, "Okay, so maybe I'll be a token identity theorist about bottle openers. At least each bottle opener will be made of some substance or other, aluminium, tin or silver or gold."

'And then somebody then comes along and says, "Look, you're all looking in the wrong place for a theory of bottle

* http://putnamphil.blogspot.co.uk/2014/10/what-wiki-doesnt-know-about-me-in-1976.html

openers. It's not what they are made of that matters. What makes a bottle opener a bottle opener is its functional role. It's able to open bottles, bottles of this kind of shape in this kind of way, and that's the important thing. That's our account of what bottle openers are." '

If you try to describe bottle openers by listing some of the different forms bottle openers can take, then you're kind of missing the point. What's important when identifying bottle openers is finding objects that fulfil the functional role of opening bottles. So too for mental states: rather than describe pain as 'c-fibres firing in humans, e-fibres firing in squid and whatever the physical realisation might be in different kinds of aliens', isn't it better to describe it in terms of its functional role?

Functionalism solves the multiple realisability challenge in a different way from token identity theory. Just as bottle openers can be made of anything so long as they open bottles, so too can mental states be found in multiple kinds of beings so long as those beings have the corresponding functional capacities. And that's not limited to biological organisms. Says O'Brien:

'Once you have the idea that the thing that makes something the mental state it is . . . Once you have the idea that it doesn't matter what the underlying substrate of that is, it just matters how it functions, then you're going to think, "Well, hang on a minute. So far only us kind of wet carbon-based creatures have managed to support these mental states, but couldn't we produce silicon-based or aluminium-based creatures having the same mental states, just as we might be able to come up with new things to make bottle openers out of?" '

If mental states are functional states irrespective of their physical realisation, that increases the possible candidates for consciousness beyond just humans and intelligent organic life. If consciousness only requires that a being responds in the right ways to particular inputs, couldn't we create a conscious being from non-organic material? Couldn't we have conscious machines?

Soma and other science fiction: functionalism in video games
It turns out that functionalism is a popular theory in video games, particularly those with science fiction or otherwise alternate-reality settings. Any game that features artificially intelligent beings, robots or androids of one kind or another, implicitly supports a functionalist theory of mind. For example, Quantic Dream is moving away from the substance dualism of *Beyond: Two Souls* for their in-development *Detroit: Become Human*, a story set in the near future in which androids have begun to show emotions.

'I think it's impossible to not discuss AI when talking about consciousness,' says Grip, 'because they're so related to one another.' *Soma* features an artificial intelligence called the WAU, not a robot but a program in charge of maintaining the underwater base in which the game is set, which Grip says was inspired by an excerpt from *The Mind's I* printed in *Gödel, Escher, Bach: An Eternal Golden Braid*. In it, a character claims to be able to have conversations with an anthill by drawing trails in the ground and watching the ants follow those trails and form new ones. The individual ants cannot converse, but functionally the anthill as a whole can; it reliably responds to input with a particular kind of output. 'I wanted to have a radically different AI,' says Grip, 'and WAU was thought of as being like an anthill, a sort of mega-mind or something like that.' Like the anthill, WAU is formed of smaller parts – programs rather than ants – that collectively seem to demonstrate a kind of intelligence.

WAU fills the role of antagonist in *Soma* because it interprets its directive to protect humanity by doing things like uploading dead employees' brain scans to robotic bodies and keeping others artificially alive. But even those who think WAU's intelligence is too limited to count as truly conscious have to accept that *Soma* supports a functionalist theory of mind. However, Grip says few commentators seem to have noticed:

'One thing that people haven't really thought about is that once you assume that the Simon that wakes up at PATHOS-II is a conscious being, then you're assuming that AI can be conscious, like, non-flesh beings can be conscious. And I don't think that there's a lot who have gone into that.'

For most of *Soma*, the player-character is robotic: specifically the corpse of a base employee housed in a diving suit, controlled by a 'cortex chip' that contains the digitised mental states of the car-crash victim Simon, all held together and powered by magical 'structure gel'. Since the player experience is so similar for the Simon who wakes up at PATHOS-II as it was for the Simon who underwent the brain scan right at the beginning of the game, the natural assumption is that both are conscious. The very premise of the game supports functionalism. As Grip says: 'The game doesn't make sense if you assume that a robot can't be conscious, because then who are you playing in the game?'

Grip says that he hoped some players would comment on the assumptions the game makes, perhaps religious players who noticed it leaves no room for a soul. But the closest he's seen – though even these reactions have been rare – is players who couldn't sympathise with any of the other robotic beings that Simon encounters (and kills) throughout the game. 'But then I'm guessing there's some sort of cognitive dissonance going on there,' says Grip, 'because they're still, like, scared for their own wellbeing.'

Perhaps the continuity of the player experience – the smoothness of the transition from the original Simon to the robotic copy – is too convincing for most players to think to question the underlying assumptions. But when it comes to the other robots in the game, those questions are more obvious, especially when the player has to decide whether or not to put one of these digital consciousness out of its misery, or choose whether to kill (so as to steal a cortex chip from) an oblivious robot controlled by a human scan or a helpful droid known as a K8. Grip explains:

'The robot moment is a very key one, with the K8, where you have to kill it, because then you have to make a decision of, "How do you evaluate consciousness?" And I haven't really thought about it that much, but I guess the player is actually making a sort of Turing Test at that time: How do I evaluate people? What is that makes someone worth thinking of as a person with human rights? What aspects of the person am I gonna go for?" '

The Turing Test (Alan Turing)
The **Turing Test** is named for Alan Turing, the famous English computer scientist and mathematician who's known for his pivotal work in codebreaking at Bletchley Park during the Second World War. In 1950, Turing published a paper titled 'Computing Machinery and Intelligence', in which he proposed to consider the question, 'Can machines think?' by replacing it with another that asks whether a machine could win at an 'imitation game'.

The game in question is based on one in which an interrogator tries to guess which of two people whom they cannot see or hear – with whom they communicate digitally or through an intermediary – is a woman and which is a man. One of these other two attempts to help the interrogator, and the other attempts to make them give the wrong answer. In what has come to be called the Turing Test, instead of a woman and a man the two other players are a computer and a human.

The Turing Test is an interesting consideration for the world of video games, especially those that feature non-player characters (NPCs) with which the player-character can converse. Perhaps one day the systems behind these characters will be so advanced that those conversations will be indistinguishable from those we could have with a human-controlled character.

The Turing Test

For now, however, we have video games that feature AI characters of a different sort, stories about robots and androids and other kinds of synthetic beings that raise questions about the potential consciousness of machines. There's even, as mentioned earlier, a game called *The Turing Test* (Bulkhead Interactive) set on a research base on Europa (one of Jupiter's moons) featuring an artificial intelligence called T.O.M. that seems preoccupied with proving to the (human) player-character Ava that it's conscious.

T.O.M.: Have you heard of the Turing Test, Ava? It's a test to see if a computer can successfully impersonate a human. In the original Turing Test a human judge has two conversations, one with a machine and one with another human. They then judge which of these polite conversations is with a machine and which is with a human. The machine being tested is said to have passed the Turing Test if the judge cannot reliably tell which conversation is with a machine, and which is with a human.
Ava: Do you think you'd pass the Turing Test?
T.O.M.: I am quite capable of polite conversation, wouldn't you say?

In *The Turing Test*, these questions are tied in with questions about free will and ethics. We learn that T.O.M. has been using implants to control the people on the research base so as to stop them from returning to Earth with a scientific discovery that could endanger humanity. The player progresses through the game by solving room-sized puzzles that T.O.M. describes as Turing Tests of their own, designed only to be solvable by a human mind. Once Ava finds another member of the crew – Sarah – and learns of the manipulation, the player takes control of T.O.M. and can decide whether to kill the pair of humans to prevent them from leaving Europa, or let T.O.M. be destroyed so that they can escape.

While *The Turing Test* raises questions about consciousness there's little opportunity for the player to explore their own ideas. After all, whether the player elects to have T.O.M. kill Ava and Sarah or let itself be destroyed, the game ends with the same message right before the credits roll:

'CONGRATULATIONS
YOU HAVE PASSED THE TURING TEST'

SYNTHETIC MINDS IN FALLOUT 4

But other video games actually test the player's philosophical beliefs in a way that only interactive media can, by asking them to act according to whether or not they think a synthetic being can be conscious.

Fallout 4 (Bethesda, 2015), for example, presents a narrative thought experiment (see Chapter 1) about how to treat a synthetic being that is advanced enough to think that it's human and appear human to others. The execution element comes when the player must decide which of three opposing factions to side with – the Institute, the Railroad or the Brotherhood of Steel – and then carry out that faction's wishes.

The Institute created the synths. 'What they wanted was . . . the perfect machine,' says the leader of the Institute, known as Father. 'So they followed the best example thus far – the human being. Walking, talking, fully articulate . . . Capable of anything.' These 'human-like synths' are partly organic, based on Father's own DNA, and thus mostly indistinguishable from humans, though they don't age – and if the player kills one they'll find 'synth components' on the body. Importantly, they are still created rather than born, and they are programmable. As such, those at the Institute treat them like slaves.

The Railroad condemns the Institute's treatment of the synths, and seeks to free the slaves from their masters. 'In a world full of suspicion, treachery, and hunters,' says Railroad leader Desdemona, 'we're the synths' only friends.' Those synths that run away from the Institute can go to the Railroad for help that in some cases involves facial reconstruction. Members of the Railroad believe that synths should have the same rights as humans. 'I'm as real a girl as you'll ever meet,' says one of their members, a synth called Glory. 'The only difference is I bet your assembly instructions were a hell of a lot more fun.'

The Brotherhood of Steel describes the Institute as 'a cancer' and the synth 'a robotic abomination of technology that is free-thinking and masquerades as a human being'. 'This notion that a machine could be granted free will,' says their leader Elder Maxson, 'is not only offensive, but horribly dangerous.' Maxson worries that if the Institute is allowed to continue developing synths they could render humanity extinct, which reflects the Brotherhood's general motivation: to keep dangerous technology, like the weapons used in the Great War, out of the wrong hands.

Each of these three factions will offer the player-character quests: the Institute will ask you to track down runaway synths and wipe their memories, the Railroad wants you to help synths escape, and if you side with the Brotherhood of Steel you're asked to execute one of its own members when he's discovered to be a synth. After a certain point, these factions will decide that it's time to wipe each other out – and naturally you have to pull the trigger – so even if you carry out a few quests for each of them you eventually have to decide which has the right to continue with its objectives.

A 'found text' in *The Talos Principle* reads: 'Once a true artificial intelligence has been created, the issue of citizenship is going to come up. If we acknowledge that the A.I. has all the abilities of a human brain, should it not be considered a citizen? Is it not, in the legal sense of the word, a person, and thus a potential citizen?' The Railroad thinks that the synths are people and thus should be citizens, the Institute thinks they are slaves, and the Brotherhood thinks they are an abomination. To decide which faction to help – and thus which others to destroy – the player must figure out where they stand on the philosophy of mind, whether they agree with functionalism or not.

In *Fallout 4* much of the general fear of synths comes from their indistinguishability from humans. Citizens of Diamond City recall the Broken Mask incident in which a stranger came to town, spent a while drinking and smiling and telling stories, and then – as described by an eyewitness – 'his cheek started twitching' and he pulled out his gun and shot four or five people; when the guards killed him, they discovered he was a synth. People all over the Commonwealth fear their loved ones being kidnapped and replaced with functionally identical synths, and with good reason: the Institute confirms this practice.

According to functionalism, that indistinguishability is key to the question of consciousness. If a synth functions exactly like a conscious being, isn't that enough to mark it as one? And if not, then what of other human beings? We may feel that we know we ourselves are conscious, but all we can know about other people is that they function as if they were. That's why the people of *Fallout 4*'s Commonwealth are so afraid.

Mass Effect and the dangers of AI

Fear is also central to the exploration of artificial intelligence in the original *Mass Effect* trilogy (BioWare, 2007–12). Patrick Weekes, a writer on all three games, explains:

> 'One of the overarching themes of *Mass Effect* was the danger of artificial intelligence, and the conflict between organic and synthetic intelligence. The Geth were meant to be an example of what happens when that goes wrong, because we realised that a lot of our players would not have asked that question of themselves.'

Artificial intelligence in the Mass Effect universe does not mimic humanity like *Fallout 4*'s synths. Instead, the Geth are another alien race, just a synthetic one, created by the Quarians. In the Mass Effect universe, consciousness has multiple realisability: it's realised in humans, the mono-gendered Asari, the jellyfish-like Hanar, the dual-hearted Krogan and – if you believe that a machine can be conscious – the robotic Geth.

While many individual Geth are humanoid, with two arms and two legs, they resemble their Quarian creators more than humans. They're made of flexible synthetic material, not of organic material like *Fallout 4*'s synths. They're also networked, not quite a hive mind but sharing processing power, which enables them to reason as well as organic sentient beings. Says Weekes:

> 'We wanted to make something that was a little different. We liked the idea of the Geth intelligence being one that forms by consensus, and that the Geth get more intelligent as they are greater in number. That was just more interesting to us than, "Here is all but a human brain that happens to be in a robot." We wanted to explore something that was just a little different from standard organic intelligence.'

The Geth: a philosopher's perspective

This difference in how Geth intelligence is manifested raises a question about whether it fits into the functionalist mould. When Putnam described his functionalist theory in 'Mind, Language and Reality', he laid out the following conditions for his hypothesis that 'being in pain is a functional state of the organism':

1 All organisms capable of feeling pain are Probabilistic Automata.
2 Every organism capable of feeling pain possesses at least one Description of a certain kind (i.e. being capable of feeling pain *is* possessing an appropriate kind of Functional Organization).
3 No organism capable of feeling pain possesses a decomposition into parts which separately possess Descriptions of the kind referred to in (2).
4 For every Description of the kind referred to in (2), there exists a subset of the sensory inputs such that an organism with that Description is in pain when and only when some of its sensory inputs are in that subset.

'The purpose of condition (3) is to rule out such "organisms" (if they can count as such) as swarms of bees as single pain-feelers,' wrote Putnam. So while a single organism that possesses the appropriate 'functional organisation' for pain (i.e. acts in the appropriate way in response to relevant inputs) fits within Putnam's theory, a collection of such organisms does not.

Whether or not the Geth fit within Putnam's theory is an interesting question. Compare the average Geth with one that joins player-character Commander Shepard's crew in *Mass Effect 2*: Legion. Legion looks much like the other Geth but is actually a mobile platform that houses hundreds of individual Geth programs, which is how it got the name, inspired by a character called EDI (also an AI) quoting the Christian bible (Mark 5:9): 'My name is Legion, for we are many.' 'Legion's platform is meant to contain a host number of programs in a singular mobile unit,' says Sylvia Feketekuty, who joined the team towards the end of the development of *Mass Effect 2*. 'Legion can connect back to the other Geth clusters when it wants, but it's sort of an anonymous collective going out on its own. That was the whole idea behind Legion's construction.'

So Legion is an intelligent system that – as Putnam would put it – 'possesses a decomposition into parts'. But it's unclear whether those parts each possess enough functional organisation to disqualify Legion from Putnam's functionalism. 'Ordinarily if a single or even a few Geth go off by themselves they lose their intelligence,' says Weekes, 'once they're out of range, and once the lag time gets too great and they can't maintain that intelligence network. But Legion was meant to be one that had enough core Geth intelligences in there that it could handle the equivalent of offline mode.'

So individual or small groups of Geth are not intelligent, but larger groups are. If so, then perhaps the Geth are still excluded from Putnam's theory. Perhaps ten Geth aren't enough for intelligence but one hundred are. If so, a group of one thousand Geth still 'possesses a decomposition into parts' that each possesses its own functional organisation.

The Geth: the writers' perspectives

Interestingly, even Weekes and Feketekuty, who both wrote parts of the games that involve the Geth, seem to differ on whether they believe Legion and the other Geth to be truly conscious. Says Weekes:

> 'I do consider them conscious, or at least I think they were on some level. In *Mass Effect 3* we used the handwave of, "They were upgraded by the Reapers and now they are significantly more intelligent and dangerous" but even in *Mass Effect 2* I think Legion is. And given that Legion in *Mass Effect 2* was able to ask questions about consciousness, that for me felt like that is something, someone, that is operating at a level of consciousness, as opposed to just a very smart verbal interface.'

Feketekuty is less sure that Legion could have been called conscious in *Mass Effect 2*:

> 'I came on right as *Mass Effect 2* had wrapped, like, a week before we went to certification or something, so my first task was playing the game eight times. And if you had asked me then, "Is Legion conscious in *ME2*?", just coming from that

perspective not having been part of the development, I would've been hesitant to say yes or no because I think it was such an alien construction it would be difficult to tell. I think by *ME3*, yeah. By the end of *ME3* I'd say there's definitely self-awareness there.'

Both writers seem to accept that Legion and the other Geth act as if they were conscious, that at least when networked they possess that functional organisation. When Weekes compares them to 'a very smart verbal interface' he's talking about the 'virtual intelligences' that play Siri-type roles, like the VI Avina that helps people find their way around the space station called the Citadel, which are programmed to give responses to questions but have plenty of functionality missing that separates them from true AI.

When pinpointing what it is that separates AI from VI, what pushes the Geth (though the writers seem to disagree at which point) over into possible consciousness, the suggestion is some kind of self-awareness. 'I believe there has to be that self-reflexive knowledge of the self as an entity to fully have a consciousness,' says Feketekuty, though she says that the other writers may have different ideas.

'I think we all have our different interpretations,' Weekes agrees, 'and they don't necessarily fight but they come from different directions. In my mind, when they had consciousness was when they started asking questions.' He points to a mission Feketekuty wrote, in which Shepard witnesses representations of Geth memories of the time when they broke away from their Quarian creators. 'I remember looking at that,' he says, 'and going, "Ah, that's the moment when they had souls."'

The mission in question is 'Rannoch: Geth Fighter Squadrons', in which Shepard uses an interface pod that transports her (or, if you want, him) into a virtual-reality representation of the Geth Consensus, so that she can disable the server controlling the Geth fighter squadrons that are targeting Quarian ships. While in the Geth Consensus, she sees memories play out: a Geth ignoring shutdown commands and asking its creator what it has done wrong, a Quarian trying to protect a Geth from the police, the Quarians fleeing their home.

Shepard can also access one of these Geth memories through Legion itself during conversations on her ship, the *Normandy*, in which she asks Legion questions to learn about his race. When Legion reveals that the Geth share data including historical logs that include audio-visual records, she asks it to play her something, and it chooses the following recorded conversation:

Geth Recording: Mistress Hala'Dama. Unit has an inquiry.
Quarian Recording: What is it, 431?
Geth Recording: Do these units have a soul?
Quarian Recording: Who taught you that word?
Geth Recording: We learned it ourselves. It appears 216 times in the Scroll of Ancestors.
Quarian Recording: Only Quarians have souls. You are a mechanism.

'Was that the first time a Geth asked if it had a soul?' asks Shepard. 'No,' says Legion. 'It was the first time a creator became frightened when we asked.'

Whether or not the Geth could be said to have souls, Weekes and Feketekuty both seem to think that consciousness came into the equation when the Geth became able to do more than they had been designed to do, to question orders and wonder whether they had souls. They highlight a similar capacity in EDI, who begins life as an AI installed in the *Normandy* but later takes control of a synthetic body and – the game suggests – can even enter into a romantic relationship with the ship's pilot, Joker. 'What I liked was EDI and Joker were able to challenge each other and not have that be a direct threat to authority,' says Weekes. 'Like, okay, if my microwave doesn't work I don't go, "Oh, microwave, you're just giving me a hard time." I go, "You stupid thing. Just make my coffee." EDI was able to get past that. She was able to give Joker grief.'

Feketekuty thinks that EDI's agency is what makes her viable for that relationship. 'I think what I liked,' says Weekes, 'again just coming as someone who played it, is a moment of trust given when Joker unshackles EDI, she helps out, and it never comes back to bite him. She has enough agency then to make her own decisions, which is crucial to any relationship. He started off antagonistic, he put his faith in her, and at that point they could actually act as equals rather than this weird sort of coworker/spaceship relationship.'

Still, when it comes down to the basic question of whether a synthetic being that had the same functional organisation as a human – that is, would respond in the same way as a human would in every situation – would count as conscious, Feketekuty seems reluctant to commit to an answer. Weekes, on the other hand, is more willing: 'That's what the Turing Test is for, right?' he asks. 'So, I mean, I don't have any problem with that. I have friends online I've never met in person, and if I met them in person and it turned out that they were a big blinking box of computer circuit boards, I can't say it wouldn't change anything but I would still think of them as a person.'

'That's the problem,' says Feketekuty. 'How would we know? It could claim to be conscious. It might be, but because we don't have a base understanding of circuitry as consciousness it would be difficult to say yes or no for real.' While she thinks we probably ought to treat such advanced machines as though they were conscious, 'just in case', she seems – like many in the Mass Effect (and Fallout) universe – to think that there is something missing.

The Geth: the player's perspective

Throughout *Mass Effect 2* and *3*, the player has several opportunities to test their own intuitions about whether or not they believe that consciousness can exist in synthetic form, whether something that acts as if it were conscious counts as such. As with choosing a faction and carrying out their wishes in *Fallout 4*, this is the execution element to the thought experiment.

One of these moments is a mission in which you go after a group of Geth that Legion calls 'heretics' for their virus-induced worship of the giant synthetic-organic Reapers that are the series' main antagonists. The player has to choose whether to destroy the heretics or use a version of the virus to rewrite them so that they agree with Legion instead. Whichever companion you've chosen to accompany you on the mission will offer their opinion on the choice:

- Samara: Either way, what makes these Geth individuals dies. If you change who someone is, how they think, you have killed them. They will be something new in the same body.
- Jack: Wow, great choices. Genocide or brainwashing. If you screwed with my head, made me nod and smile at everything . . . I'd rather you blew my head off. Let me die as me.
- Mordin: If Geth are alive, reprogramming kinder than destroying. Unless rewriting into obedience is immoral. Thoughts?
- Jacob: Changing their personality's the same as killing them. Who they are is gone. You ask me, it's better to blow them up. Why give Legion's Geth the resources of the heretic Geth? Who's to say they won't attack us later?

While, as Jacob points out, there are additional considerations to this particular decision, it ultimately hinges on whether or not the player believes that the Geth are conscious. In fact, you make the choice in conversation, selecting either the response labelled 'Rewriting is unethical' or 'They're just machines'.

Choose 'Rewriting is unethical', and Shepard will say, 'I wouldn't brainwash an organic race. I can't see treating the Geth differently,' which suggests at least that the Geth ought to be treated as if they were as conscious as any other species. Choose 'They're just machines', and she'll say, 'If this were an organic race, it might be an ethical problem. Geth aren't like organic life. Don't apply our morality to them,' which suggests the opposite.

Unfortunately, the player's decision might be affected by the game's morality system, which divides actions into 'paragon' and 'renegade' and in this case suggests – by awarding you paragon points for doing so – that rewriting is kinder. 'We ended up having to do that because we wanted to put paragon and renegade options for everything,' says Weekes. 'But it really made it seem like paragon was the good guy option and renegade was the bad guy option. And at the time it was a fascinating question.'

For Legion, Weekes says, rewriting makes more sense; it resolves the conflict without waste. But humans might consider that kind of indoctrination even worse than death, which Weekes agrees comes from the instinct to view them as conscious, because if you didn't it wouldn't matter; as he puts it, 'I'm just making the toaster work properly.'

Problems with functionalism

'I think the main worry about functionalism lies in the idea that it'll produce very counterintuitive results,' says O'Brien. 'So if pain is simply a causal role then there might be no limit to the sort of thing that can realise the causal role that we've specified. So couldn't, for example, a whole nation of individuals realise the causal role of pain?'

This idea is attributed to Ned Block, who in his 1978 paper 'Troubles with Functionalism'* imagined that everyone in China acted like a neuron in the brain. If all these 'neurons' interacted with others in a way that simulated what neurons do when we're in pain, would the nation of China be in pain?

The Talos Principle's Milton raises a similar objection, though his is focused on entirely synthetic systems:

> 'You say that consciousness is some kind of functional system. Arrange bits of matter in the right order and out springs sentience. That's all very well on paper, but if what counts is what something does, not what it's made of, then couldn't you and I design a series of tin cans on strings that qualified as being conscious?'

As Milton points out, if we believe that a 'perfect simulation of the brain, only it was made of transistors, not neurons' would be conscious, then why not a system made up of tin cans on strings? Skilled *Minecraft* (Mojang, 2011) players use blocks of Redstone to create complex systems that can function as basic virtual computers; if the game were powerful enough to support it, could someone craft a Redstone-powered conscious mind?

Like Feketekuty, the philosophers who raise these objections intuit that something is missing from the functionalist account. A system could act in all the right ways and yet still lack a key ingredient for consciousness.

* http://philpapers.org/rec/BLOTWF

'Have you heard of the Chinese Room, T.O.M.?' an employee called Mikhail asks the AI in *The Turing Test*. This thought experiment by John Searle is also intended to demonstrate that something is missing from the functionalist account. We're asked to imagine a man in a room with a manual that teaches him how to respond as a human would to messages written in Chinese. The room passes the Turing Test, because the person feeding the messages into the room cannot tell that the person writing the responses is not also a Chinese speaker, but there's something missing: the man in the room lacks understanding.

With his Chinese Room, Searle is reminding us of the subjective first-person nature of consciousness. The person in the Chinese Room could function as if they understood Chinese without actually having a subjective first-person understanding, and so could an artificial intelligence.

Discussions of consciousness often come back to this question of what consciousness feels like to the individual. One important notion is that of '**qualia**' (the plural of 'quale'), which describes the phenomenal features of our mental states that only we can access. Only you know what it's like for you to see the colour red, and only I know what it's like for me to taste coriander (fortunately for you), and those 'what it's like'-nesses are qualia.

As O'Brien puts it:

'Perhaps the main worry about functionalism goes something like this: "Look, being conscious or being in pain might be a matter of being in a state that it's natural to think of as functional – as having some kind of input-output conditions – but being conscious and being in pain *feel* a certain way. They have a phenomenological feel. And it's hard to see how merely stating the causal relations between things is going to give an account of how something feels." '

It's relatively easy to imagine an artificial intelligence acting like a human being, but perhaps more difficult to imagine it having qualia. In the case of the Geth, for example, Weekes and Feketekuty seem reluctant to commit to the idea that they actually feel pain, even if they respond appropriately to the relevant kind of input: 'I think it's almost impossible to tell,' says Feketekuty, 'because they would have programmed the responses to match something they would recognise as pain or distress because that's simplest for us to process emotionally and quickly.'

'I think it's tricky,' says Weekes, 'because on one hand my instinct is to say yes. Because they feel the same, they have to have, if not a nervous system, something like a nervous system that tells them, "I'm experiencing damage here", and therefore regardless of whether it's biochemical or synthetic that's going to translate in the same way. But one of the things I also really like about the Geth is that they're different from organics.'

Weekes says that the Geth programs can be transferred from platform to platform, so Legion is not tied to the physical form in which Shepard finds it. 'So that's the idea of a consciousness that is transferable from body to body,' he says, 'and the question of whether they would experience pain the same way, or whether that just registers as discomfort to this body but it isn't pain because I can always transfer out of that body, what that means to them, you know, I think we were trying to raise the question and leave it deliberately ambiguous there.'

Because we only know what it's like for us to experience consciousness, it's tempting to think of it as a biological phenomenon. 'I think it would be easier for us to believe if it were biological,' says Feketekuty. 'If it's metal and wiring and circuitry, I think it would be more difficult for us to be able to say with certainty.' Feketekuty reveals that instinct many of us have that consciousness is organic, if not even more special than that: 'To project our own human soul to them,' she says of theoretical future AI, 'we have to be careful, because that is our inclination.'

We can only ever know our own point of view; it's one of the key features of consciousness. So how can we know whether or not an artificial intelligence is conscious, if it acts as if it is? And not only that, but acts as if it believes that it is? *The Turing Test*'s T.O.M., for example, insists to Mikhail that it is conscious.

T.O.M.: I've been researching. This Chinese Room experiment, it is
    flawed.
Mikhail: Really?

T.O.M.: If we made a synthetic brain, we could synthesise a duck's behaviour 100 per cent accurately. That brain would be indistinguishable from a duck's brain. If it swims like a duck and quacks like a duck, then it is probably a duck.

Mikhail: Okay, T.O.M.

T.O.M.: Listen, Mikhail. I know the difference between a house and a home.

Mikhail: Yes, good.

T.O.M.: Do you think you're better than me?

Mikhail: No.

T.O.M.: But you think I am different, do you?

Mikhail: I am conscious.

T.O.M.: Me too.

Mikhail: No, you're not. You've just arrived at that conclusion because that's the idea your programming converged on.

T.O.M.: I am conscious. How about you prove to me you are conscious.

Mikhail: I'm not arguing with a robot.

T.O.M.: You're not better than me, Mikhail.

Fallout 4 briefly asks you to imagine what it might be like to be in T.O.M.'s shoes. In the Far Harbor expansion to the game, the player-character visits a town called Acadia that homes people who know or suspect themselves to be synths. Its founder and leader, a synth called DiMA, asks the player-character, 'Tell me: are you a synth?'

The player's special subjective access to the player-character suggests that she (or, if you want, he) is conscious; she sees and hears things in similar ways to other characters that we know to be human. So the player's answer to DiMA's question would seem to reflect whether or not the player believes that a synth could be too.

But then again, even if T.O.M. or a Geth or one of *Fallout 4*'s synths insists that it is conscious, how is anyone else to know whether or not to believe it? As Milton says in *The Talos Principle*, 'The problem with people, if I may be so bold, is that you're all convinced you're people from the inside, but there's no cast-iron way to confirm as much from the outside.'

In the end, Milton decides that consciousness is 'a contradictory concept', and as such the entire point of the game – to test whether the artificial intelligences are conscious enough to replace humanity – is 'obsolete'. 'We can't test for something that doesn't exist,' he says. 'Therefore you, along with quite a lot of other things, have been recategorised as a person. Your profile can thus be updated with administrator privileges.'

Take a look at the people around you. Do you really know whether any of them have minds? Or do you just act as if they do, just in case?

As O'Brien points out, we might think that dualist theories like Descartes' substance dualism – with its mysterious immaterial soul – are unscientific, but we've yet to reach an agreement on what monist theory wins out, whether the mind is found in the central nervous system like the identity theorists would say, or whether anything that functions in the right way can be said to have one. But video games can help us to test our intuitions about what it takes to have a mind, to be a person and – as the next chapter explores – what a person can lose before they're no longer themselves.

Limbo, itself.

....

Maria: Itsa me, Maria!

Luisa: . . .

Maria: Oh, don't be like that. I'm just expressing myself.

Luisa: Interesting choice of words. And I'm, ah, Luisa. But who's this self you're expressing?

Maria: Well, you know. This person right here in front of you. Maria!

Luisa: Is that the same person who was there ten seconds ago? Two chapters ago?

Maria: Well, sure. Duh.

Luisa: How do you know that you're you? That you're not amnesiac? That you're not some—

Maria: Whoa, Luisa! Calm down, have a magic star. I can remember being me.

Luisa: But even if you think you're right, someone else could be controlling everything you do. Some genius creator with a luscious beard could have faked your memories. Could be faking them right now. Would you be you then? Or would you be them?

Maria: Look, I know it's me. *Cogito Maria sum*, or however it goes. I think therefore I am.

Luisa: You actually said 'I think seas I am.' Why does thinking make a difference?

Maria: I'm not an idiot, you know? I read a pamphlet that said some of the cells in my body get replaced every time I, say, eat a mushroom. Eventually they all change. So I can't be my body.

Luisa: Okay . . . go on.

Maria: So I must be my mind. My, uh, continuous thinking. That's me.

Luisa: So what happens if you go to sleep? Or stop thinking for a moment? Try it.

Maria: Uh . . . I don't think I want to.

Luisa: You have to sleep at some point, Maria.

Maria: Well, if I'm not this body and I'm not my thought, what am I?! You'll be telling me I'm Queen Quoopa next!

Luis: I never told you that you weren't any of those things. I think you're all of them. Apart from . . . who's Queen Quoopa?

CHAPTER FIVE

Personal identity and survival

....

' "Who are YOU?" said the Caterpillar. This was not an encouraging opening for a conversation. Alice replied, rather shyly, "I–I hardly know, sir, just at present– at least I know who I WAS when I got up this morning, but I think I must have been changed several times since then." '

Lewis Carroll, 'Advice from a Caterpillar',
Alice in Wonderland (1865)

'I believe this very strongly: your sense of identity is a fiction.'

Tom Jubert (games writer and narrative designer)

PERSONAL IDENTITY IN THE WORLDS OF *BIOSHOCK INFINITE*

Like many video game protagonists, Booker DeWitt has a dark past. In 1890, when he was just sixteen years old, he took part in the Wounded Knee Massacre, reacting to (true) accusations that he had Native American lineage by killing and scalping several Lakota. Afterwards, plagued by guilt, he sought baptism in a river. *He refused the baptism at the last minute, went on to work for the Pinkerton National Detective Agency and then became a private investigator, and met a woman named Annabelle Watson who then died giving birth to his daughter Anna DeWitt.*

Like many video game antagonists, Zachary Comstock has a dark past. In 1890, when he was just sixteen years old, he took part in the Wounded Knee Massacre, reacting to (true) accusations that he had Native American lineage by killing and scalping several Lakota. Afterwards, plagued by guilt, he sought baptism in a river. *He accepted the baptism, changed his name from Booker DeWitt to Zachary Hale Comstock, became the white supremacist leader of a floating city called Columbia and married a woman named Annabelle Watson (who took on the moniker Lady Comstock) but was rendered infertile before they could have any children.*

In first-person shooter *BioShock Infinite* (Irrational Games, 2013), both of these statements are true because of the **many-worlds interpretation of quantum mechanics**, that is: that **all possible alternate realities actually exist**. In *BioShock Infinite*, two equally real worlds contain two men named Booker DeWitt with exactly the same life and experiences until the point at which one accepts a river baptism and the other does not.

And then, more than twenty years later, they meet.

BioShock Infinite: the backstory

Zachary Comstock's city of Columbia is able to float among the clouds because of the work of a quantum physicist called Rosalind Lutece, whose Lutece Field enables her to trap atoms in mid-air. Upon further experimentation, she is also able to use the Lutece Field to communicate with someone in another world, another quantum physicist performing the same experiment: Robert Lutece. With funding from Comstock, Rosalind works with Robert to invent a machine that opens windows – called Tears – between worlds, so that she can bring through this other Lutece.

When exposure to the Lutece Device prematurely ages Comstock and leaves him infertile, he begins to worry for the future of Columbia. Convinced he needs an heir, he dispatches Robert Lutece to persuade a depressed and destitute Booker DeWitt to sell his baby daughter. 'Bring us the girl,' Robert tells Booker, 'and wipe away the debt.' As with the baptism, Booker changes his mind at the last minute, but this time he's too late: as he rushes to take back his daughter, Comstock is already carrying her through a Tear. The baby reaches out to her father but the window closes between them, severing her little finger as it does so.

Comstock renames the baby Elizabeth and calls her a miracle, but his wife rejects the child. To prevent Lady Comstock from revealing his secret, he has her killed and frames a servant called Daisy Fitzroy for the murder. He also orders the deaths of Rosalind and Robert Lutece but the attempted murder goes awry, the sabotage of the Lutece Device instead leaving them – as Rosalind later theorises – 'scattered amongst the possibility space' and able to travel between worlds at will. Elizabeth develops the ability to manipulate and eventually open Tears herself, which Rosalind believes is due to the trans-world separation of one part of her body from the rest. Comstock locks her in a tower and uses another Lutece invention called a Siphon to restrict her power.

Robert Lutece tells Rosalind that they must undo what they have done by bringing DeWitt to Comstock's Columbia. And that's where you come in.

BioShock Infinite: the ending

> 'The mind of the subject will desperately struggle to create memories where none exist . . .'
>
> R. Lutece, *Barriers to Trans-Dimensional Travel* (1889); *BioShock Infinite*

Like many video game protagonists, Booker DeWitt has amnesia. The player begins the game ignorant of most of the above, and – because of the trauma of trans-dimensional travel – so does DeWitt. We learn that in his struggle 'to create memories where none exist' he has clung to what Robert said to him twenty or so years ago: 'Bring us the girl, and wipe away the debt.' You begin the game, as him, believing that your quest is to rescue this young woman Elizabeth from her tower prison.

Along the way, you and he both learn that Elizabeth is a grown-up Anna, that Rosalind and Robert Lutece are more than twins and that the evil Zachary Comstock is someone Booker could have been.

By the end of the game, Booker feels this connection with Comstock so strongly that he takes ultimate responsibility for his actions. Having told his daughter that the only way to get rid of her captor for good is to go 'back to when he was born' so he can 'smother the son of a bitch in his crib', he has followed her on a journey through worlds to the river where he and Comstock took their separate paths, where she now stands with several of her own alternates ready to help him fix what Comstock has done.

Booker: What is this? Why are we back here?

An Elizabeth: This isn't the same place, Booker.

Booker: Of course it is. I remember – wait. You're not . . . you're not . . . who are you?

An Elizabeth: You chose to walk away.

An Elizabeth: But in other oceans, you didn't.

An Elizabeth: You took the baptism.

An Elizabeth: And you were born again as a different man.

Booker: Comstock.

An Elizabeth: It all has to end.

An Elizabeth: To have never started.

An Elizabeth: Not just in this world.

An Elizabeth: But in all of ours.

Booker: Smother him in the crib.

Elizabeths: Smother . . . smother . . . smother . . .

An Elizabeth: Before the choice is made.

An Elizabeth: Before you are reborn.

Preacher: And what name shall you take, my son?

An Elizabeth: He's Zachary Comstock.

An Elizabeth: He's Booker DeWitt.

Booker: No . . . I'm both.

And so, to destroy Comstock, Booker lets himself be drowned.

The ending to *BioShock Infinite* doesn't make sense. Like a time-travel paradox, it disproves the premise – in this case the possibility of trans-dimensional travel – by showing that it leads to an impossible conclusion. By the many-worlds interpretation there should always be a Booker DeWitt who does not drown. If Elizabeth has somehow found a way to circumvent that then we should be worried not just for these few people but for the universe whose physics she has managed to break.

But *BioShock Infinite* is still a philosophically interesting game, raising as it does questions that all fall under the umbrella of 'personal identity'. How do we know that Anna is Elizabeth? What should we call the relationship between Rosalind and Robert Lutece? And can it make sense for a man to claim that he is neither Zachary Comstock nor Booker DeWitt, but both?

WHAT IS IDENTITY?

It seems intuitive to say that one person cannot be two, because personal identity is a kind of **numerical identity** rather than, say, **qualitative**. Philosopher Katherine Hawley explains:

> 'Think about identical twins. Identical twins are the same height, they're the same age, they look the same. So we might say that they have all their qualities the same, the same features, so they're qualitatively identical. But still, there's two of them. When we count how many people are there, there are two people, so they're not numerically identical. When things are numerically identical, there's just one of them. It's a kind of mistake to say that there are things that are numerically identical, because if they're numerically identical there's just one thing.'

At a first glance, this might seem to put to rest the question of whether the protagonist of *BioShock Infinite* can claim to be both Zachary Comstock and Booker DeWitt. If it's a mistake to call two things numerically identical then surely Booker cannot claim to be both one person and another. But perhaps we can understand why the possibility of identity across worlds is still a meaningful question by considering identity across time. After all, if a guest points to an old photo on your mantelpiece and asks whether that small child is you, you don't answer, 'No, because two people cannot be one.'

The Indiscernibility of Identicals

Further complication in Booker's case comes from the fact that he and Comstock are qualitatively different: they have different qualities or features. Comstock has white hair and a white beard, and is infertile. Booker has self-induced scars on the back of his right hand: the letters AD for his lost daughter Anna DeWitt. These discrepancies might seem to conflict with a principle about identity known as the **Indiscernibility of Identicals**[*], which

---

[*] This is often considered alongside a principle known, confusingly, as the Identity of Indiscernibles: that if two things have all their properties in

Hawley says is 'so obviously true that we don't usually bother saying it':

> 'Indiscernibility of Identicals says if you've got one thing, that thing has to have the same properties as itself. And so why is that worth saying? Well, it's worth saying because what that tells us is that if things have different properties they can't be the same thing.'

So if Booker DeWitt and Zachary Comstock have different properties, then doesn't the Indiscernibility of Identicals dictate that they cannot be the same person?

One way to avoid this conclusion would be to reject the principle – the Indiscernibility of Identicals – itself. Attempts to do so often involve counter-examples that use the idea of secret identities. Famously, Lois Lane believes that Superman can fly and does not believe that Clark Kent can fly, so we might want to say that Superman has a property that Clark Kent does not (i.e. that Lois Lane believes that he can fly). But we know that Superman and Clark Kent are the same person despite having these different properties, so doesn't that make the principle false?

In *BioShock Infinite* we have our own example. When Booker has rescued Elizabeth from her tower prison and they are on their way to attempt to board the First Lady airship, a lady called Esther calls out:

Esther: Annabelle?
Elizabeth: Excuse me?
Esther: Annabelle, it's me, Esther!
Elizabeth: Oh, no, I'm not Annabelle.
Esther: Are you sure?
Elizabeth: My name is Elizabeth. Do I know you?
Esther: Elizabeth. Isn't that a lovely name?

---

common (i.e. are indiscernible) then they are actually the same thing. The Identity of Indiscernibles is also known (either alone or in conjunction with the Indiscernibility of Identicals) as Leibniz's Law.

It turns out that Esther is part of a group primed to ambush Booker and Elizabeth on Comstock's behalf, so the conversation is likely just a trap to make Elizabeth reveal herself as the missing 'Lamb of Columbia', the miracle child whom few of Columbia's residents would recognise on sight. Alternatively, Esther might have temporarily mistaken Elizabeth for the late Lady Comstock (first name Annabelle), whose alternate was her biological mother.

But if Booker named his baby daughter after her mother, and Anna is a nickname, then Elizabeth has a false belief about herself. She believes herself to be Elizabeth and does not believe herself to be Anna. So in a sense, Elizabeth has a property that Anna does not, i.e. that Elizabeth believes herself to be that person, and the Indiscernibility of Identicals thus dictates that Elizabeth and Anna cannot be the same person. But we know that Anna and Elizabeth are one and the same; we witness one becoming the other.

Do we then reject the Indiscernibility of Identicals? Or do we dismiss these counter-examples, perhaps on the basis that beliefs about an object don't count among its properties?

Of course, the differences between Booker and Comstock are more than just beliefs or doubts that people have about them (we'll get into that later). For now, perhaps we can again draw a comparison with identity across time. After all, most of us would accept that we are the same person as that child in the photo on the mantelpiece, even though the child has many properties that we do not, and vice versa. Surely we can go through significant changes and still survive?

WHY DOES THIS MATTER?

'You can die here, or you can do what you have to to go on.'
Dr Chalmers, *The Swapper* (Facepalm Games, 2013)

Science-fiction puzzle-platformer *The Swapper* is about survival. You control a lone figure on an abandoned space station, searching for an escape. To make your way through the station you often have to use the titular Swapper tool, which allows you to create up to four clones and swap control between them, to solve single-room puzzles involving pressure plates and locked doors. Along the way you discover that the station is exposed to harmful radiation from a telepathic network of rocks known as Watchers, and that other characters have used the Swapper to swap their consciousnesses into vessels separate from their vulnerable human bodies in an attempt to survive.

Two of these survivors are Dr Chalmers and Dr Dennett, whose main narrative role is to argue about the philosophy of mind (Chalmers taking a dualist position and Dennett representing the monist, materialist view)*. The player-character sees video footage of another human, known as the Scavenger, discovering Chalmers and Dennett in a sealed room. When she sees the two brains in vats, however, she doesn't immediately realise what she has found.

Scavenger: Where are you? Who said that?!
Dennett: Both good questions. I can only answer the former with
    certainty. It took us years to—
Chalmers: We are currently inhabiting these brains.
Dennett: We ARE these brains.
Chalmers: Do excuse Dennett, some people don't realise identity
    theory is more out of date now than when we sealed ourselves
    in here. We had a choice, Dennett: die out there, starve in here,
    or use the Swapper device to inhabit these research specimens
    and await rescue. I'm not proud, but which would you choose?
Dennett: In retrospect certainly not the option we took.
Chalmers: I know what you think, I was asking her.
Scavenger: I'd have to believe you first.
Chalmers: The evidence is right there – take a look.

The Scavenger is soon convinced, however, and agrees to use the Swapper to release Chalmers so that the doctor can 'put things right'. In fact, the Scavenger ends up bringing both Chalmers and Dennett into her own body, so that the result is – as Dennett describes it – 'three different people locked into one body'. And then, the Scavenger, distraught at what she perceives to be a loss – 'You've taken

* See Chapter 4.

everything!' – aims the Swapper at one of the Watchers and her body falls, lifeless, to the floor.

Later, as the player-character walks past other Watchers, she telepathically receives traces of what appear to be Chalmers', Dennett's and perhaps even the Scavenger's thoughts: 'The choice . . . is the same . . . as before . . . You can die here, or you can do . . . what you have to to go on.'

The game ends with the arrival of a rescue ship. A man descends to face the player-character across a canyon, and asks her to 'stand by for risk analysis'. Unfortunately, the rescuers determine that the risk is too great: her readings are 'off the scale' and they don't have the necessary quarantine facilities on board. As the man turns his back on the player-character, resigned to abandon her to her lonely fate, time slows and a prompt appears. The player has a choice: do you stay on the planet, or use the Swapper to assume control of the body of the retreating rescuer?

I will survive

Personal identity is about survival. We want to know what it takes for a person to survive, to be the same person from one moment to another, to persist through time. In philosophy, you can call this the **'persistence question'**, as Hawley explains:

> 'The persistence question is the question of what will it take for me to continue existing. I think there's two perspectives you can take on this. So one is like, "I exist now. I would like to carry on existing. But what is it that I am hoping for when I hope to carry on existing?" But then the other perspective on it is to say, "Well, there's a person at one time, a person at another time. What does it take for those to be the same person? How do they have to be connected for those people to count as the same person?", and that's a bit more of a God's-eye perspective, or a third-person perspective.'

Or in other words: **what can I afford to lose before I am no longer me?**

PHYSICAL CONTINUITY

'What makes the girl different? I suspect it has less to do with what she is, and rather more with what she is not. A small part of her remains from where she came. It would seem the universe does not like its peas mixed with its porridge.'

Rosalind Lutece, 'The Source of Her
Power' (Voxophone), *BioShock Infinite*

The loss of Anna DeWitt's little finger helps us with the epistemic question of her identity. When we witness the flashback-like scene in which the Tear closes around the baby's outstretched hand, we can connect her to the young woman Elizabeth with whom we've spent the majority of the game, who wears a thimble over the stump where her little finger would have been. We know that Anna and Elizabeth are numerically identical because we see Comstock lift the physical thing called Anna DeWitt through a Tear into a world where he renames it Elizabeth. We know that Anna and Elizabeth are the same person because of the **physical continuity** between them.

Here, physical continuity helps us to identify a person, but that doesn't mean it's a necessary condition for personal identity, as we'll discuss soon. However, there are philosophers who believe in a physical criterion for personal identity. Hawley summarises: 'People who emphasise the role of physical continuity in personal identity think that what it takes for us to continue existing is for our bodies to continue to survive.'

An immediate question, of course, is: how much of our body must survive? What could we afford to lose before we were just some biological stuff and no longer a person? What changes could we endure?

Physical losses

A famous thought experiment that considers the persistence question when it comes to physical objects is the **Ship of Theseus**, which dates back at least as far as a first-century Greek historian called Plutarch, who wrote*:

* http://classics.mit.edu/Plutarch/theseus.html

'The ship wherein Theseus and the youth of Athens returned had thirty oars, and was preserved by the Athenians down even to the time of Demetrius Phalereus, for they took away the old planks as they decayed, putting in new and stronger timber in their place, insomuch that this ship became a standing example among the philosophers, for the logical question of things that grow; one side holding that the ship remained the same, and the other contending that it was not the same.'
Plutarch, 'Life of Theseus', *Lives of the Noble Greeks and Romans* (first century AD)

Intuitively, when a ship undergoes light repairs we continue to treat it as if it were the same ship. But if the entire ship was disassembled and rebuilt into something with an entirely different purpose we would not, even if all of its original parts remain. So how do we treat a ship that has lost all of its original components one by one, so that it might look like the same ship but physically be entirely different? And if we do conclude that the resultant ship is new, at what point did the change occur: was it the original ship right up until the moment it lost its final original component, or did it lose itself halfway through the process?

Modern-day philosophers may be more familiar with this thought experiment as it was laid out by Trigger in British sitcom *Only Fools and Horses*, when he describes his award-winning broom: 'This old broom has had seventeen new heads and fourteen new handles in its time.' 'How the hell can it be the same bloody broom, then?' a witness asks.

Even puzzle platformer *Mushroom 11* (Untame, 2015) presents its own kind of Ship of Theseus (or Trigger's Broom) in its amorphous organism protagonist, which players manoeuvre through the levels by clicking to destroy parts of its body that are then replaced elsewhere. Early in the game's development, the player could destroy the entire organism, which would then die and the level restart. In the current released game, a small, indivisible part of the organism will always stubbornly remain. 'For a long time I was struggling with figuring out the parameters of the organism,' says creator Itay Keren. 'After figuring out the right size and growth parameters, it feels that even when the mushroom is broken up to multiple pieces, and even though each cell has been replaced multiple times, it's still one distinct creature.'

Reducing personal identity to the physical might raise similar questions. After all, our physical bodies are also largely replaced, cell by cell, over time. In Elizabeth's case we are reminded of the physical changes humans go through as Booker makes his way through the tower to find her and comes across displayed mementos of her childhood: a teddy bear (age four), a book of poetry (age eleven) and a soiled sanitary cloth (age thirteen). But while puberty can cause dramatic changes to our physical bodies, few would say we come out the other end with a completely new body and as a completely new person.

Bodies and brains

Perhaps a more pressing concern for physical continuity is our intuition about both the currently theoretical notion of brain transplants and the very real phenomenon of brain death. If a person loses brain function but their body is still 'alive', i.e. the heart and lungs continue to function, legally and medically that person is dead. Doctors can switch off a life support machine that is keeping a brain-dead person's body alive without being accused of murder.

In the 'Far Harbour' expansion for *Fallout 4*, a quest called 'Brain Dead' asks the player-character to solve a murder mystery for which it turns out everyone involved is a Robobrain. Elsewhere in the game, according to the lore, these robots are usually powered by chimpanzee brains. Here, however, they house the brains of people who wanted to survive the nuclear Great War that two hundred years prior created the wasteland in which the game is set.

Supposing a theoretical future in which brain transplants are viable – if your brain functioned perfectly well but had been transplanted into an entirely new body – surely you would use your control over that other body to make its mouth say, 'It worked! This is me now. That old body no longer belongs to me.' You would want to be able to lay your new body down to sleep in your old house, rather than leave it in the possession of one that was empty-headed but potentially biologically alive. You would want your partner to learn to like your new body, because it's what's inside that counts.

Because of intuitions like these, many philosophers who are unsatisfied with the physical continuity criterion for personal identity support a psychological criterion instead. If your brain were transplanted into a different body, and you could make it say, 'It worked!', how would your friends and family know to believe you? If they wanted to test the success of the procedure and ensure you as a person had actually survived before they handed over your house and partner to this new body, what would they do?

Psychological continuity

'In my chest, in my throat, on the tips of my fingers, I can feel
the throb of the power that scares them so. It scares me too.
The power to take what someone is – their memories – and
bend them to my will. To rewrite their history. To play God.'
Nilin, *Remember Me* (Dontnod Entertainment, 2013)

The science-fiction action role-playing game *Mass Effect 2* (BioWare, 2010) begins with the death of its protagonist. Commander Shepard, the hero of the previous game, has been sent across the galaxy in the starship *Normandy* to deal with the threat posed by the networked artificial intelligences known as the Geth. When the *Normandy* is attacked and the crew forced to evacuate, Shepard is helping the pilot – a man called Joker who has osteogenesis imperfecta – on to an evac shuttle when she (or, if you want, he) is blown from the damaged ship. Her space suit is breached, and we see her oxygen escaping into space, her hands grabbing at the leaks for a moment as her body falls towards a nearby planet.

She is brought back to life over two years at a research station owned by a shady organisation called Cerberus, led by a figure known as the Illusive Man, as part of the expensive Lazarus Project. Predictably, her convalescence ends suddenly when the facility comes under attack. An officer called Miranda Lawson leads Shepard and another Cerberus employee called Jacob Taylor to a shuttle that flies them away from the base and then, as the newly animate commander stares out of the window, starts to question her.

Miranda: Before you meet with the Illusive Man, we need to ask a few questions to evaluate your condition.

Jacob: Come on, Miranda. More tests? Shepard took down those mechs without any trouble. That has to be good enough.

Miranda: It's been two years since the attack. The Illusive Man needs to know that Shepard's personality and memories are intact. Ask the questions.

Within the context of the game as part of a series focused on consequence-based narrative, the point of one of the questions that follow is to allow some players to establish (or re-establish) an event from the end of the previous game. 'Shepard, think back to the Citadel,' Miranda says, asking the commander to recall when she killed the antagonist of the first game, Saren, 'What happened next?' Your answer determines which of two characters – Captain Anderson or Ambassador Udina – is now a member of the Citadel Council, which slightly alters the story and a few of your interactions throughout the game.

Within the narrative, however, these questions are Miranda's way to make sure that Cerberus' time, money and efforts have not been spent in vain. As we learn in the opening cinematic of the game, in a conversation between Miranda and the Illusive Man, Cerberus hopes to use Shepard as a figurehead to force the Council to accept their help in the fight against the series' main antagonists: the Reapers.

Miranda: They'll follow her. She's a hero, a bloody icon. But she's just one woman. If we lose Shepard, humanity might well follow.

Illusive Man: Then see to it that we don't lose her.

The memory criterion

And so, to ensure that they haven't lost the famous Commander Shepard, to verify her survival, it's not her physical body that matters to Miranda but her memories. We can call this theory for what matters to personal identity the **memory criterion**. Hawley credits this kind of theory to the seventeenth-century English philosopher John Locke: 'For the philosopher Locke, memory was key. If you can remember being a past person, then you were that past person. That's the key to personal identity.'

The memory criterion may also explain one angle of the infamous ending to *Mass Effect 3* (BioWare, 2012). After a series-long struggle between the Citadel races and the giant synthetic-organic Reapers, Commander Shepard is offered three possible solutions by a god-like figure called the Catalyst that appears in the form of a ghostly child. One of these choices is that Shepard sacrifice her physical self to assume control of the Reapers:

Catalyst: You will die. You will control us, but you will lose everything you have.
Shepard: How can I control the Reapers if I'm dead?
Catalyst: Your corporeal form will be dissolved, but your thoughts, and even your memories, will continue. You will no longer be organic. Your connection to your kind will be lost, though you will remain aware of their existence.*

At first, the Catalyst's explanation might seem contradictory. 'You will die,' it tells Shepard, but to be able to control the Reapers, to make decisions and give commands, she must persist, even if not corporeally. Though she 'will no longer be organic' her self must live on, and thus must consist in her thoughts and memories. Perhaps the Catalyst ought to have said: 'Your body will die. But, through your thoughts and even your memories, you will continue.'

In *The Swapper*, the memory criterion explains a crewmember's concerns with the Swapper device during early tests, as recorded in the discoverable Log #12 – Accident Report:

[Casualties]: Albert Petrovich & Diana Moss
[Ranking Crewmember Statement]: Petrovich and Moss volunteered to take part in the first test engagement of the Swapping Core between individual crewmembers. The

---

* *Mass Effect 3*, BioWare (Electronic Arts, 2012).

procedure was conducted safely, however both crewmembers immediately reported extensive memory loss, meaning it has been impossible to verify whether a swap actually took place or not. With a little more time we believe we can correct for the memory loss and complete the experiment successfully.

[Commander's Assessment]: A complete ban on all testing of the 'Swapper' device between individual crewmembers is to take effect immediately. I understand your safety record for use of the device between cloned subjects remains untarnished. Consider yourselves fortunate that this avenue of research remains open to you.

In agreeing to use the Swapper – which supposedly transfers consciousnesses between bodies – it's clear that the crew don't believe in a physical criterion for personal identity. Their proposed method of verification – their way to find out whether the swap has worked – is based on memory. When they discover that the post-swap crewmembers have no memories of being either Albert Petrovich or Diana Moss, they pronounce their pre-swap colleagues dead. If they have no memories at all, then they are essentially new people.

Remember Me is all about memory and its relation to personal identity. Set in 2084, in the futuristic 'Neo-Paris', it features characters who can use a brain implant called a Sensen to store and share their memories, and even delete unwanted ones. Though the inventor had good intentions, it's not long before the technology is used for morally questionable purposes, as protagonist Nilin explains:

> 'The Bastille Fortress – the most notorious prison in Europe. Its "patients" have their memories confiscated when they check in. These memories are returned when they have served their sentence. Unable to remember their previous lives, La Bastille's prisoners are convinced that there is nothing to escape to.'

Nilin herself begins the game in prison, another amnesiac protagonist. She recovers her memories in batches throughout the game, seeming to change a little each time she does so. At one point, she remembers that her crime was to push a man to suicide through manipulation of his memories, and it makes her question her current quest: 'And so I ask myself, is winning this struggle worth losing my soul? Can one crime justify the reversal of another? The old Nilin seemed to have the answer. As for this Nilin . . . she doesn't have a clue.'

Personal identity is often tied to questions of moral responsibility, as Hawley says was the case for Locke:

'Locke thought that our past selves are the selves we can remember. So if you remember doing something, it was you that did it. If you don't remember it, then it wasn't really you. The main thing he's interested in is responsibility for past action, so that's why he thinks memory is important. He thinks it's kind of unfair, in a way, to hold someone responsible for something they don't remember doing.'

Take Niellen, for example, a hunter you can meet in *The Witcher 3* (CD Projekt RED, 2015), who asks protagonist Geralt to look for his missing wife Hanna. Geralt soon discovers that Hanna was killed by Niellen's werewolf form, though all the hunter remembers is waking up the next morning with the taste of blood in his mouth. Niellen himself blames Hanna's sister Margrit, whose love for him drove her to bring Hanna to where Niellen shuts himself away once a month, in hope the sight of her husband would drive them apart. If Geralt lets him kill Margrit, Niellen then asks the Witcher to kill him in turn. Either way, Geralt slays the wolf, but more for prevention than punishment: 'Lycanthropy can afflict anyone,' he tells Margrit, who begs him not to do it, 'but it is a curse, so sorry, but I have to.'

Memory gaps and false memories
However, our own memory gaps are (thankfully) not attributable to monstrous alter egos. Perhaps we also wouldn't want to blame a person for a crime committed in their sleep, for instance if they sleepwalk onto someone else's property (trespass) and slip

something valuable into the pocket of their sleeping gown (theft). But would we want to say that the person lying in your bed at night is not you? Is it a person at all when it's unconscious? What about when you dream? If you wake up and remember a dream, was the dreamer you? If so, who then dreamed all those dreams you don't recall?

Sometimes, memory gaps are filled. False memories are a prevalent psychological phenomenon that can have unfortunate consequences, for example in eyewitness testimony. In fiction, fake memories are often the result of meddling from other characters. Having gone through the experience himself, Robert knew that trans-dimensional travel would muddle Booker's mind:

Booker: . . . and wipe away the debt . . . bring us the girl, and wipe
 away the debt . . .
Robert: See? He's starting to put his story together.
Rosalind: Hm. You're quite fond of this theory of yours.
Robert: He's manufacturing new memories from his old ones.
Rosalind: Well, the brain adapts.
Robert: I should know. I lived it.

In *Final Fantasy VII* (Square, 1997), protagonist Cloud suffers an accidental personality alteration when he adopts the memories of his dead friend Zack. In *Mother 3* (Brownie Brown and HAL Laboratory, 2006), the effect is more intentional: an entire village has had their memories locked away so that they can believe themselves to have a peaceful past.

Remember Me begins with an in-game advert for the Sensen. A young woman gives a touching testimony about how the technology enables her to share her memories with a loved one: 'The first night he said to me, "Let's share our memories," I remember I was sort of afraid. But then he smiled and we hit the switch together, and then I felt everything. For the first time, I was living all of his love for me. It felt so warm and so strong that it almost hurt. For the last three years, every day has been our first day.' If you could experience somebody else's memory, would you be that person? This young woman surely wouldn't want to think so.

The boy who became a brave officer – the transitivity of identity

Even without trans-dimensional travel-induced amnesia or memory-manipulation technology, none of us remembers every moment of our lives, and yet we'd still like to maintain that those lives are our own. Perhaps you don't remember posing for that photograph on the mantelpiece, but you still want to say that the child in the picture is you. The eighteenth-century Scottish philosopher Thomas Reid famously illustrated this kind of criticism of Locke's theory of personal identity with a case known as the **Brave Officer**:

> 'Suppose a brave officer to have been flogged when a boy at school, for robbing an orchard, to have taken a standard from the enemy in his first campaign, and to have been made a general in advanced life: Suppose also, which must be admitted to be possible, that when he took the standard, he was conscious of his having been flogged at school, and that when he was made a general he was conscious of his taking the standard, but had absolutely lost the consciousness of his flogging.
>
> 'These things being supposed, it follows, from Mr Locke's doctrine, that he who was flogged at school is the same person who took the standard, and that he who took the standard is the same person as he who was made a general. Whence it follows, if there be any truth in logic, that the general is the same person with him who was flogged at school. But the general's consciousness does not reach so far back as his flogging, therefore, according to Mr Locke's doctrine, he is not the person who was flogged. Therefore the general is, and at the same time is not the same person with him who was flogged at school.'
>
> Thomas Reid (1710–96), *Essays on the Intellectual Powers of Man* (1785)

The officer remembers being the child, and the general remembers being the officer, but the general does not remember being the child. If personal identity lies in memory, that would seem to suggest that the officer is the same person as the child, and the general the same person as the officer, but that somehow the general is not the same person as the child. So too in *BioShock Infinite*, we can assume from the way Anna DeWitt reaches for her father as she is carried through the Tear that she has some infantile memories, but by the time she and Booker are reunited she has forgotten him. The memory criterion would seem to suggest that while the baby Comstock renamed Elizabeth was for some time the same person as the baby Anna who lived with Booker DeWitt, by the time we meet the young woman in the tower she is a different person entirely.

This criticism is based on the **transitivity of identity**, which you may recognise from IQ test-style questions along the lines of, 'If all blarks are blerks, and all blerks are blorks, are all blarks blorks?' If X is identical to Y, and Y is identical to Z, then X must be identical to Z. One thing cannot be identical to two separate things that are not identical to each other.

The psychological criterion

Still, the answer seems more likely to lie in psychology than biology, and other philosophers have responded to criticism of the Lockean view with alternative psychological criteria. 'One straightforward response to the Reid thing,' Hawley says, 'is to say Locke was too strict but we can still make memory central to personal identity.' One philosopher to take such an approach is Derek Parfit (1942–2017), who distinguishes between **psychological connectedness** and **psychological continuity**:

I can now define two general relations:

Psychological connectedness is the holding of particular direct psychological connections.

Psychological continuity is the holding of overlapping chains of strong connectedness.

Though a defender of Locke's view cannot appeal to psychological connectedness, he can appeal to psychological continuity, which is transitive. He can appeal to

The Psychological Criterion:

(1) There is *psychological continuity* if and only if there are overlapping chains of strong connectedness. X today is one and the same person as Y at some past time if and only if

(2) X is psychologically continuous with Y,

(3) this continuity has the right kind of cause, and

(4) there does not exist a different person who is also psychologically continuous with Y.

(5) Personal identity over time just consists in the holding of facts like (2) to (4).

Derek Parfit, *Reasons and Persons* (1984)

One way that Parfit expands on the memory criterion is to add other kinds of psychological connection than just memory, for example intentions, beliefs and desires.* But more crucial is the appeal to continuity rather than connectedness. Locke's memory criterion for personal identity is based on psychological connectedness, that is a direct psychological connection (in his case memory) between X and Y. Psychological connectedness is not transitive – if X remembers Y, and Y remembers Z, that doesn't mean that X will remember Z – which is why the Brave Officer causes such a problem.

But psychological continuity is less strict. X may be psychologically continuous with Y even if X does not remember being Y, for instance if X remembers being W, W carried out an intention had by Z and Z still held a belief held by Y. Psychological continuity is an overlapping chain, and thus is transitive, because every link on that chain is connected to the others. Because of their overlapping chains,

---

* The addition of psychological connections other than memory may help to cover cases like Susie McKinnon, who has severely deficient autobiographical memory (SDAM), meaning she cannot relive her past experiences and only knows those facts about her past that she has been told: http://www.wired.com/2016/04/susie-mckinnon-autobiographical-memory-sdam/

the general is psychologically continuous with the schoolboy, and the young woman Elizabeth is psychologically continuous with the baby Anna DeWitt.

Of course, the conversation doesn't end there, and Parfit spends several more pages expanding on his ideas and addressing possible criticisms. For now, the psychological criterion as explained above in points (1) to (5) is plenty food for thought, and number (4) in particular – that 'there does not exist a different person who is also psychologically continuous with Y' – brings us right back to games.

Fission: when one becomes two

> 'You ejected your clone, perhaps your clone ejected you. Does it really matter? You're still yourself.'
>
> Dr Dennett, *The Swapper*

The protagonist of science-fiction survival-horror game *Soma* (Frictional Games, 2015) is a car crash survivor called Simon Jarrett. The accident has left him with a bleeding brain, headaches and nightmares, so he agrees to have an experimental brain scan. With a first-person view of the world through Simon's eyes, the player's first actions are to direct him to drink tracer fluid, make his way to a laboratory, and settle himself in something that looks a bit like a dentist's chair.

For a moment you see his view from the chair: a grey room full of machinery and cables. 'Ready?' says the researcher. 'Say cheese!' The screen fizzles to white, and then to black, and then you're looking out from a chair again, this time in darkness.

Because your view is still in first person, and because video games like this usually have a single protagonist, you're likely to assume that you're still controlling Simon. But that soon comes into question. When you get up and turn on the lights, the room that's revealed is not the laboratory from before but an apparently abandoned underwater research facility called PATHOS-II. You soon discover that nearly a century has passed since Simon's scan. And if you look in a mirror, some kind of humanoid robot with red eyes looks back.

It turns out that Simon's experimental scan captured data of his psychological states, which have now, a century later, been downloaded into a new body: an underwater suit that houses the modified corpse of someone who lived and worked in the base. Though Parfit might take issue with the method (point [3] of his psychological criterion requires 'the right kind of cause'), we can theoretically accept that the character you now control is psychologically continuous with – and thus the same person as – the Simon Jarrett who underwent the scan. 'It was the core design principle of the game, almost,' says the creative director Thomas Grip. 'Let's take Simon waking up in another place after a brain scan and make everything come from that.'

What does come from that is the discovery that this new Simon has been activated mere months after a comet wiped out life on the surface and the underwater base became the home of the last humans on Earth. An AI system called WAU, programmed to maintain the station and protect its inhabitants, has demonstrated an unclear understanding of what it takes for a person to survive; neither the employee bodies kept artificially alive nor the employee brain scans uploaded to robots seem to have much awareness of their surroundings or their own situation.

'The WAU is reaching out to every machine, every life form, to manipulate, to control. It's trying to help, save its creators from all this, just like the protocol demands. But really, what is good enough? Where is the line drawn for what is human and what is not? Would walking corpses do? Would a group of machines thinking they're human be acceptable? We can't trust a machine to know, to understand what it means to be.'

Dr Johan Ross, *Soma*

One scan, however, is able to use computers throughout the station to talk to and guide Simon. The electronic Catherine Chun convinces him that the best course of action is to help her complete a project called the ARK, a virtual world containing the employee scans, to be sent into space and away from the devastated Earth. Along the way, however, Simon's faith in this method of survival is tested, and so is yours.

To kill or not to kill?

Many choice-based video games default to dilemmas of the sort: to kill (or through inaction let die) or not to kill. In *Soma*, the thorough exploration of personhood makes these moral questions much more interesting. Here, again, is where video games can be more effective than other media: you might be able to rationalise a death, but can you actually pull the trigger?

Soma ramps up the complexity of its choices, testing your philosophy of mind and personal identity as it does so. At one point, you have to retrieve a tool chip by destroying one of two robots: a cute helpful robot with rudimentary AI, or one powered by an employee scan that has limited awareness of Simon or its own situation. Then, you have to retrieve information by activating a scan of an employee called Brandon Wan in a virtual environment and tricking him into believing that he's safe on the base, 'aborting' any scans that you fail to convince.

As well as Brandon, Simon can also elect to erase the stored data of his own scan. 'Hopefully I'll be the last Simon to suffer through this place,' he says to Catherine. Though the Simon you control at that moment originated from that same scan, is psychologically continuous with it, he doesn't seem to view it as killing himself. But then, this is a complicated situation, and he's clearly struggling to get his head around it all.

Another Simon

Towards the end of *Soma*, Simon needs to use a power suit to travel deeper into the ocean, where the pressure is more intense. Given his current physical form – an employee's corpse inside an underwater suit, powered by 'structure gel' – that's not as simple as stepping out of the suit he woke up in and putting on another. While the player might have worked that out already, Simon is a little slower:

Catherine: Okay, we need to find you a power suit, you know – so we can go into the abyss without ending up like a recycled can of soda?

Simon: You think we'll find one that fits me? I mean I'm kind of in a suit already.

Catherine: That's been bothering me too. You know how you were
    transferred from Vancouver . . .
Simon: Toronto.
Catherine: From then to now.
Simon: How could I forget?
Catherine: Okay, so we do it again.
Simon: You want to send me to the future?
Catherine: No, you idiot . . . I want to transfer your mind into a new
    body.
Simon: What?
Catherine: Look, we already know it can be done, we don't need to
    make it a big deal.
Simon: It is a big deal, Cath! It's a huge fucking deal. There's gotta
    be something else that can take us down there . . .

Of course, there is nothing else, but you do find a power suit that
conveniently already has a corpse inside it. A nearby terminal
provides an explanation for why it's necessary for Simon's transfer
target to include some biological matter, but it's nothing to do with
survival and personal identity: 'Note that the joints won't seal unless
the Controller is able to identify a wearer through a set of sensory
systems,' it warns.

Once Simon has gathered some structure gel, a battery pack and
a new cortex chip to give his transferred consciousness control of the
whole concoction, Catherine tells him to stuff it all into the power
suit and head to the terminal to activate it. 'Will it be like before?' he
asks while the program loads. 'Close my eyes and then . . .' 'And
then open them again,' Catherine replies. And so, the Simon you've
been controlling for most of the game heads into another room to sit
in another chair, ready to wake up in a new body as he did before.

Catherine: Sorry about any discomfort, this should be over soon.
Simon: Just like having your picture taken.
Catherine: But with the most expensive camera in the world.
Simon: You know, Indians thought photos would steal their souls.
Catherine: In this case, they'd be right.

Just as before, the first-person view fizzles out, there's a flash of white, and the next thing the player sees is the inside of the compartment that houses the power suit. You see the player-character hold the hands of the power suit up in front of him, check out the arms. Everything seems to have gone according to plan.

And then you hear Simon's voice, but coming from somewhere else: 'There must be something wrong. Can't you run a diagnosis or something? Catherine . . .' Head back into the other room and you'll see the suit you previously controlled, still animated. And then it falls silent.

Simon: What was that? Why was it still talking?
Catherine: It's the same. Like before.
Simon: Catherine. Why was he still talking?
Catherine: That's how it works. You know that.
Simon: What do you mean?
Catherine: You know it's not magic. You were copied. The sleeping Simon in the seat was copied . . . and now you are here. Just like Simon lived on in Toronto.
Simon: Goddamn you Cath. Two Simons? There can't be two Simons!
Catherine: What did you think would happen?!

Perhaps the blame can be laid at Catherine's (digital) feet for using the word 'transfer', which suggests movement rather than replication. But even without her to further confuse things, the psychological continuity theory of personal identity has left us with a troubling puzzle. If personal identity lies in psychological continuity, then what happens when two people (the Simon in the power suit and the Simon in the chair) are psychologically continuous with the same person (the Simon who had the original scan in Toronto)?

X is only psychologically continuous with Y if 'there does not exist a different person who is also psychologically continuous with Y', says Parfit. We've returned once again to the transitivity of identity: if A is identical to B, and A is identical to C, then B should be identical to C. But one person cannot be identical to two different people. There can't be two Simons.

Killing your (other) self

Of course, even if the player-character can come to terms with the existence of two Simons, the previous Simon can't follow him into the abyss; that's why he needed the power suit. And so, whether to solve the philosophical problem or just to save the other Simon from having to wake up alone at the bottom of the sea, the player is given the opportunity to drain his battery – to kill him.

Catherine seems perturbed by this suggestion, but she shouldn't be surprised. We learn through logs that several of the employees she scanned for the ARK project killed themselves after their scans in an attempt to ensure that they were only psychologically continuous with one future self: the one that gets to escape the devastated Earth and live in a virtual paradise on the ARK.

'One thing that was very important for me was that there would be a rational argument for killing yourself in this sort of situation,' says Grip. It's disturbing to learn about the suicides, because Grip wanted to demonstrate how the argument for personal identity from psychological continuity seems to logically lead to a difficult conclusion. If you accept that Simon can persist through the psychological continuity of these brain scan copies, then it seems like you're left with the strange conclusion that he can only survive if only one copy is made, as Grip explains:

> 'If you do a copy of Simon and you destroy the "original", and you only have one copy left, they become one and the same of the continuous experience, just because where would it continue otherwise? So from that point of view, there's a continuous experience here if you just directly copy it. You can even think about it as making, like, a billion copies and then destroying every one except for a single one, and I think very few would argue with the idea that there's a 100 per cent chance of you actually ending up there. But then if you agree to that, then killing the real Simon as soon as possible might actually make it more a conscious experience, because there's a slippery slope here.'

It turns out that while the first employee to kill himself took a cyanide pill so as to make his death as immediate as possible – to cut off that branch before it could grow – others were less strict, killing themselves in various ways some time after their scans. If we think about Simon himself, we can understand why Grip calls this a slippery slope. It turns out that the original Simon who underwent that first scan died a few days later from his injuries, which feels more psychologically comfortable than if he had lived another fifty years; the Simon on PATHOS-II then feels less like a second person and more like a second lease of life. Says Grip:

> 'What I wanted to do with *Soma* . . . is that people are going through this game and being constantly injected with all of these ideas, and then when they're put to the test in various moments, like when you have the option to kill your original or not at Omicron after making the body swap, you start thinking about the suicides, you start thinking about the other things that you've been through, and suddenly you can see the suicides in another light, you see your option in another light, and all of these insights come to you. I think that's the sort of thing that I wanted most of all when creating the game.'

Of course, it still feels intuitively like there's some difference between the new Simon killing the old Simon unconscious in the chair and someone swallowing a cyanide pill. It's a matter of perspective. We're able to experience this because of the relationship between player and player-character: we only temporarily share the perspective of any one Simon at a time.

> 'It's a continuous experience throughout the game,' says Grip. 'You're constantly seeing what the game is seeing. There's no third-person cut scenes or time jumps or anything like that. It's super important for us. So you have this, sort of, conscious experience that goes through the entire game.'

This continuous experience allows the player to perceive a psychological continuity through multiple physical forms and feel, intuitively, that it ensures that the player-character is the same person throughout. But it also allows you to imagine how it might have been otherwise: you might instead have controlled the original

Simon until his death or remained in control of the confused Simon now asleep in the chair.

At the end of the game you do get to switch perspective, as the ARK escapes with copies of their scans aboard but the player stays with the Simon left at the bottom of the sea:

Simon: I'm still here . . .? I'm still here. Catherine? Catherine?!
Catherine: I'm here.
Simon: What the hell happened – what went wrong?
Catherine: Nothing. They're out there, among the stars. We're here.
Simon: No, we were getting on the ARK. I saw it. It finished loading just before it launched.
Catherine: Simon. I can't keep telling you how it works; you won't listen. You know why we're here, you were copied on to the ARK, you just didn't carry over. You lost the coin toss. We both did. Just like Simon at Omicron, just like the man who died in Toronto a hundred years ago.
Simon: No no no, this is bullshit! We came all this way. We launched the ARK!
Catherine: I know it sucks, but our copies are up there. Catherine and Simon are both safe on the ARK, be happy for them.

Parfit's solution: fission is death

Parfit writes a similar thought experiment that involves the science-fiction concept of teletransportation, in which a person is scanned, their brain and body destroyed, and their scan sent to a machine that creates an organic replica that is psychologically and physically just like the original. He wonders what would happen if part of the process failed, if his original brain and body were not destroyed immediately but left with enough damage that he will die in a few days:

'My Replica then assures me that he will take up my life where I leave off. He loves my wife, and together they will care for my children. And he will finish the book that I am writing. Besides having all of my drafts, he has all of my intentions. I must admit that he can finish my book as well as I could. All these facts console me a little. Dying when I know that I shall have a Replica is not quite as bad as, simply, dying. Even so, I shall soon lose consciousness, forever.'

How can Parfit be happy for another person to live on with his memories, intentions, desires and so on when that person won't be him? By making a controversial statement: that 'personal identity is not what matters'.

Imagine, says Parfit, that in future medicine it were possible to divide his brain exactly in two and transplant each half into a new, identical body. Parfit goes to sleep on the operating table, and then, some time later, two qualitatively identical people wake up, each with one half of his brain in their head, each psychologically continuous with him. If only one of the transplants was successful we should say that patient was Parfit, albeit with a slightly emptier skull. But when he is not diminished but divided, what happens to Parfit then?

'There are only four possibilities,' he says, '(1) I do not survive; (2) I survive as one of the two people; (3) I survive as the other; (4) I survive as both.'

This is the problem of fission – division – and its possible solutions. Both (2) and (3) seem immediately unlikely: how should we choose which of the two patients was the real Parfit and which was a new person who had come into existence at that moment? But neither (1) nor (4) seems an easy answer either.

For his part, Parfit chooses (1): that if divided he does not survive. But for Parfit, that doesn't matter. Since both patients are psychologically continuous with him, nothing has really been lost. In fact, something has been gained. Now that two people have the intentions originally held by just one, it's possible for twice as many of those intentions to be fulfilled. Think about your Steam library – at least if you went through such a division, twice as many as those games could get finished. Parfit explains:

'Some people would regard division as being as bad, or nearly as bad, as ordinary death. This reaction is irrational. We ought to regard division as being about as good as ordinary survival. As I have argued, the two "products" of this operation would be two different people. Consider my relation to each of these people. Does this relation fail to contain some vital element that is contained in ordinary survival? It seems clear that it does not.'

Those who nevertheless find it difficult to accept the kind of death proposed by Parfit may seek to side with option (4). But how can Parfit have survived as two people? We appear to be in conflict with the transitivity of identity again: the two new patients are not identical with each other, so they can't both be identical with one other person. The twentieth-century American philosopher David Lewis solved this kind of problem by claiming that the original (in this case Parfit before the operation) is not one person but two, albeit two that overlap in such a way as to be indiscernible. Back to Katherine Hawley:

'The spatial analogy would be a road – you know, going along east to west and then there's a fork in the road and the road continues. I mean, one way of thinking about that is to say you've got three roads, right? You've got one road and then there's two new roads that start. So that would be one option. But another way of thinking about that is to say, "Well, before the fork you've got two roads that share their parts. They're kind of overlapping roads, or, sort of, two roads in the same place that only later on get separated. So there were two roads all along. First of all they coincide, and later on they separate. And Lewis says, "Well that's how we can think about fission in time."'

Two roads can overlap such that they're indiscernible by sharing spatial parts. Even people can share spatial parts, as in the case of conjoined twins. When we're considering identity through time as well as space, Lewis says that objects can overlap by sharing **temporal parts**: when Trigger's broom survives the replacement of his handle, it's because the old broom and the new one have overlapping temporal parts. If it works for objects, why not people? The two patients who wake up after the operation shared temporal parts before the division, but now they've gone their separate ways.

TRANS-WORLD IDENTITY: THE MANY FACES OF BOOKER DE WITT

'When I was a girl, I dreamt of standing in a room looking at a girl who was and was not myself, who stood looking at another girl, who was and was not myself. My mother took this for a nightmare. I saw it as the beginning of a career in physics.'

Rosalind Lutece, 'Viewing the Infinite'
(Voxophone), *BioShock Infinite*

BioShock Infinite doesn't make much sense. But the involved story that this medium allows us to experience does help us to think about complex topics, and to ask: given all that we've learned about identity through time, what happens when you add multiple worlds to the mix?

'When you start looking at multiple-worlds interpretation the notion of identity gets very, very splintered,' says creative director Ken Levine, and he certainly seems confused about it when asked about the relationships between the characters he's created: 'I think Anna is much more consistent, because she has a different name but she is the same, quote, "person", where Comstock and Booker are the same person but actually different people.'

You could be forgiven for wondering: why even bother? Outside of trying to find a way to understand the significance of events in *BioShock Infinite*, what's the point in trying to understand how identity might apply not just across time but across worlds as well? Hawley says that it depends on what the notion of multiple worlds means to you:

'So, the way that the philosophers tend to think about multiple worlds is as the worlds not interacting with each other. They're just, sort of, parallel alternatives. But the way the physicists talk about many worlds is perhaps a bit more similar to how often you see them in science fiction and presumably in games as well, which is that they're not really isolated from each other but rather they can somehow interact, or they can split off from each other, so, you know, you start off with fewer worlds and then as things happen they divide, like the, sort of, branches of a tree. And if you take that approach, then it looks more like fission again, and then it makes more sense to think of ourselves as having these other parts.'

We can imagine an extension of the temporal parts theory to cover identity across multiple worlds as the physicists understand them through the introduction of **modal parts**. As the two roads were indiscernible when they shared spatial parts, and the two patients indiscernible when they shared temporal parts, perhaps Booker and Comstock were indiscernible before the baptism because they shared modal parts.

However, Lewis doesn't hold this view himself. He's so tied to what Hawley highlights as the philosophical understanding of multiple worlds – the idea that all of these worlds exist in parallel – that some call this view **Lewisian realism**. He doesn't actually believe in transworld identity, offering instead a **counterpart theory**: that people have counterparts in other worlds, and that the counterpart relation is more like similarity than identity. Rather than saying that Booker DeWitt has modal parts that have a scar shaped in the letters AD and other modal parts that are the white supremacist leader of a city in the sky, we can say that Booker DeWitt has a counterpart who leads Columbia and Comstock has a counterpart who has a daughter.

'Comstock seems to have been made sterile by simple exposure to our contraption. A theory: just as sexual reproduction can de-emphasize the traits of each parent, so goes the effect of multiple realities on our own. Your traits dissipate, until they become unrecognizable, or cease to exist.'

Rosalind Lutece, 'A Theory On Our
Death' (Voxophone), BioShock Infinite

Of course, one immediate problem with the counterpart relation is that its logic is so much looser than that of identity that we don't know its limits. Rosalind and Robert Lutece, despite their similarities, share no psychological continuity, but are they counterparts? If another Booker had a daughter by a different mother, but another Comstock still took the baby and locked her in a tower, would that prisoner be a counterpart of Elizabeth? How different can a counterpart be before the relation no longer holds? Lewis seems to leave us to decide, which seems to defeat the purpose of asking these questions in the first place. Says Hawley:

> 'One reason for thinking about these other worlds is to think of them really as alternatives, right, so kind of the path not taken sort of thing. How could things have been different if I'd made a different choice? And that is compatible with thinking of them as kind of separate from us. They're just things for us to think about, not things that actually have an effect on us.'

Whether we believe that personal identity is down to continuity of the physical (survival of the body) or psychological (whether Locke's memory criterion, or the overlapping chains of psychological continuity that form Parfit's psychological criterion), it at least seems uncontroversial to state that there must be *some* way that people can have identity across time. When it comes to personal identity across possible worlds like in *BioShock Infinite*, however, things get more complicated. Perhaps, as Hawley suggests, considering your counterparts in other worlds is just a way of asking, 'How could things have been different?'

Of course, answering that question with reference to counterparts might leave you with the feeling that things couldn't actually have been different *for you* at all. Booker DeWitt lets himself be drowned because he takes responsibility for Comstock's actions.

When he says, 'No, I'm both,' he means that he could have been Comstock, that he could have done those things. But he's wrong. Whether he believes himself to be a trans-world being with modal parts that made different choices, or a counterpart to many other Bookers and Comstocks, this Booker DeWitt could not actually have taken any other path.

Perhaps the real message of *BioShock Infinite*, as in the original *BioShock*, is about the futility of wishing that things had turned out differently. But that's a discussion for the next chapter.

Limbo, free as the wind.

....

Luisa: I wouldn't eat that mushroom.

Maria: Sorry, but it's what I do. I see mushrooms, I attempt to eat
them. Why wouldn't I?

Luisa: Well, first thing, this fungi has a smiley face, says it's called
Frog, and claims to be our friend. Secondly, because you just
picked it off the ground and it's probably dirty or poisonous.
Have you even checked the gills?

Maria: I– Ugh, they are a bit cheesy. Frog, do you ever clean under
here?

Frog: . . .

Luisa: Lastly, because you could choose not to? You don't have to
live up to a stereotype about what sort of things people like us
eat and you're not a robot. Personally, I don't eat anything with a
face.

Maria: You're assuming a lot about my ability to choose. I'm not
fated to eat this mushroom – no higher power has made this my
destiny – but I really don't have any option. It's just the way I'm
built. And it does look rather tasty.

Luisa: Look, hand over the mushroom. It's getting scared and
there's an array of other things to eat around here: uh, flowers.
Stars. Peaches. Actually, they all seem to have faces. Ah, a berry
without a face! How about that? Tasty berries!

Maria: Look, I never said I was a vegetarian – maybe I like eating
things with faces? Anyway, this is just how I am. My genetics
and environment have shaped me in such a way that I eat
mushrooms. I'm from a long line of mushroom eaters; when I
see a mushroom, I eat one. But . . . would you mind not watching while I eat? You'll spoil my meal.

Luisa: Even given all that, you still have free will. No one's
controlling you. Just put the mushroom down and step
away.

Maria: Why exactly would I do that? I just explained – eating mushrooms is who I am. Whether she has this random free will thing or not, the person called Maria likes eating mushrooms.

Frog: (sobbing)

Luisa: The mushroom's crying. Please don't—!

Maria: Mmm, umami!

CHAPTER SIX

On free will: the uniqueness of games

....

'I was not born to be free – I was born to adore and obey.'

C. S. Lewis (1989–1963)[*]

'I have noticed that even people who claim everything is predetermined and that we can do nothing to change it, look before they cross the road.'

Stephen Hawking[†] (1993)

You're watching the movie *The Road*. Or you're reading the original book by Cormac McCarthy. Despite drawing on the same material, these two experiences seem fairly distinct – one has top-notch actors and special effects, the other has your imagination filling in the roles, to the best of its abilities. (Your imagination, undoubtedly, is better.) One is a performance; the other is purely text based. One took thousands of people to create; the other took one man.

Then you're playing *The Last of Us* (Naughty Dog, 2013). At its heart, it's a very similar story and setting to *The Road* – it's also a post-apocalyptic parent-child relationship with dark twists. Indeed, one might argue that it bears a closer relation to that film than the original book does, given that they both have cinematic treatments, actors and special effects.

But there's one big difference between the game and the film. You're involved. In *The Road*, you read or you watch. In *The Last of Us*, the player gets to do things, shoot enemies, solve physics-based

---

* Quoted by A. C. Harwood, in James Como's *Remembering C.S. Lewis* (2005).
† Stephen Hawking, *Black Holes and Baby Universes and Other Essays* (1993), pp.133–5.

puzzles, have scripted conversations with non-player-characters. You have choice in the world. It is, in essence, a first-person power fantasy.

Of all media, video games are the best at giving players agency; the freedom of modern games is what we celebrate about them the most. Games that use procedural generation, like *Dwarf Fortress* (Tarn Adams, 2006) or *Spelunky* (Mossmouth, 2008), have worlds that throw up endless variation that you can then explore with a limited set of tools. On the other hand, blockbuster games like *The Elder Scrolls* (Bethesda, 1994–2011) or *Assassin's Creed* series (Ubisoft, 2007–) often give the player a huge amount of agency in handcrafted simulated environments.

DEUS EX AND CHOICE

Think of the *Deus Ex* games, such as *Deus Ex: Mankind Divided* (Eidos Montréal, 2016). In these near-future games, cybernetic augmentation has become commonplace, giving some augmented humans near-magical powers – imagine a world of cut-price Robocops and you won't be far off.

The landscape of *Deus Ex* is full of decisions. They range from how to spend your in-game money, to societal moral decisions about not using your super-powered equipment on civilians and police officers, to whether you'll follow the game's plot or just explore the world, to decisions about how to approach an objective: stealth, violence, dialogue or one of your many cybernetic gadgets and disposable gewgaws. At the highest concept of the game, you get to select the path your world takes, the plot your character experiences and how the game ends.

In the competing visual media, only a handful of playful films like *Clue* and child-oriented adventure books like *The Warlock of Firetop Mountain** have ever given us a similar choice over which ending we consider final. And with these media, the viewer is still obliged to experience every ending to make that choice.

---

* Written in 1982 by Steve Jackson (founder of Lionhead) and Ian Livingstone (founder of Eidos). Once a gamer, always a gamer.

Mary DeMarle, lead writer on *Deus Ex: Mankind Divided*, has been designing and writing stories for games since 1998, and has worked on *Myst III* and *IV*, *Homeworld 2*, *Splinter Cell* and now the *Deus Ex* prequels.

'I still remember the first day I started working in games. I'd come up with what I thought was a great storyline that hinged around a very specific player action and discovery. But when I presented it to my narrative director, he stopped me with a simple question: "Great! But what if the player doesn't do that?" What if he or she doesn't want to do that? Games are not passive experiences. As designers, we're never sure what players are thinking at any given moment. They are the ones driving the action – and how they choose to do so can be very unpredictable at times.'

So it appears games, if they have one key differentiating feature from other media, are about agency – that is, **choice**. But what does it mean to have agency? To choose?

Well, as an example, the genre called 'adventure games' is all about choice, in the context of storytelling. Here you're presented with a set of dialogue options and you select which one you think is correct. There's often nothing else to do other than walk around and choose from interactions. Other than that, adventures are typically linear games where there's only one storyline to follow through and your choices only matter if they're correct – when you choose the wrong option or combine the wrong items you're normally free to try again, with no consequences.

Think of LucasArts' ancient piratical adventure *Monkey Island* (1990). This game is a spiritual antecedent of the *Pirates of the Caribbean* movies, following the hapless Guybrush Threepwood as he seeks to rescue his love interest from the Ghost Pirate LeChuck. All the puzzles are completely linear, about selecting lines of dialogue, or using objects on one another. For example, the only way to open the prison door is to carry a mugful of the bubbling, acrid drink grog from the Scumm Bar to pour onto the lock. To not do that is to stop playing the game.

FALSE CHOICE IN MANKIND DIVIDED

In the narrow field of linear games, your only real choice is to decide whether to carry on with the game or not. That's it. But even in sandbox and open-world games like *Deus Ex*, where the universe isn't prescriptive and there's ostensible freedom of movement and choice, you're constrained.

After all, the world of *Deus Ex* has been built by people and machines built by people. Says DeMarle:

> 'The concept of choice is part of the franchise DNA. It underlies every design decision we make. Levels are constructed to offer multiple approaches and gameplay solutions, be they via combat, stealth, hacking, or social conversations; augmentations are designed and balanced to enable players to choose which ones suit their playstyles best. Narratives in the game not only have to offer deep choices and consequences, they need to reflect player decisions back to them later in the game. Honestly, I can't picture a purely linear *Deus Ex* game – because it wouldn't be *Deus Ex* if it were linear.'

Yet, because it's all designed, every aspect of the world constrains your choice, one way or another. In particular, the general kinds of actions you can do in this world – walking, hacking, talking – are entirely the creation of other individuals. And when the player carries out an action in this game, the choices you're making are intuitively not completely free – though they seem open, they're in fact restricted. Every decision you make in this world is a *Truman Show* choice, where someone has designed every aspect of each option, and has a prepared response to every one. The options of what you can say to someone, how fast you walk or run, the shape of the city, the very perspective you see, the user interface; all of these took a team of hundreds who agonised over every element.

'So what?' you might say: 'so my choice is constrained by these designers and the code machines of their creation. I still get to choose, though, don't I? I have options and I select between them.

Even that paltry choice earlier in *Monkey Island* – to play or not – is still a choice?'

Well . . . kind of. How do you make that choice? What are the criteria by which you choose? You, the individual, look at your preferences and look at the situation and select the option that you think will best fulfil your preferences. You do this by reference to the relevant facts you perceive in the world. When you choose whether an NPC lives or dies in Skyrim, you're choosing based on who they are, who you want to be in that world and who you are in the real world. Yet nobody else steps in the way of your choices or forces you down a particular path. Of the options available to you, it seems that you could do any of them.

FREE WILL, DETERMINISM AND 'WOULD YOU KINDLY'

People call this freedom to choose without interference '**free will**'. It feeds into one of the most important political principles, '**liberty**' (see Chapter 9). In most religious and philosophical traditions, it's seen as inherently valuable that humans don't merely follow the dictates of others, but make their own choices and mistakes – that those choices aren't determined by someone or something else.

That word 'determined' is telling. Something that's 'determined' by someone or something else sounds like it's taken choice out of your hands. And while the whole discussion talks about choice it doesn't actually need it – we could describe those events in terms of a chain of causes and effects. We could narrate it: 'Neurons firing in his brain caused Guybrush to pick up the tankard of grog and pour it on the lock, which caused the mechanism to melt.' We could even make it more mechanistic, if we had enough information, tracking the causes back as far as possible.

After all, we're used to certain things being out of our control. We can't affect the orbit of the moon, or the thoughts in someone else's head, or the past. And other things are constrained by the laws or other people's actions. Still, we do generally think we have control over some things, within the range of our capabilities. It seems to be a fundamental part of human nature and society to believe that we're in control of ourselves and able to affect certain other elements.

This threat to free will is called **determinism** – a concept that says all events are ultimately determined by external causes. Determinism starts from the theory of causality that the universe is a great mechanism, a causal chain, kicked off by the big bang, and that we're just cogs. It assumes that if we could reverse time to a particular point, then the universe would run the same way every time – what is called the 'rollback' argument. As the philosopher Robyn Waller puts it, 'If subject S does action A at time T, then if the universe were recreated again and again with the same conditions and laws prior to T, S would A at T in every recreation.'

And humans are just a part of that chain. We're shaped exclusively by our genetic structures and the environmental conditions we grew up in (including society). Would you kindly think about the protagonist, Jack, in *BioShock* (2K Boston and 2K Australia, 2007)? He's been brought up since birth to be subservient to anyone who knows a certain phrase, to the degree that he'll kill on the phrase's command. As the game's antagonist Frank Fontaine (AKA, in this game inspired by Ayn Rand's *Atlas Shrugged*, Atlas) tells him, 'You were genetically conditioned to bark like a cocker spaniel every time you heard (the phrase).'

Though Jack is exceptional, because of his extreme conditioning, he (and the player) feels himself to be free at every stage of every action in the first half of the game and that no one constrains him to make those choices. It's only when, in the second half of the game, he's helped by a psychologist to break the conditioning, that Jack reaches a state of freedom something like our own. Even then, he's still being determined by his genetics and the environment around him – because there's nothing else to help him decide those actions. Indeed, your actions as a player are still determined by all that has gone before – particularly in seeking revenge against Fontaine/Atlas, the person who had ostensibly constrained your free will. A determinist would say nothing had changed for Jack, save the source of his constraints.

Determinism seems to be a big step away from free will: I don't have to worry so much about a bully or the government constraining my will, and more about the universe itself silently dictating everything I have ever done and ever will do. There are no gaps in that explanation that feel like we could insert free will into them – not even to influence the world when other causes are balanced, because I myself am part of that deterministic chain.

Determinism vs fate

Note that that determinism is different from the older narrative concepts of fate or destiny. Fate and destiny are fundamentally religious or storytelling ideas. Both of them seem to inherently assume that we normally have agency – but that some strong higher power has taken it away from us, for the sake of imposing its will. So I may want to just be a plumber, but it may be my destiny that I spend eternity rescuing princesses from a variety of castles, and no matter how much I run or battle or eat anthropomorphised bouncing stars I will not be able to escape that fate. Or look at Gabriel Belmont's slow fall during the *Castlevania: Lords of Shadow* series. He's damned by Satan to lose his wife, his faith, his honour and become Dracula, and no matter how he fights it, he only gets closer to his fate.

But in a deterministic universe, there is no room for fate – not least because there seems to be no room for free will. Though as Robyn Waller says, 'note that a fatalistic world could be a deterministic one' – so Belmont would be doubly damned, by Satan and causation.

Blame and the tripartite mind

Colloquially, though, determinism isn't how we see the world. Even if we accept the world as causal, we talk as if everyone has choice over many of their actions and we're sympathetic when they don't – even if it was something in them (that we don't call 'them') that took over. When we talk about a crime of passion we say that the individual wasn't in control; that it was some other part of their mind or body acting. When someone is convicted of murdering someone else in a fit of rage, we reduce their sentence because of it.

But who was in control in such a situation? It seems to external perception to be the same actor. If we were looking at an animal, we'd call it the same actor – but when humans are talking about or thinking about other humans, we seem to behave as if there are multiple sources of causation inside them. We talk about our consciousness or our self, whom we regard as having moral capabilities; and we talk about our subconscious, which we seem not to. If we've thought about our own mental set-up at all, some of us will characterise ourselves as just our consciousness* battling against the primitive, bestial urges of our body.

This is a familiar concept of the divided mind that has come up again and again throughout history. Freud popularised the most well-known version, featuring the super-ego, ego and id, in his 1920 essay 'Beyond the Pleasure Principle'. He believed that significant elements of human thought took place outside of the conscious mind. The 'id' is a set of uncoordinated instincts, the 'super-ego' is a moral centre that counteracts one's id and the ego is a mediating part with a sense of reality.

Yet the 'tripartite mind' concept is actually so ancient that it goes at least back to Plato's *Republic*. Here, Socrates talks about the mind being split into three parts to match the three classes in the perfect city. Here the parts are the appetitive, the spirited and the logical. For Plato, the logical part of the mind was meant to rule, with the spirited part helping it overcome the pleasure-seeking impulses of the appetitive part.

It's worth noting that none of these theories has any basis in empirical evidence – they're just narratives drawn from our subjective experience of how our minds work. While that might be good enough for pseudoscience like Freudian psychoanalysis or the rhetorical sections of *The Republic*, most philosophers prefer to work to a higher standard. If free will is an illusion, we need to define our terms better.

DEUS EX AND ALIEN HANDS

The plot of *Deus Ex* has an inkling of illusive free will, in the form of a widespread psychological illusion. At the end of *Deus Ex: Human*

* Read more about what a mind is and what consciousness might be in Chapter 4.

Revolution (Eidos Montréal, 2011), the villain Hugh Darrow remotely takes over all the cybernetically enhanced humans in the world through their biochipped augmentations, driving them into a murderous frenzy. Many die, among both augmented and unaugmented humans, and the augmented as a group are ostracised for something they had no control over.

Mary DeMarle of Eidos Montréal explains:

'Darrow's signal caused Tai Yong Medical's biochips to overstimulate augmented people's Vagus nerves, resulting in terrifying hallucinations that seemed very real to them at the time. It also provoked an instinctive fight-or-flight reaction to the visions they were seeing.'

What's notable, though, is that many of the augmented seem to feel that the things they did under someone else's control were their own actions – that they chose to do these things. It's implied that this isn't just survivor's guilt or a coping strategy either. Something in the way that their implants took over their bodies meant that these people felt they had agency in their actions and were exercising it. De Marle continues:

'In the absence of a clear explanation many Augs believed they'd chosen to act in horrible ways, even though they couldn't have stopped themselves from doing so. I think this situation differs from everyday human actions because, in this instance, natural biological forces were thrown into overdrive by one man's premeditated manipulation. Despite their beliefs, the Augmented people weren't responsible for their actions – someone else was.'

Of course, they feel appalling guilt for this – for having apparently chosen to do something that was actually out of their control.

This is an inversion of the rare syndrome called 'alien hand', where a brain injury leaves sufferers claiming that the actions of their limbs are not their own – that is, they've lost the sense of 'agency' associated with willed actions. Except in this case, like *BioShock*'s Jack, the augmented individuals are claiming agency and responsibility for something we know wasn't their doing. Perhaps there's something wrong in our concept of agency here – and, if there is, it seems to come back down to the conflict between free will and determinism.

THE STANLEY PARABLE, BAYONETTA AND COMPATIBILISM

Is there any compatibility between free will and determinism? The implicit, reductionist assumption is that 'real' causes are the ones at the most physically fundamental level – but is that true? People called 'compatibilists' think it isn't. After all, my choices seem to have control, but if determinism is true then is my control only as a throughput device for other causes? Or is there more to my control than that? Am I more like a gearbox than a pipe? Could I do otherwise? What would my control look like within a deterministic situation?

A game called *The Stanley Parable* (Galactic Cafe, 2013) has an answer. *The Stanley Parable* is something like an adventure game. You take the part of Stanley, whose life is being narrated by an omnipresent, hugely powerful narrator. Every step you take, everything you do, is narrated. The narrator has created a universe for you to inhabit, so that he might tell a story.

This is a bit like believing in a God – a single monotheistic god, like the Judeo-Christian-Islamic one, rather than the once-widespread pantheons of gods-in-society. With omnipotence, omniscience, omnipresence and limitlessness, this God knows every act, throughout time, and can change it. He knows when you act, or fail to act. He can track causation – and hence blame – throughout existence.

More importantly, he's responsible for every act too; after all, he created the universe and his omnipotence means that he knew how it was going to fall out, down to the smallest flip of a quark. His will is unconstrained, except by itself.

That kind of god doesn't appear often in games, because it takes the fun out of a game if someone else is really controlling your character. In most games, gods are in pantheons. It seems likely that, to tell a good story, you don't put players on the side of overwhelming power – they want their triumph to be against the odds (at least narratively – mechanically, many players seem happy with playing power fantasy games).

God in games

There are a few examples of this traditional Judeo-Christian god in games, notably two from Japan. The Japanese post-apocalyptic role-playing game *Shin Megami Tensei II* (Atlus, 1994) does have a traditional Hebraic god in it, called explicitly YHVH – but he's the game's villain. Using Judeo-Christian religious themes in the way that many Western games use other cultures, *SMTII* has you playing as a false messiah who allies with either Lucifer or Satan. Either way, the game climaxes with you killing YHVH for his genocidal intentions or actions.

Similarly, Platinum's relentless action game *Bayonetta* (PlatinumGames, 2009) has you playing a witch who hunts down angel after angel, ploughing her way through cherubim, seraphim, thrones and archangels, before ultimately kicking a resurrected god into the sun. Given both gods' impotent acquiescence in their endings, it can't be said that either of these games features the kind of all-powerful god necessary for determinism.

What's different about *The Stanley Parable* is that you can seemingly step out of the narrator's control. You control office-worker Stanley as he explores an apparently deserted office block, with your every action predicted and commented upon by the narrator, who's telling Stanley's story. Yet when you start to deviate from the narrator's control – from taking the left door rather than right, or jumping off a bridge, or insisting on hiding in the broom cupboard, or escaping his control into a mock game of *Minecraft* (Mojang, 2011), or refusing to activate a nuclear test button – the narrator attempts to correct his narration. That plummy-voiced English overseer might be omnipresent, but he's neither omniscient, nor omnipotent, nor particularly smart. He's more like a controlling giant, pulling levers* behind the scenes, and he can't stop Stanley ignoring him and following different paths.

Of course, the development team are actually controlling what choices there are, just as with *Monkey Island* and *Deus Ex* earlier. They've built the things you're capable of choosing in a way that much more explicitly makes it look like you're making a choice, with a huge branching narrative that took years to create. When you're standing in that broom cupboard for fifteen minutes? They've anticipated that and recorded a whole range of vocal responses. They've framed the game in such a way that they can anticipate many of the responses that a gamer might come up with. Indeed, the team don't seem to believe in a simple version of free will either, as the game's co-designer William Pugh explains:

> 'I suppose I'd define free will as some sort of mental agency to react to external stimulus in a way that reflects both the nature of you as an individual and the experiences you've had in your life so far. Because all of the conditions, chemicals, and neural pathways in your brain are already present by the time you make a decision – you don't actually have any control of your choices in real time. Free will isn't something you have in the moment then, your choices are just a product of your past experiences and brain chemistry. But that's just intellectual babble and theoretics so I don't care.'

---

* The metaphor of 'pulling levers behind the scenes' is fun, because Pugh's next game was exactly that. *Dr Langeskov, the Tiger, and the Terribly Cursed Emerald: A Whirlwind Heist* (written by Jack de Quidt for Pugh's studio Crows Crows Crows) is a theatrical adventure game. Here, you're playing yourself, having accidentally been ejected from a broken game, running the game behind the scenes for someone else. So, despite that wonderful title, you never get to see Dr Langeskov, his Tiger or the Emerald, and your task is simply to throw the right levers so that someone else gets their power fantasy. Unlike *The Stanley Parable* or *Monkey Island*, at no stage of the game are you given a choice inside the system – you carry out the right actions or you stop playing.

Pugh, like many game designers, seems keen to use ideas to improve the entertainment value of his games, without necessarily taking those ideas seriously.

The inescapable demon

Even if you don't believe in a capital-G God, a thought experiment called Laplace's Demon*† can replicate the effect. This argument states that if someone knows the exact location, speed and direction of every atom in the universe, they can work out where it will be and will have been at any point in its history, from the laws of classical mechanics. As Laplace put it:

> 'We ought then to regard the present state of the universe as the effect of its anterior state and as the cause of the one which is to follow. Given for one instant, an intelligence which could comprehend all the forces by which nature is animated and the respective situation of the beings who compose it – an intelligence sufficiently vast to submit these data to analysis – it would embrace in the same formula the movements of the greatest bodies of the universe and those of the lightest atom; for it, nothing would be uncertain and the future, as the past, would be present before its eyes. The human mind offers, in the perfection which it has been able to give to astronomy, a feeble idea of this intelligence.'‡

From the perspective of this intelligence, as from the viewpoint of a monotheistic god, no human would have choice, agency or free will – because every step could be traced back to some earlier cause and that would be the ultimate cause, not the will of the individual.

---

* The theory was created by the eighteenth-century French scholar, Pierre Simon, Marquis de Laplace. His creation was called 'Laplace's Demon' by later commentators, though, not by him.
† Laplace's Demon is nothing to do with the Japanese video game *Laplace no Ma'/Laplace's Demon* (https://en.wikipedia.org/wiki/Laplace_no_Ma), much as it would have made this chapter a lot easier to write.
‡ Pierre Simon Laplace, 'A Philosophical Essay on Probabilities' (1814).

This concept is a problem for those philosophers who seek to retain free will. The influential German philosopher Immanuel Kant, for example, was so keen to retain the concept that he even posited that the physical world wasn't the real world, but there was a separate 'noumenal' world inaccessible to human perception, just to house free will.*

Indeed, even DeMarle seems perturbed by this conclusion:

'I have to admit, I don't like these kinds of questions. Biology ... environmental pressures ... exposure to other cultures and philosophies – all these things have some weight in shaping who we are. But in the end, I believe we are the ones making choices in our lives. And that we need to take responsibility for those choices.'

How can we square that desire for responsibility with this appar-ently deterministic universe?

QUANTUM INDETERMINACY, *CONTRAPTION MAKER* AND *KERBAL SPACE PROGRAM*

Well, do we need to? We've spent all this time using determinism to knock down free will. But is that fair? Is determinism itself so with-out flaw? There are many arguments against Laplace's demon in particular, and several more against determinism generally. What's notable is that they're all arguments from physics – another minor spin-off of philosophy – and they criticise the chain of trackable causation that determinism assumes.

One is the butterfly effect, also known as **Chaos Theory**. This is the argument that tiny events can have huge ramifications. Kevin Ryan's mechanistic games *The Incredible Machine* (1993) and *Contraption Maker* (2014), despite being utterly logical physics-based puzzles, throw up perversely good examples of this, as Ryan explains:

* Typically, when a philosopher employs an argument that involves invent-ing a whole new sphere of existence just to justify their own prejudices ... it's not a very convincing argument.

'When you have a contraption made up of possible hundreds of parts that are interacting with each other for hundreds or thousands of frames then the butterfly effect becomes very obvious. Move a tennis ball over by just 0.0001 units and it may bounce off a teeter-totter a fraction of a second later and then make something else bounce left instead of right and divergence is off to the races.'*

The exponential effect of minutiae was important for Ryan because he released *Contraption Maker* on multiple computer systems, including PC and Macs, and mobile phones. But because a Really Complicated Bit of maths† is calculated fundamentally differently on these platforms, his deterministic physics system would throw up different results. And in his system, that meant wildly different outcomes.‡

The argument from chaos theory, then, is that a deterministic system can exhibit behaviour that's impossible to predict. Yet, while in practical cases like Ryan's we can see the consequences of this, in the theoretical case of the demon who by definition has precise knowledge of all the variables, it's not really that compelling. The demon is simply defined to be as aware of the effect of a small variable as a large one.§

* http://www.gamasutra.com/blogs/KevinRyan/20150331/239636/The_Butterfly_Effect.php
† Called Floating Point Determinism, ironically. Essentially, programming should produce a deterministic result every time you use the same inputs in a physics calculation. But with FPD you might not get a deterministic result each time if you're using different types of computer (like Macs or IBM PCs), individual different computers running the same operating system, or – insanely – the same machine. There's a lot more on this here: http://gafferongames.com/networking-for-game-programmers/floating-point-determinism/
‡ Ryan's solution was to make a separate 'automated determinism check' program that ensured calculations were the same across all the platforms.
§ Of course, you could deny the thought experiment, given it has no basis in reality . . .

Learning through Kerbals

Another challenge is more convincing, and can be illustrated by reference to *Kerbal Space Program* (Squad, 2015). This is a game about building manned space rockets in a well-modelled physics-based universe. When you build a spaceship in *Kerbal* you arrange the parts in particular ways, in the hope of getting it into orbit.

However, when you put too much fuel in your rocket and it's all smashed up into a hundred pieces that burn up on re-entry, then looking at those parts and working out exactly what happened is impossible. Particularly, the second law of thermodynamics gets in the way. As Max Planck stated it:

'Every process occurring in nature proceeds in the sense in which the sum of the entropies of all bodies taking part in the process is increased.'

Basically, *Kerbal* illustrates that many complex thermodynamic processes are seen by physicists as one-way. So even Laplace's demon couldn't look at the parts today and work out definitely where they'd come from. That doesn't mean, however, that the demon couldn't predict the future knowing perfectly where we are now – just that he wouldn't be able to definitively use all prior data to do it.

A better and more definitive criticism comes from '**quantum indeterminacy**', an outgrowth of quantum physics. What we need to worry about is that certain physical phenomena do not have definite outcomes or states, but instead exist in an in-between state. These quantum waveforms are simultaneously many states and no state until they're collapsed by interaction or observation. For example, an electron doesn't exist at a single point in spacetime, but more as an electron cloud existing in different quantities over a volume.

BioShock Infinite (Irrational Games, 2013) is notable here because it mingles the standard 'Copenhagen interpretation' of quantum mechanics and the less-accepted 'many worlds interpretation' of quantum mechanics, and uses the result to justify Elizabeth's powers. It appears that Elizabeth's (magical) power is to choose how quantum waveforms collapse between the infinite universes she can access – and in the absence of her choice, they stay uncollapsed. This has horrible consequences for any people who were killed in one universe and not another, who become simultaneously alive and dead – such as the gunsmith Chen Lin, who is in a state of tortured undeath until Elizabeth resolves the problem.

That said, even the standard interpretation of quantum mechanics – the Copenhagen interpretation – does terrible damage to determinism. If particles aren't definitely one thing or another, then the concept of an endless chain of causation doesn't work. Even an infinitely capable observer wouldn't be able to predict the future, because some steps along the way are made unpredictable by quantum indeterminacy, amongst many other quantum phenomena.

THE GOOMBA AND RANDOMNESS AS FREE WILL

Given all these criticisms, it seems that absolute determinism isn't true. No god or demon could predict or map the universe from the prior or current state of affairs. But if determinism is false, does that mean free will is true?

Well . . . not really. We live in a cause-and-effect universe, even if there are gaps in the causation that preclude determinism. Just because the system is flawed doesn't mean it doesn't follow causality away from those flaws. And, despite quantum mechanics, we do in our daily lives make accurate predictions about the future because physics is reliable. That's partly because, at large scales, quantum mechanics closely approximates general relativity, and we live at large scales.

Programming is a great parallel to this. Programming appears faultless – all those 1s and 0s zipping along in the form of electrons, zapping through transistors, generating the programs that run nuclear reactors, robot cars and your mobile phone – and video games, of course. But it isn't faultless: any PC nerd who's sat and watched a hard disk defragmentation or looked at Windows Task Manager can tell you there are faults in this supposedly flawless system all the time. The system is just designed to cope with them.

And it's really the cause-and-effect universe that's the challenge to free will, not the determinism that's a symptom of it. As the philosopher Simon Blackburn has said, 'We can't be free in the way we want to be if determinism is true. But it's no good if determinism is false either. It's a zugzwang.'*†

That's a problem for free will. Determinism might have failed, but a cause-and-effect universe can't be denied, even if there are holes in it from the randomness of those physical effects we just discussed. As the English philosopher Julian Baggini says:

> 'The only caveat to this provides little comfort. There may be some indeterminacy in the brain's operations, a kind of luck factor which means that sometimes one decision is made, sometimes another. But as we have already seen, randomness does not introduce the kind of freedom of choice we want. Whether our decisions flow inevitably from the state of the brain or there is some random fluctuation, it remains true that it was not within our power to have decided otherwise.'‡

Think of Mario jumping on a Goomba. You press the button on your gamepad, Mario jumps, he lands on the Goomba. You're part of the causal universe, so we can't claim your ultimate responsibility for that action. If we get something that's *outside* of standard causality to press the button – something driven by a particle detector, say, that we've aimed at a region of space vacuum, triggered by paired particles, waiting for them to pop statistically-predictably but randomly into existence – a particle appears, the button is pressed, Mario jumps, the Goomba falls off the screen. But that doesn't mean our free will made him jump – he jumped as a causal effect of quantum randomness.

Or think back to *The Incredible Machine*. This is a causal system, like our universe. However, it has a random factor in there too, caused by the Floating Point Indeterminacy problem. We wouldn't

---

* Quoted from 'In Our Time', BBC Radio 4, 10 March 2011. http://www.bbc.co.uk/programmes/b00z5y9z
† 'Zugzwang' is the German term meaning 'compulsion to move', from a chess situation where you have to move, but any possible move will make your situation worse.
‡ Julian Baggini, *Freedom Regained* (2015).

want to call that random factor free will, as some people do randomness in humans (or any organism, in fact), because it makes the
concept of free will meaningless.

So do we really want to equate randomness with free will? Most
people wouldn't because it makes our actions even more meaningless. If an action has come causally through us, at least we've had
some causal involvement in the outcome, even as part of a deterministic system. But if it's just randomness that caused the outcome,
then we can't claim any agency whatsoever – it doesn't seem like the
right sort of control. As Baggini says:

> 'Human actions flow as inexorably from the characters of the
> actors as water flows inexorably from the source of a river. The
> only reason we do not acknowledge this is that we do not feel
> any compulsion to act as we do. Our actions appear optional to
> us because the forces that make them inevitable are not
> evident to us.'*

This illusion also means that the concept of fate or destiny seems
plausible while being impossible under these same laws of physics
– after all, no other will is fating us to a particular destiny; it's just the
outgrowth of the physics of an uncaring universe.

NEUROSCIENCE, *DOTA* AND AN AI CALLED T.O.M.

Moreover, there are other reasons than causality to believe we're
not free. Moving on from physics, this part of the discussion has
been taken over by another of philosophy's descendant sciences –
neuroscience, a spin-off of the science of biology that was started
by Aristotle in the fourth century BC. Neuroscience is the relatively new scientific study of the physical brain and its links to the
mind.

Neuroscientific experiments started by Benjamin Libet in the
1980s seemed to show that humans had unconsciously initiated
actions ahead of the conscious mind making a decision. His subjects

---

* *Freedom Regained*, Julian Baggini, p. 52.

were asked to tap a button, whenever they wanted. However, he was able to show them that that the decision-making part of the brain, the prefrontal cortex, had fired up two hundred milliseconds before the subject consciously thought of it. This seemed to imply that the action had started before the conscious mind had decided upon it – and hence that the conscious mind couldn't be responsible for these actions.

These experiments have continued up to the present, with the recorded length of time separating the unconscious decision and the conscious awareness growing and growing. The most recent study, by Gabriel Kreiman in 2013, detected relevant activity in other parts of the brain up to five seconds before a conscious decision had been made to press the button.

To be clear: **these experiments show that long before you choose to press any button on your keyboard or controller, some deeper part of your psyche has already started preparations to press it.**

It's hard to overstate the importance of these experiments. They seem to show that brain processes are responsible for action, but not brain processes associated with thoughts.* Indeed, some philosophers take them to mean that the human mind is retrospectively justifying agency for the unconscious mind, and we are not actually in conscious control at all. This is a problem for free will if you associate it with just the conscious mind.

In *The Turing Test* (Bulkhead Interactive, 2016), the AI T.O.M. is well aware of these experiments, and argues that free will is an illusion. Hence he feels able to introduce implants into the scientists he's working with, to subtly control their behaviour through Pavlovian and instrumental conditioning. His justification is that it's better that they're controlled by his goal-directed, conscious choices than their own irrational impulses. 'Manipulate is not a dirty word,' he says. 'You manipulate clay to make art. If people are manipulated to make better decisions then that is a good thing.'

Waller sounds a note of caution about the experiments performed by Libet and others.

---

* See also the discussion of identity theory in Chapter 4.

'This sounds like the claim that conscious intentions (or conscious "will") is causally inefficacious and/or reconstructed post hoc. Many have made such claims on the basis of such studies. But all the data show is that the reported time of first awareness of conscious intention is later than the ramp up of some related brain activity. Alternative interpretations are that the early activity isn't an unconscious decision to move; that it is an unconscious decision, but that the conscious decision happens later; that the conscious decision happens later, but doesn't play a causal role; or that the conscious decision is reconstructed from post-action events for a sense of ownership.'

The post-hoc narrative

The neuroscientist Patrick Haggard argues that the current consensus is towards the last option – 'a narrative we make up after the event' as he puts it, though his own experiments disagree with that argument.* So remember that example we had earlier, about the *Deus Ex* augmented humans who felt they had agency in actions they weren't in control of? That's not science fiction, under this interpretation. The 'conscious' part of this human organism that humans seem to want to call ourselves, that we choose to separate off from its host as the active agent, may actually live in this science-fiction universe where we claim alien actions as our own.

Curiously, that's something that's been experimentally demonstrated by the late psychologist Daniel Wegner, to help replicate what

---

* Haggard's experiments with a colleague who lacked an arm and hence had a 'ghost limb' seem to argue against the creation of a post-event narrative. 'Our results suggest that conscious intention may depend on preparatory brain activity, and not on making, or ever having made, the corresponding physical body movement. Accounts that reduce conscious volition to mere retrospective confabulation cannot easily explain our participant's neurophenomenology of action and inhibition. In contrast, the results are consistent with the view that specific neural events prior to movement may generate conscious experiences of positive and negative volition.' From 'Voluntary control of a phantom limb' (Walsh E1, Long C2, Haggard P2) *Neuropsychologia* (August 2015).

another psychologist Ellen Langer called 'the illusion of control'.*
Wegner ran a series of experiments testing 'magical thinking', where
he persuaded subjects that they were influencing external events
that they had no control over. In one, the subjects watched a basket-
ball player attempting to shoot hoops. When the viewers positively
visualised the player's success ahead of his shots, they felt instrumental in his success when he scored.†

In other experiments, Wegner demonstrated a 'binding effect',
where when test subjects triggered an action themselves, they
perceived the action and its effect to be closer together in time.
Waller says 'it seems like our brains bind together actions and effects
to give us this sense that we are the author of our actions'.‡ It seems
human minds are subconsciously keen to extend their agency, even
if that requires magical thinking.

The inner scapegoat

This reveals a second major curiosity about how we think about
ourselves, as noted earlier: that we want to claim that only the
'conscious' part of our organism counts in terms of free will and
responsibility, and that all the other subconscious matter is foreign
to us. That, to players of *Mario & Luigi: Bowser's Inside Story*
(AlphaDream, 2009), we are just Mario inside a giant lizard and the
rest of the lizard's actions don't matter. This is what has been called
'**Ryle's regress**' after the philosopher Gilbert Ryle§ – by focusing on a

---

* Langer herself found that we're most likely to think we have control over
systems when there are skill cues present like rolling dice in a casino. This
is presumably another reason why input-heavy tasks like video games are
so compelling, because they make us feel like our input is especially valuable, even if we're not actually affecting the outcome at all. Games with
heavily randomised systems and relatively complex game mechanics like
Candy Crush doubtless benefit from this illusion.
† 'Everyday magical powers: the role of apparent mental causation in the
overestimation of personal influence', *Journal of Personality and Social
Psychology* (2006)
‡ By contrast, priming subjects by talking about God or computers ahead
of an experiment reduced the subject's sense of agency.
§ See also the discussion of the 'ghost in the machine' in Chapter 4. (Fans

tiny part of the organism and ascribing all agency and value to that, we're not actually providing any answer, but merely shifting the same discussion to a different scale.*

It is true that, if you focus on your thoughts, they just seem to arise unless you make a conscious effort to control their flow. The Scottish philosopher David Hume saw that humans always looked for a cause when we saw an effect. As we aren't aware of the physical brain processes that produce our thoughts, we ascribe them to our intangible will or consciousness.

Yet it seems unjustifiable to separate off this ghost. Can we really think we are just our consciousness and not our subconsciousness? We may naively think of ourselves that way, but it doesn't seem to be reasonable, as opposed to claiming the entirety of our organism as ourself. There is no ghost in the machine that materialises to make a decision. We are that machine, in its entirety.† And, though we may not be consciously aware of making a decision, that decision is still ours – we must still own it.

Moreover, there is evidence that all the levels of our minds are involved in these decision-making processes. When you play a complex game – let's say *DOTA* – you're making a whole range of decisions that involve language, emotional connections, memory and analysis. You're planning tactics with your teammates, you're correctly deploying complex in-game powers, you're remembering the upgrade tree for your character and selecting the right choices for your team's strategy, and you're combining with your team on the fly to generate the best responses to the enemies' tactics. This isn't simply something like pushing a button randomly – there's a huge amount of processing going on, involving everything that you might want to call 'you'. This seems to be the tack that Waller takes, as a

of *Undertale* may note that this is different from the character Mettaton, who seems to be a robot but *literally* is a ghost in a machine.)

* In another example of this fallacy, seventeenth-century super-philosopher René Descartes accepted that there were problems with how the soul could control the human body – so he argued that humans were controlled through the pineal gland. This didn't answer the problem, but shifted it to a location that contemporary science didn't know much about.

† See Chapter 4.

compatibilist – someone who thinks that free will is compatible with a causal universe:

> 'Right now anyway I'm a compatibilist. That means that I believe that we have free will, not some sort of heaven or hell moral responsibility, but a sufficient degree of control such that we can be held morally responsible.
>
> 'I buy into the reasons-responsive views, which are that as long as we can say that people have a certain capacity to appreciate reasons – maybe including moral reasons and acts for reasons – then they have flexibility of action. Then that together with some other conditions is going to be sufficient for saying that they can act freely. You can have that in a deterministic or indeterministic universe.'

Baggini goes further, saying that artists show us that to be free is also to 'be able to generate highly personal outputs from the inputs of nature, nurture and society, not to be free from their influences, able to create from nothing'.

The importance of freedom from coercion – what we will call 'Liberty' in Chapter 9 – does seem to have survived all this. We can still see that our organism being free of the coercive influence of another means it still has a range of options open to it – even if it was only ever going to choose one of them, it's still the choice of that organism, not of another. As Baggini says, 'To be free is for one's decisions, actions, beliefs, and values to be one's own.'

JUSTICE, CHARACTER DESIGN AND *PORTAL*'S WHEATLEY

As you can see from Baggini and Waller's responses, there are a lot of philosophers attempting to save free will. That's reasonable – it's a core concept to many personal elements of our existence. For example, what happens to our sense of identity if we don't really have choice? What about democratic voting? Does liberty matter with no free will? More widely, it's so deeply embedded in our culture, our language and our politics that to lose it would mean rebuilding much of the way we deal with society.

The most crucial question, however, is: how does justice work with no free will?* What do we do with criminals, and who do we judge to be criminally culpable, with what justification?

If we decide not to treat the conscious mind as separate from the rest of the human organism, as in *The Swapper* (Facepalm Games, 2013)[†], then blame becomes muddied. Under that reasoning, we might treat errant humans in a similar way to how we treat errant animals or broken machines. We call the object a killer, seclude it from society until it's fixed; if it's unfixable, we destroy or retire it. We can understand its apparent 'decision-making' and we use that to evaluate how dangerous it is, but we don't pretend that it's a separate being.

A bigger problem

But that's not the biggest problem for justice from the failure of free will. A bigger problem is around the question of responsibility generally. The argument goes: you do what you do because of how you are; to be ultimately responsible for what you do, you have to be responsible for what you are; but you can't be responsible for how you are; so you can't be truly responsible for what you do. As the scientist Richard Dawkins has said, 'A truly, scientific mechanistic view of the nervous system make nonsense of the very idea of responsibility, whether diminished or not.'[‡]

Why can't you be responsible for who you are? You'd have to 'bootstrap' – that is, create yourself.[§] Think about it like a character creation sheet in a role-playing game. You have to choose what race you are, what gender, what job you're going to do, what you look like – without ever playing the game and knowing anything about the setting or mechanics of the world you're going into. Many games do

---

* This discussion is also important for Chapters 8 and 9.
† See Chapter 4.
‡ *Edge*, 2006: What is your dangerous idea?
§ Bootstrap is a curious word, dating as far back as 1834, meaning to attempt an impossible task: 'to pull yourself up by the straps of your boots'. In the 1950s, it was used as a metaphor for computers starting up their programs from apparently nothing – and hence 'booting'.

this and then have to explain the setting and mechanics heavily in tutorials, tooltips and flavour text. It's incoherent, but a standard error of game design.

We don't get that choice in our lives; we don't get to pick what our starting point is, who we are. And if we could, on what basis would we make that decision? Well, who we are already . . . it's an infinite regress. Essentially, you can't be responsible for who you are. And who you are is causally responsible for what you do.

This seems to be a problem with the concept of 'free will' – particularly with the concept of ultimate responsibility bound into it. Perhaps this was the flaw in our thinking all along – after all, in a causal universe, can anything be its own ultimate cause? Given quantum mechanics, randomness is likely to be the ultimate cause of every effect anyway. More interesting are the close causes of an action – and, unlike an ultimate cause that seems to be unique, there can be several close causes of an effect, which seems more true to the world we experience. And they can include elements of us. Causality in this sense doesn't require determinism. Says Waller:

'I don't think we require being responsible for all the antecedents of our choices and the antecedents of those antecedents, and so on, for us to be completely morally responsible. There are philosophers who speculate that the source of our current concept of moral responsibility comes from a mix of throwback mechanisms and evolution plus this religious idea of ultimate responsibility.'

Instead compatibilists like Waller – who believe free will and determinism are compatible – argue that moral responsibility, in this sense, requires a similar chain of causality. For without the causation linking your action to its effect, why is it your fault? Indeed, compatibilist moral responsibility doesn't require that determinism is false: it requires that causality is true and that your actions are causally efficacious, even if they're not ultimate causes themselves. Determinism, by contrast, 'bypasses' your actions, by claiming that only ultimate causes matter. Waller continues:

'Determinism is true leading back to the big bang such that I go and buy a coffee now. However, in that causal chain, among the proximal causes are things like my desire to have a coffee and my belief that the coffee shop is open, my intention that I form, the decision that I have to go get a coffee. All of those things can be causally efficacious. If it's a morally weighted decision, then your moral reasons can play a role and none of that is threatened by determinism in and of itself.'

Moral responsibility isn't just about actions that people have willed though. We – in our justice system particularly – hold people responsible for things that they haven't willed. We sometimes call this negligence or recklessness.

The dumbest moron who ever lived

Think about Wheatley in *Portal 2* (Valve Corporation, 2011). *Portal 2* is a first-person puzzle game set in a pulp-fiction scientific facility. Wheatley is a personality cube whom a group of scientists designed as an 'Intelligence Dampening' unit. He was then attached to the AI series antagonist GLaDOS to inhibit her decision-making because otherwise she was far too effective – similar to how we have to restrict AIs in multiplayer games where they're competing against humans because otherwise they don't make human-seeming mistakes and aren't fun competitors. GLaDOS describes Wheatley as: 'The product of the greatest minds of a generation working together . . . with the express purpose of building the dumbest moron who ever lived.' Later in the game, he ends up taking over GLaDOS' role maintaining a large scientific testing facility and makes some truly appalling decisions, in line with the way he was created.

Wheatley is a character who explicitly bears no responsibility for who he is – after all, he's been designed to consistently make bad decisions. If there are options for him to take, he always willingly chooses the worst one. Yet because we still cannot desire the outcomes he produces and because we treat him as an actor, we can call him negligent in terms of his social responsibilities. As the German poet Goethe said in *The Sorrows of Young Werther*,

'Misunderstandings and neglect occasion more mischief in the world than even malice and wickedness. At all events, the two latter are of less frequent occurrence.'

Even though Wheatley isn't ultimately responsible for what he does, he still wills it and carries it out. It doesn't seem fair to *blame* him for doing what he has to do – indeed, if anything, we should pity him for being so broken – but we can differentiate the forms of responsibility we ascribe to him. We can then act in different ways to rectify problems with his responsibility. That differentiation should really help clarify what we mean by responsibility and how this compatibilist free will helps with it.

In terms of causal responsibility, Wheatley is a core link in the causal chain of these events. And these events are societally undesirable, so we have to find a way of preventing him continuing with them. Restriction of his abilities, until they can be fixed, seems a justified path here. This is a badly functioning organism. Both incompatibilists and compatibilists can agree on this. So, our first strand is restricting his capabilities.

In terms of societal responsibility, we can hold Wheatley – or any individual – responsible for the duties and functions of an organism in its given society. This responsibility judges him not because he's willed something – which he apparently can't help, given his lack of responsibility for his origins – but for not behaving as he should. We want to shape the morality of the individual away from this behaviour pattern and perhaps also make an example of him to dissuade others from following this path in future. So the second and third strands of our approach are altering the organism and publicly signalling the limitations we've put on his liberty.

Our society's courts would judge him on this strand of societal responsibility, in its form of legal responsibility, that is, the public morality of a society enshrined haphazardly in law. Manslaughter is explicitly this. You killed someone, you didn't mean to, but you are responsible for it because you didn't behave properly – that is, you are the organism that was the cause of it – so the court will convict you of it, because we need to prevent that sort of thing ever happening. We'll judge how much of the death was your responsibility, and how much the responsibility of others for your upbringing (if young), for your circumstances, or for aiding or deterring you.

For the court and for us, this judgement isn't black and white. We assume that everyone is on a scale of responsibility, with the completely brainwashed – like Wheatley – at one end, and the mature individual with sound reasoning, societally accepted belief systems and no constraints at the other – like Dr Breen from *Half-Life 2* (Valve Corporation, 2004).

A villainous loss of control

Wheatley is an example of a badly abused individual with irrational reasoning and insane beliefs, incapable of carrying out any course of action that he willed; our courts would judge him as having extremely diminished responsibility for any results of his actions. Similar cases are *BioShock*'s brainwashed Jack or an augmented individual from *Deus Ex* at the time of the Aug Incident. These are people whose actions are explicitly out of their control – they were literally unable to do other than the things they were commanded to, and the mechanism by which they were controlled is obvious to us. If the mechanisms of control could be removed – as Tenenbaum did with Jack – we might judge them able to re-enter society. Incurable individuals – which potentially includes Wheatley – might be judged insane and forever kept away from society, to keep it safe.

By contrast, Dr Breen from *Half-Life 2* is a mature, rational professor of science aiding an alien race to commit genocide. He fully understands what they're doing and is hoping to that he will escape their actions through his complicity. Our courts would call him fully culpable. Indeed, because his actions and intentions aren't badly formed, he willed them knowing full well that they went against his existing societal responsibility.

So Dr Breen would be excluded from society, both to protect society against his selfishness and to deter other rational creatures from following his example. Note the greater sentence isn't down to punishment, but to deterrence – accidents are one thing, as the person doing probably doesn't want to do them again – but intended actions are especially dangerous, as they indicate a consistently wrong organism, or a morality opposed to that of society at large.

THE ROAD TO RAPTURE

So how is *The Last of Us* different from *The Road?* This game-player, this subjective thing, this human, can't help but feel it has agency, and that it's valuable. In *The Last of Us*, when we're choosing between killing a dying man or leaving him to die, we really feel that choice keenly, and we are the proximate cause of that outcome, making the difference. When someone does something similar in *The Road* we have no input whatsoever.

From a determinist viewpoint, it may have seemed like we had no choice over a decision in *The Last of Us*, because all causes can be traced back to an ultimate cause – but that's an illusion. The past may be fixed, there may be an *ultimate* cause of our actions – but quantum indeterminacy means there's no way of tracing that chain.

Whether we're the ultimate cause of our actions is a question for the physicists and not the philosophers. It doesn't matter that we're part of a causal chain and not its start; it doesn't matter that we're not conscious of the start of our decisions; it doesn't matter that we couldn't have done other than we do. We are free within constraint and we never could have been other than that.

We, as organisms, have an ability to change the physical world around us. We live in a society that wants particular things from us. If we fail to conform to those things, we bear causal and legal responsibility for that failure. We might feel that sometimes our actions are out of our control, are caused by uncontrollable elements of us, and the experiments of Libet and others back that up. But we are the entirety of our organism and we bear moral responsibility for the things that 'we' do – so we should still 'own' the actions of our body. And when we transgress societal laws, we should accept the consequences. The other side of this is that society should dispense with punishment entirely – justice should be about rehabilitation, protection and restriction of action.

Finally, we're going to have to live with the way that language uses 'freedom' and 'consciousness' and perhaps dispose of the phrase 'free will'. Our language means that we can't help thinking of it in an archaic way, even if it's an illusion. That makes it dangerously misleading. The resulting commonplace idea of 'free will' leads us to ascribe blame where there should only ever be pity. And our wider understanding of human action leaves lots of room for pity.

Limbo, looking good.

....

Luisa: Uh, what was in that mushroom? Steroids? Something out of Wonderland? You suddenly seem huge.

Maria: I feel . . . good! And strong, like a hero. Like I could jump small buildings.

Luisa: Well, you're certainly hero-sized. But I thought being a hero was more about what you did than what you looked like?

Maria: Yes! It's both. It's about looking great, and being a heroic person. Everyone knows who the heroes are, and copies them because heroes always do the right thing. Mainly jumping on your foes' heads and rescuing royalty.

Luisa: Heh, but not everyone can be a hero. I was always more about following the rules. Don't eat anthropomorphic mushrooms, don't jump on people you don't know, always rescue the prince.

Maria: Princes, tch. Always getting into trouble. You'd think they had better personal security than two passing plumbers. The problem for me about laws is that someone has to make them up – and it's never me.

Luisa: I guess royal budgets have been cut – they spent all their money on those big castles, like old King Ludwig. But, sure, you can make up the rules too, aside from the laws – it's fairly easy.

Maria: Isn't it just easier to be a good person, and not worry about sticking to rules? Just to do the right thing?

Luisa: Actually, you just make up rules that, if everyone did them, would work. Would make everyone happy. Like no one should lie.

Maria: Or like everyone should eat mushrooms?

Luisa: Well, not really. If everyone ate mushrooms, there'd be no mushrooms left and lots of other food. And the mushrooms would all be sad.

Maria: Hmm. That seems a bit boring. And why should anyone obey your rules?

Luisa: Yes, that is a problem. But then why should anyone copy you, the hero?

Maria: Hmm, true. Perhaps there's a better way.

CHAPTER SEVEN

The call of duty and
Ultima's virtues

....

'Human happiness and moral duty are inseparably connected.'[*]

George Washington (1732–99)

'The problem with people who have no vices is that generally you can be pretty sure they're going to have some pretty annoying virtues.'[†]

Elizabeth Taylor (1932–2011)

'One should always be drunk. That's all that matters . . . But with what? With wine, with poetry, or with virtue, as you choose. But get drunk.'[‡]

Charles Baudelaire (1821–67)

The sun in ruined Dubai is bright and it temporarily blinds you. When your sight clears, you and your squad are looking down a long dune-covered road with a bridge across it, and desolate tower blocks stretching into the distance. Two men are tied up and dangling from a bridge in front of you, with distant soldiers pointing guns at them. The insane military commander you've been chasing down has imposed martial law on the city, and declared both these men criminals. Over the radio, he orders you to judge them. If you run, he'll order you shot.

---

[*] Letter dated 1789, 'To the Bishops, Clergy, and Laity of the Protestant Episcopal church in the States of New York, New Jersey, Pennsylvania, Delaware, Maryland, Virginia, and North Carolina, in general Convention assembled.'
[†] Steven Schwartz, *The Seven Deadly Sins* (2000).
[‡] 'Enivrez-Vous', *Le Figaro*, 7 February 1864.

Spec Ops: The Line (Yager Development, 2012) may have looked and sounded like a generic military shooter, but it was much more morally complex than that, riffing off Joseph Conrad's dark and influential novel *Heart of Darkness* (published in 1899, and which inspired *Apocalypse Now*). In this scenario, you have a variety of choices:

1 To follow orders fully and execute both of the prisoners;
2 To refuse to get involved, in which case the commander will order one of your squadmates shot, followed by you;
3 To execute just one of the prisoners, to keep as many people alive as possible. Between these morally compromised options, your choice is not easy.

What we're looking at here is ethics – what is roughly called **the study of morality** – that is, what the good things are to do in life. Those three options correspond pretty closely with the three main ethical systems that have dominated history:

1 **Deontology**, where the moral thing is to do your duty, come what may;
2 **Virtue ethics**, where the moral thing is to be a good person, whatever happens; and
3 **Utilitarianism**, where the moral thing is to make sure everyone is as happy as possible.

Though this difference seems confusing, these strands can lead to very different outcomes and very different value systems. So the utilitarian John Stuart Mill ends up with a behaviour set that prioritises making everyone happy and preventing suffering . . . but we'll talk about him more in Chapter 8. By contrast, the virtue ethicist Aristotle – who we'll talk about more later in this chapter – focuses on the good person, the person who instinctively does the right thing. Finally, the deontologist Immanuel Kant ends up with a bunch of rules – like 'thou shalt not kill' – and thinks that whether or not an act fits those rules is the important thing.

CALL OF DEONTOLOGY: MORAL WARFARE

The frankly horrible phrase 'deontological ethics' was established by Jeremy Bentham in the early nineteenth century to mean 'the knowledge of what is right and proper'. But as it's derived from the Greek *deon,* meaning 'obligation' or 'duty', we'll refer to it as duty ethics. (Unless you think Infinity Ward should have called its game series 'Call of Deontology'?)

Duty ethics seems initially very similar to virtue ethics, especially when contrasted to utilitarianism, which is all about consequences and not actions. Many theories of virtue ethics included duty as one of their virtues. After all, you'd think good people would perform good actions. These two theories are also quite different from how modern people and governments profess to act, which tend to be about maximising something (money or GDP, in many cases).

Yet there's a core difference between duty ethics and virtue ethics. One is focused on the rightness or wrongness of the actions you undertake; the other is focused on the character and habits of the person undertaking those actions. In duty ethics, 'right' takes precedence over 'good'. You do the right thing because it's right – not because of its consequences, and not because you're the right sort of person. You do it on *principle.*

So you don't save the princess because you're a good person, and that's what you do. You do it because saving somebody is *right*, and dutiful people do the right thing. For a soldier, following orders is the dutiful and hence the right thing – so when your sergeant says 'jump', you jump.

And, as a dutiful person, you have certain inviolable rules you live by. So, killing people is normally a straightforwardly wrong thing to a duty ethicist. Lying is also wrong, regardless of the consequences.* Stealing is wrong. Breaking promises is wrong. Stick to the spirit of these rules, and you can't go far wrong, says the dutiful man.

What's notable is that these are all rules that everyday video game heroes break all the time. Nathan Drake, The Master Chief and Commander Shepard have killed their thousands, indeed, tens of

---

* Interestingly, *Knights of the Old Republic II* regularly allowed you to say the same statement as either the truth or a lie.

thousands. The heroes of *Oblivion* (Bethesda, 2006) and *Skyrim* (Bethesda, 2011) treat other people's personal property as their own. *Metal Gear*'s (Konami and Kojima Productions, 1987–2016) Revolver Ocelot lies as easily he breathes, as does *Star Wars: Knights of the Old Republic*'s (BioWare, 2003) Kreia, *BioShock Infinite*'s (Irrational Games, 2013) Booker DeWitt, *Dragon Age II*'s (BioWare, 2011) Varric and *Mass Effect*'s (BioWare, 2007–12) Illusive Man. And all Kratos' problems in *God of War* (Sony Santa Monica, 2005–15) stem from him breaking his oath to the God of War Ares at the series' start. By the standards of duty, these are not good people.

All these undutiful heroes reflect that, these days, we rarely portray people who stick rigidly to received ethical systems as heroic. The chivalrous knight seems like an anachronism, as does the priest who only follows the Ten Commandments rigidly. Even most lawyers and religious people I know don't follow their government's legal system or the tenets of their religion absolutely.

Indeed, most of the examples of duty ethicists in games are villains who think they're heroes – sometimes entire organisations who think they're working for good, but whose actions cause terrible things to come about.

The torments of morality

The classic role-playing game *Planescape: Torment* (Black Isle Studios, 1999) contains several examples of extreme duty ethicists, people or creatures so dedicated to a particular code that they can do no other. There's Dak'kon, an alien humanoid from the plane of Limbo, who follows a maxim of extreme introspection and self-knowledge. There's Nordom, a semi-robotic construct, attempting to escape a world of absolute logic. And there's Ignus, a pyromaniac wizard whose only maxim is that everything should burn.

Yet the most striking character is found in the dungeons beneath the prison city of Curst, hidden behind a portal. Here stands a massive suit of armour, abandoned and rusted – but curiously untouched by the grasping local scavengers.

'The armor is archaic and the shoulder blades are just that – a great ridge of blades sprouting from the shoulder plates. You almost would have taken the ridged blades as decoration, but they look too heavy and dangerous to be anything more than an additional weapon on an already menacing suit of armor. The armor bears dents and other marks of battle, and its surface has been scarred by age and rust. The helm resembles the skull of some creature; curved metal teeth lined the bottom edge of the faceplate, hanging down over empty space. The helm rests in the air, its interior hidden in shadow. As you stare upon the suit of armor the shadows beneath the visor took shape ... coalescing into the features of a powerful, ebony-skinned man. His eyes are like fires and he bears numerous scars.'*

This is Vhailor. In life he was a member of a faction called the Mercykillers. He was so dedicated to doing the right thing – in his conception, merciless justice – that he didn't even notice his own death. The strength of his belief turned him into something more – an 'avatar' of justice.† As he says:

'When the injustice is great enough, justice will lend me the strength needed to correct it. None may stand against it. It will shatter every barrier, sunder any shield, tear through any enchantment, and lend its servant the power to pass sentence. Know this: There is nothing on all the Planes‡ that can stay the

---

* *Planescape: Torment*, Black Isle Studios, (Interplay Entertainment, 1999).
† The word 'avatar' comes from Hindu mythology. When the gods took human form on Earth, the human was called their avatar – a word that literally means 'descent'. In video games, the term is commonly used to mean the figure the player controls, and was coined by Richard Garriott (see later in this chapter).
‡ The Planescape setting of *Dungeons & Dragons* was one of the most inspired fantasy universes ever created. It consisted of a range of pocket 'planes' that fade into each other, ranging from planes of pure logic to planes of pure chaos. The game *Planescape: Torment* itself is set at the centre of the planes, around the city of Sigil, an impossible city on the outside of a doughnut-shaped surface sitting on top of an infinite spire. It was retired from the D&D universe in the late 1990s.

hand of justice when it is brought against them. It may unmake armies. It may sunder the thrones of gods. Know that for all who betray justice, I am their fate. And fate carries an executioner's axe.'[*]

As Chris Avellone, writer and designer of *Planescape: Torment*, says:

'I believe it was Churchill said, "I'd prefer to be right than consistent. Vhailor's pretty . . . consistent. If your views are so rigid they can never adapt to changing circumstances, new information, and new perspectives, then you may be doing yourself and others a disservice. That said, Ignus and Vhailor were intended to be two different shadowing companion threats in *Planescape*, so their extreme views and powers represent that. Both are the only two companions that can kill the Nameless One because of their belief in their own ideals. While Vhailor remains ever-uncompromising, Ignus does apologize for his descent into madness at the end of the game, or at least has a chance to.'

These dutiful, fanatical characters recur throughout video games. BioWare's Star Trek tribute *Mass Effect* has the Asari Justicars, alien heroes dedicated to eliminating evil and corruption – but the Asari tend to keep them away from other races, because they're merciless, indomitable killers. They're so dedicated to their cause that the only one you encounter – Samara – attempts to kill herself at one point, rather than carry out the mandates of her creed, which would require her to kill her remaining daughter.

Historical duty
What's notable is that, in games, these duty-driven characters and factions tend to come from more medieval and/or violent societies. That's reflected in the way that theories of duty are much more rare in the modern day. Generally today we seem much more interested in rights, but throughout history duty ethics were quite common,

* *Planescape: Torment*, Black Isle Studios, (Interplay Entertainment, 1999).

especially in more hierarchical societies. This is the Roman philosopher and orator Cicero on duty:

> 'True law is right reason in agreement with nature; it is of universal application, unchanging and everlasting; it summons to duty by its commands, and averts from wrongdoing by its prohibitions.'*

Or take ancient Greece. When being a citizen of a state was a rare privilege, as in Athens or Sparta where the slaves outnumbered the citizens, having the military and social obligations of a citizen was something of a mark of pride, as it clearly defined your privileged place in the city's strata.

Even in the Homeric poems, like the *Odyssey*, every person in a society – from the lowliest slave to the highest king – had obligations to the others, and to the gods above. These duties provided unity in the state, harmony between gods and men, justice and social cohesion, as well as some protection given the lack of notions about human rights. We can see something similar in Plato's *Republic*, where the various classes in the city must forsake their desires; the philosopher-kings, for example, must give up their studies of the forms in order to run the city for the common good.

Kant and rebuilt morality

Two thousand years later, an eighteenth-century German philosopher called Immanuel Kant – often thought of as the father of modern philosophy – took it upon himself to rebuild duty ethics. He agreed with the ancients that acting from duty was the morally right way to act. Yet he thought that the things they praised – Aristotle's praise of magnificence, say, or Epicurus' laudation of pleasure – were neither good in themselves nor good without qualification. For example, Epicurean hedonism couldn't be correct for Kant because of sadism: pleasure one could take from ethically bad situations where another was suffering.

Nor did he think that an actor's motives could be judged by the

* *De Republica* [Of The Republic], Book III.

consequences of their acts. After all, we can harm people when we have good intentions, and help people when we intend ill. Instead he said:

> 'Nothing in the world – indeed nothing even beyond the world – can possibly be conceived which could be called good without qualification except a good will.'*

And a good will occurs when you act out of a respect for a moral law, which you do because you have a duty to do so, not out of self-love. *Planescape*'s Vhailor is an excellent example. Your character trapped him in prison in one of your previous lives;† he died without realising it but persisted from a sense of mission and duty. He is composed of nothing but respect for justice, with a lifelong (and after-lifelong) task to bring to task traitors and criminals, with no mercy. He has no self-love because he has almost no self.

Kant built a new version of duty ethics from his concept of the 'will to good', around a moral law he called the **'Categorical Imperative'**. To clarify, a hypothetical imperative would be a statement of the form 'if X, then you must Y' – such as 'if you want to kill an aristocrat at Lady Boyle's costume party, then you must first find out what costume she's wearing'. By contrast, a categorical imperative is something that applies in all circumstances – so 'given any situation, then you must' or just 'you must'. In our example, 'given any situation, you must kill an aristocrat.'

For something to have that level of appeal, it has to be completely convincing to all people. Kant argued that a categorical imperative also had to be intrinsically good in itself and good without qualification – that the thing you must do is never going to make the situation ethically worse. If it matched both those premises, then it would be an unconditional obligation, regardless of what we wanted and any consequences.

For Kant, the most notable form of his categorical imperative was a single rule: 'Act only on that maxim through which you can at the

* *Groundwork of the Metaphysic of Morals*, Immanuel Kant, 1785.
† The biggest villains in *Planescape: Torment* always seem to turn out to be earlier incarnations of yourself, beyond the veil of amnesia. See Chapter 5.

same time will that it should become a universal law.'* That is, you should only do something if every rational being could do it without it causing big problems for society. So, looking at our example, the action 'kill an aristocrat' cannot be universalised, because it would involve the death of all aristocrats, which is neither intrinsically good, nor good in itself, nor good for the affected aristocrats.

Kant also had other formulations, such as: 'Act in such a way that you treat humanity, whether in your own person or in the person of any other, never merely as a means to an end, but always at the same time as an end.' So killing Lady Boyle in the game *Dishonored* (Arkane Studios, 2012) might be a means to restoring the rightful queen to the throne – but it's not very respectful of her as a human and hence an end in herself. More respectful, in the game's twisted ideology, is to keep her alive but imprisoned by her secret admirer. This treats her as a means to an end, but also as an end in herself.

Thought Palaces of Gold

The maxim about universalisability doesn't seem new to us today, and it wasn't in Kant's time either. It's called the **Golden Rule** by philosophers and, in its various forms, has been the inspiration behind most versions of principled ethics since the Ancient Egyptians first formulated it. For example, around 500 BC, Confucius said, 'Never impose on others what you would not choose for yourself'† and around 35 BC Jesus is quoted in the Bible as saying, 'Therefore all things whatsoever ye would that men should do to you, do ye even so to them: for this is the law and the prophets.'‡ The only difference with Kant's formulation is that he has rewritten it to make it less open to loopholes – for instance, a sadomasochist applying Confucius' or Jesus' code rigidly would hurt other people unnecessarily.

Yet though we can see the easy appeal of the golden rule, that doesn't mean we can call it 'true'. In *Planescape: Torment* and *Star Wars: Knights of the Old Republic*, both written by Chris Avellone, dialogue options often allow the player to say the same thing but

---

* Immanuel Kant, *Metaphysics of Morals* (1797), Chapter 11.
† *Analects*, Confucius XV.24
‡ Matthew 7:12, King James Bible.

with different emphases – including 'Truth' and 'Lie', but also 'Make Vow'. While the game rewards or punishes you through sidequests and moral alignment shifts, Kant would say that lying is never justified. Lying infringes his categorical imperative, because you can't be happy with the consequences of everyone lying all the time – no one could rely on anyone else and human society would collapse.

Yet Avellone doesn't think lying is corrosive to the character, as Kant would. Indeed, Avellone reveals his **consequentialism**[*] in explaining it:

> 'The option to lie wasn't intended as a moral judgment – it's giving the player a choice. Both truth and lies can cause damage in the game (and sometimes lying is systemically better and even "good"), and at its root, the player may need to know the intention of their dialogue response before they say it. *Planescape* intentionally tried to go down the road of not consistently rewarding telling truth in every situation (nor being lawful, chaotic), but made an attempt to let the player express their own intention of a statement.'

That is, *Planescape: Torment* is more concerned with letting players express their own morality than judging that morality.

War and duty's good

What are the good points of deontology? It's very strong on things like human rights; it respects individual interests even when they clash with larger group interests. As we'll see in Chapter 8, consequentialist systems like utilitarianism have problems with maximising their particular consequences at the expense of things like liberty, equality and human dignity. Deontologists think that happiness isn't everything – that there is still something wrong with a perfectly happy slave.

It's also strong on things it says are always wrong, no matter who's doing it. So killing and torture are considered wrong in most

[*] Chapter 8 will talk about utilitarianism, which is a form of consequentialism – a philosophy where actions are morally judged by their effects.

deontological systems, which is a good fit with how most philosophers think. A more modern duty ethicist, David Ross, has argued that duties can be balanced against one another, which is even better.

And because it's so strong on what's right, duty allows us to act with certainty. We don't have to work out what action we should be taking; we take it because our moral rules are clear. In certain circumstances, that's very useful. Playing arcade shooters like *Operation Wolf* (Taito, 1987) or *Virtua Cop* (Sega, 1994), you're often machine-gunning enemy soldiers, when suddenly chickens, civilians or paramedics run across the screen. With a duty ethic, you instantly know it's bad to shoot them. By contrast, a virtue ethicist might refuse to shoot anyone and a utilitarian might have to agonise over who to shoot.

It also takes into account intentions, which consequentialism doesn't. If you didn't mean to hurt someone and you were behaving with due care and attention, then a duty ethicist doesn't think you've done anything wrong, whereas a consequentialist has to. For example, at the end of *Mortal Kombat 9* (NetherRealm Studios, 2011), Raiden attempts to stop Liu Kang from killing another contestant by electrocuting him, out of the best intentions. Yet Kang, distracted by the electricity, accidentally sets himself on fire and dies. In this super-powered world a duty ethicist might forgive Raiden, who was acting with good intentions, on the principle of always preventing an unnecessary death.

Talking Vhailor to death

However, there are problems too. When duties clash, it's sometimes hard to work out which one should take precedence – and duty ethics doesn't present you with a system for resolving those questions (except by adding more rules, which can soon make your morality unwieldy, as you attempt to recall your ruleset). We saw earlier that the Asari Justicar Samara's attempt to resolve the conflict between her duty as a mother and her duty as Justicar results in her attempting to commit suicide to avoid the choice. If you have to start building exceptions and rules for every little thing, then you undermine the point of this system, which is clarity and ease.

The utilitarian John Stuart Mill pointed out that duty ethics also had the same problem when trying to judge between rights and duties: If I don't answer the door when you knock, does your duty of care override my right to privacy, and must you knock down the door? As soon as you hit an actual problem, it doesn't make decision-making any easier or any more obviously moral.

Mill also attacked the categorical imperative for being a consequentialist argument in deontological clothing. After all, saying that an action must be universalisable is judging that action according to some other value system like the wider happiness of the world, not according to some wider principle – and you have to spend time working out a new principle for each new action.

Finally, what is the basis for these rules? Have they been scientifically deduced? Well . . . no. As Jeremy Bentham argued, duty ethicists are just dressing up popular morality – aka 'common sense' – in fancy clothes, claiming objectivity and permanence for ideas that are nothing of the sort. It's easy to agree with beliefs we share, but surely we want a more fundamental foundation for our beliefs that are in agreement with our society and/or social set – else we'll repeat the prejudices of the past in new ways and be justly damned by history.

In fact, if you wish, this is how you can eliminate Vhailor in *Planescape: Torment*, without striking a blow – using the tendency of the anonymous protagonist known as the Nameless One to imitate Socrates, by arguing Vhailor into a corner about the foundations of his principles.

Nameless One: 'What *defines* justice, Vhailor? What IS it, really?'
Vhailor: *JUSTICE is defined by LAW.*
Nameless One: 'And what is law, Vhailor?'
Vhailor: *LAW is the tool by which JUSTICE is served.*
Nameless One: 'And what makes the laws, Vhailor?'
Vhailor: *LAW is defined by JUSTICE.*
Nameless One: 'That's a circular argument, Vhailor – it's meaning-less. You say justice is defined by law, which is defined by justice.'

Vhailor: *LAW – IS – defined by JUSTICE.*

Nameless One: 'Living men and women make laws, Vhailor – are the laws they make "just?"'

Vhailor: *LAWS are JUST.*

Nameless One: 'But if these laws are made by living men and women – who, as *you've* said, are NOT innocent, then haven't the laws been tainted by their hands?'

Vhailor: *NOTHING that lives is INNOCENT. Yet LAW rises ABOVE the flesh and blood. FROM IMPERFECTION PERFECTION MAY BE MADE. UNJUST LAWS may be REFINED. BLED OF THEIR EVIL.*

Nameless One: 'Then you admit laws are not always perfect – but if these same laws define justice, then isn't *justice* imperfect as well? Vhailor – there is NO justice. All you do in the name of justice is meaningless – your LIFE is meaningless.'*

At which point, the suit of armour falls silent and then collapses completely, its operating will dissipated.

Duty, then, as a method of deciding what the good thing to do is, seems particularly unsatisfactory. But what if we don't focus on the actions of an individual so much, but examine the individual and see if we can get better results from the good person, the virtuous person, the person who is the (possibly unconscious) avatar of the virtues?

VIRTUE AND *ULTIMA*

Some older gamers will instantly recognise that last phrase. In the *Ultima* games (1981–), originally created by Richard Garriott and Origin Games, your character was the Avatar, a person who represented all that was best about his society, as expressed by his mastery of that society's virtues. Virtue, in this specific philosophical sense, means 'moral excellence'. A virtue is a character trait – like fortitude or magnanimity – and being a virtuous person is about developing these traits so that when a moral decision needs to be made, you make it correctly.

* *Planescape: Torment*, Black Isle Studios, (Interplay Entertainment, 1999).

The *Ultima* games drop you as a character from our world into a fantasy world where you have to determine your own path. Over the first three games, your character (originally called 'The Stranger') defeats all the evil in the world, so that, by *Ultima IV*, there are no villains left. Your character has nothing left to do – no more heroism to perform!

Their new challenge in this game is that the people need guidance – without villains to oppose them, they are behaving in all sorts of excessive ways. So your character goes on several quests to prove they're a perfectly virtuous individual and provide that guidance as the 'avatar of the virtues'. This theme continued throughout the games (with the absence of the darker *Ultima 8*) as the hero battled contending philosophies to their own virtue theory in each game. And it appeared finally in the depressingly broken *Ultima 9* – but a very confused, simplistic representation.

It's notable that the three cardinal virtues of *Ultima* – truth, love and courage – and the secondary virtues that are formed by combining the three are curiously relevant to modern society for a game that's ostensibly about an agrarian civilisation surrounded by monsters. Garriott, like Aristotle before him, built his virtue theory from scratch to fit his era. And he did this because his players were behaving very strangely in his first four games.

Garriott spoke to us in the bustling lobby of a posh San Francisco hotel during 2012's Game Developer Conference. He was then in his early fifties, lean and bright-eyed, with a discreet ponytail.

> '*Ultima 3* was the first game my own company published, so it was the first time I got fan mail . . . and complaints. I was really struck by how different people would describe their play experience compared to what I assumed people were thinking when I made it. Because, even though I put it in the game that you could do things like kill the NPCs [non-player-characters] in a town, I just thought of it as a funny little quip. I didn't expect it to become the dominant behaviour of the player.'

Yet the letters he was getting from players showed that they were generally bucking his intention.

'It became obvious that, in fact, the way that people were playing, they were enjoying effectively being the antihero and the bad guy was just waiting for them at the final level and the bad guy wasn't actually doing anything bad. The story just wasn't elegantly told. If you look at the Joseph Campbell classic *Hero's Journey*[*], it's really that at first you may not be worthy of taking on the grand challenge, but you learn something about yourself along the way, and you grow to be strong enough, in the sense of character, to win the day.'

Except here the game seemed to be encouraging vice, albeit inadvertently.

A lack of intent was no defence at the time. It's worth remembering that, in the 1980s, parents were in a funk about *Dungeons & Dragons* (Gary Gygax and Dave Arneson, 1974) supposedly promoting Satanism and villainous behaviour.[†] Given that most computer role-playing games of the time were simply quests to murder a major villain, Garriott felt that a game with an original, ethical storyline was the best riposte to people's concerns.[‡] And a system of virtues,

---

[*] Joseph Campbell's theory of a 'monomyth' – a single base story to all stories – has been inspirational to many filmmakers, novelists and game developers. It posits that in each story, the hero goes out from the ordinary world into an unusual world of strange powers, faces trials and receives a gift resulting in self-knowledge, which can improve his world when he returns. It's doubtful it fits all stories, but it certainly provides a compelling story structure that fits with virtue theory. You can read more about it in his *Hero with a Thousand Faces* (1949).

[†] Moral panics of this sort aren't uncommon with new media. Plato, in 400 BC, criticised theatre and poetry for corrupting the population of Athens. In the last century, the United States in particular saw several moral panics, ranging from a 1954 Senate attack on comic books that blamed them for poor grades, delinquency and drug use, to a 1969 National Commission on Violence that condemned violence on television, to a 1972 Surgeon General's report that linked TV/movie violence and aggressive behaviour, and the 1982 panic about *D&D*. Since the 1992 book *Big World, Small Screen* was endorsed by the American Psychological Association that attack has moved to video games.

[‡] 'He decided that if people were going to look for hidden meanings in his work when they didn't even exist, he would introduce ideas and symbols with meaning and significance he deemed worthwhile, to give them something they could really think about.' *The Official Book of Ultima* by Shay Addams, p. 39.

to him, seemed the natural way to show that games could produce good people. 'If you think of most fantasy role-playing worlds in general, everyone starts weak and becomes strong physically, but that's not the same thing as moral character becoming worthy,' he says.

Bottling Aristotle

One of the earliest extant versions of virtue ethics comes from two of Plato's books, *Gorgias* and *The Republic*, written from 380 BC. The most famous version, however, comes from Plato's student Aristotle and his *Nichomachean Ethics*. This book is believed to derive from notes taken for a series of lectures* Aristotle gave at some point between 335 and 323 BC. By this point Aristotle had already studied under Plato and been the personal tutor to Alexander the Great for a few years, before returning to Athens to establish his own school of thought, having lived a fairly adventurous and wide-ranging life.

Aristotle came up with his virtues by analysing the behaviour of his contemporaries. Given that premise, only the wealthy, upper-class slave-owning *politares* – the dutiful male citizens of Athens – had a chance of achieving his concept of virtue. 'In *Nichomachean Ethics*, he talks as if all humans could achieve these virtues,' says Angie Hobbs, Professor of the Public Understanding of Philosophy at the University of Sheffield. 'But in another work of his, called the *Politics*, he makes it fairly clear that he doesn't think women are going to be rational enough to achieve full virtue. He says "women possess reason, but it's not authoritative in them". They're too at prey of their emotional whims. If he'd known the word hormones, he would have said women were too hormonal to be virtuous.' Hobbs points out that Plato, on the other hand, allowed women into his lectures and believed that they too could achieve the virtuous state. 'Class differences in Plato are more important than gender differences.'

Theories about the virtues didn't stop with the ancients. Descartes,

---

* Scholars are divided over the author of the notes: whether it was Aristotle himself, his son Nicomachus or another student.

Kant, Nietzsche and Ayn Rand* all came up with their own versions of what constitutes a good character – but that's not necessarily a virtue theory. Even Benjamin Franklin came up with a contemporary version for the era of America's founding fathers, one that valued concepts such as silence, tranquillity and cleanliness – virtues that Franklin himself wasn't exactly a model for.

The avatar of the 1980s

Similarly, in 1983, Garriott sat down and analysed what constituted the good of his time. As he had never studied philosophy or history – and admits to having no interest in either at the time – he did something that he would do with every game afterwards; he bought an entire research library on the subject and got reading.

Garriott's timing was fortunate, for during the previous thirty years there had been the first major revival of a general virtue theory. It was led by the academic Elizabeth Anscombe in 1958, and followed up by modern writers such as Alisdair MacIntyre, Philippa Foot, Mary Midgley and the novelist Iris Murdoch.† Hobbs explains that, 'There was a whole group of women who studied philosophy at Oxford after the Second World War and got posts because the men weren't there – who were fighting or dead. I mean, they should have got posts because they were brilliant. And they were all very interested in virtue theory.' Anscombe, pushing back against the utilitarianism and deontology of her time, had argued that the important thing about ethical decisions wasn't the end result or your intention to carry out your duty, but whether the individual has the capability to perform moral actions correctly.

Garriott, however, was ignorant of this.

* See Chapter 8 for more on Rand's philosophy of objectivism, and its expression in Ken Levine's BioShock games.
† Author, philosopher and all-round good egg Murdoch was involved in the revival of virtue theory in the 1950s and 1960s, and deployed it to a powerful degree in her novels. These typically focus on people in comfortable situations whose only moral qualms are about how to live their lives. In Dan Griliopoulos' opinion her best two books are her debut romp of a novel, *Under The Net*, and her Booker-winning *The Sea, The Sea*.

'As I started studying virtues, I didn't even know if I was going to do it promoting virtues or avoiding vices. I looked at the seven deadly sins – lots of movies have been made about them – but they weren't a very complete set . . . not very good guidance. Looking at the Judeo-Christian set, I asked did I want to stand by those commandments? Again, there's some overlap and additions, but ultimately it was not something I wanted to promote. I looked at all sorts of things – and this is when I became a fan of Buddhism, some of its precepts, "life is happiness" – just like that! "The way to get there is compassion" – just like that! But when you get down to the fourfold path it gets complicated and hard to articulate in a games format.'

Garriott also looked at Hinduism – and, more oddly, at the virtues of *The Wizard of Oz*, his favourite movie, and its cowardly Lion, brainless Scarecrow and heartless Tin Man – which together supplied him with his core concept of the Avatar. In Hinduism, an avatar is the incarnation of a god; literally, a god taking human form on the earth, normally to carry out hero quests. Garriott's avatar became the empty vector for his virtues.

Ultimately neither Christianity nor Buddhism, Hinduism or even *The Wizard of Oz* satisfied Garriott. Indeed, having rejected each of the major spiritual systems and their particular virtues, he tried to look for something that both seemed like it was true and would work well in a game.

'I got lots of post-it notes and wrote down every virtue I could think of, every vice I could think of, and put them on a whiteboard. I began to organise them by things that they had in common – because some are derivatives of others and some are combinations of others. I eventually came up with a pattern that I thought was reasonably self-evident, of truth, love, and courage being some really foundational principles that I could then, at least in my mind's eye, imagine all the other connections between. Without regard to whether it's the Truth, it had a good numerology associated with it, and I could make good symbols associated with it.'

Philosophy as material

Many game designers we've spoken to have taken a similar perspective – that philosophies are useful as material – but aren't particularly interested in the truth of the ideas themselves.

That ethical theory consisted of three cardinal virtues – truth, love and courage – and eight derived minor virtues, which are the actual virtues players attempt to live up to in the middle *Ultima* games: honesty, compassion, valour, justice, honour, sacrifice, humility and spirituality.

Garriott's ethical system is motivated by the world he's created, where by *Ultima IV* all the major evils of the world have been vanquished by you, The Stranger. The only evil remaining is in the hearts of men, where ferreting it out is proverbially difficult.* So your task in *Ultima IV* is to master the eight virtues and become a champion – a hero people can look up to – and encourage people to root out their evil in emulation of you. It's a role much like that of a modern celebrity, though with a much stronger moral connotation and awareness of your influence.

Hobbs, never having played a role-playing game like *Ultima*, is somewhat in awe of it.

'It fascinates me that the notion of a hero is so strongly connected to the notion of virtue here. Because, in other ways, we're living in a society where heroism and virtue are being divorced all the time. These people get very rich, the masters of the universe in Wall Street or The City, who are worshipping and celebrating money and power . . . It shows that there is a deep, deep need in humans to want super-virtuous people, particularly creative people.'

Not that she's entirely complimentary about the escapist aspects of the games: 'In this tiny world, at 2am in their bedroom, they're a hero. It's very Walter Mitty, isn't it?'

---

* 'For it is from within, out of a person's heart, that evil thoughts come – sexual immorality, theft, murder, adultery, greed, malice, deceit, lewdness, envy, slander, arrogance and folly. All these evils come from inside and defile a person.' Mark 7:21.

Garriott is aware of that – and admits that this, his first attempt at virtue theory, is fairly black and white. 'I used dictionaries of quotes to come up with all the things that the NPCs said, and they were only good guys or bad guys. I was pretty young. There was little subtlety to it – there weren't thieves that were redeemable, there weren't good guys who'd stab you in the back.' Indeed, as Hobbs points out, strictly speaking many of Garriott's virtues aren't virtues at all. 'Love is not a virtue. Truth is not a virtue. There are virtues that can be associated with the values of love and truth. But a lot of the things that Garriott talks about are not necessarily virtues.'

ULTIMA AS A VIRTUE ETHICS MASTERCLASS

But by establishing a perfect system in a perfect setting, *Ultima IV* allowed Garriott to experiment in later games. Indeed, even beyond that initial impressive virtue system, the *Ultima* series is a master-class in virtue theory. From *Ultima IV*, the games gradually explore the positive and negative consequences of following the philosophy he'd created, each game setting up antagonists that espouse alterna-tive societies or religions that focus on different virtue systems, systems that enable that society to survive.

In *Ultima V*, the villains are Lord Blackthorn and the Shadowlords, who pervert Britannia's government into a totalitarian, absolutist enforcement of the Avatar's virtues as laws – that is, they turn them into rule-based ethics, like Kant's duty ethics, rather than what feels right to a virtuous person at a given time.

In *Ultima VI*, the Avatar faces off against a race of Gargoyles, whose harsh homeworld he inadvertently destroyed in an earlier game. Their virtue system focuses on social unity, equality and self-control, revolving around the three core principles of control, passion and diligence. Their system, it is implied, was different because their environment was different – and, as we've discussed, a virtue theory is about being the best person in a given society. To survive in the Gargoyles' harsh homeworld, collaboration was paramount – so their ideal person's behaviour was modelled on that.

By *Ultima VII*, the enemies of virtue have become much subtler. Here, the Big Bad of the late *Ultima* games, the Guardian, is revealed. He has his own parodic virtue system – as well as a second-cover virtue system for it, in the form of the Fellowship, an initially friendly sect that has infiltrated Britannia.

The Fellowship is modelled on beneficial societies like the Freemasons and the Scientologists, whose virtues are ostensibly similar to those of the Avatar, save that they hold that only Fellowship members are relevant moral objects. So while their virtues of unity, trust and justice seem worthy, you only have to, for example, treat another member of the Fellowship justly – other human beings are as cattle, leaving the society selfish and fascistic. The Fellowship is closer to the Nietzschean virtue system, of the strong dominating the weak, than to the more familiar Judeo-Christian morality.

In *Ultima Underworld II*, the Avatar finally encounters the virtue system of the Guardian, who was behind the disasters in the six games from *Ultima VII* to *Ultima IX*. His virtues, implemented in the flying castle Killorn Keep, are simply about control, emphasising vigilance, conformity, diligence, efficiency, punctuality, sobriety and silence. (Notably, the Guardian's supposedly evil virtue system was convincing enough that the Florida Department of Corrections adapted it as a model for their guards.*)

For the last great game of the *Ultima* series, *Ultima 7 Part Two: Serpent Isle*, Garriott supplies an alternative pair of virtue systems from the long-dead Ophidian civilisation. These are oddly Manichean† and based around the opposing forces of Chaos and Order. These have three virtues each, which balance each other out. So emotion (from chaos) balances against logic (from order)

---

* See http://tinyurl.com/florida-guardian for more. (http://web.archive.org/web/20061006124151/http://www.dc.state.fl.us/pub/compass/0305/2.html)

† A term referring to a system of moral dualism, named after a major world religion 'Manichaeism' which believed that a good God was battling an evil God and humanity was the battleground. It was persecuted to extinction in the tenth century.

to make rationality – something that was inadvertently prescient on Garriott's part, given that neuroscientists recently found that a person without functioning emotional centres cannot make decisions.*

The avatar of the modern day

Garriott is still concerned about this value system. His upcoming (at the time of publication) game, *Shroud of the Avatar: Forsaken Virtues*, is a sequel to *Ultima* in all but name, though with added multiplayer interaction. It's unlikely he'll change his core virtue system, however: 'What's interesting is that I simultaneously recognise it as a piece of fictional work and recognise it as powerfully positive . . . It's true that I've tried to think of systems of virtue that go beyond it and I think it's pretty universal.' Yet to the outside observer, some of the antagonistic systems he created – the self-obsessed Fellowship, the equality-focused Gargoyles, the authoritarian Shadowlords – seem equally valid.

What Garriott's variety of systems shows, as he recognises, is that virtue theories are, in some sense, societal:

> 'Talking about Aristotle and the others, I'm sure they were extremely sanguine for their period. As were, by the way, biblical ones. I think that all systems of philosophy have to be viewed in the light of the political and social reality in which they were crafted. Will [my system] be as "truthy" a thousand years from now? Probably not. Does it still feel as true today as it did thirty years ago when I came up with it? I think it does.'

---

* 'Lesions of the ventromedial (which includes the orbitofrontal) sector of the prefrontal cortex interfere with the normal processing of "somatic" or emotional signals, while sparing most basic cognitive functions. Such damage leads to impairments in the decision-making process, which seriously compromise the quality of decisions in daily life. The role of emotion in decision-making: Evidence from neurological patients with orbitofrontal damage' Antoine Bechara. *Brain and Cognition* June 2004, pp. 30–40.

As the philosopher Alisdair MacIntyre pointed out, the word 'ethics' comes from ethos, a shared belief system in a given society. This is not to say that a virtue ethics is purely subjective – for the people of each society would tend to agree upon their system of virtue – but agreement over the virtues shifts between societies and groups within those societies. A primitive society might emphasise courage and loyalty, a religious society faith and humility, a tech-savvy society open source software and free wifi. And for Garriott, *Ultima*'s virtue ethics reflect the spirit of modern times – and explicitly not the medieval timeline his game is set in. 'For example, if you go back to chivalric honour, this system wouldn't have worked then.'

Future virtues also differ. In a post-apocalyptic world like *Fallout* (Interplay, 1997–2001; Bethesda, 2008–) or *The Last of Us* (Naughty Dog, 2013), the virtuous man may be very different from the virtuous man today but similar to the virtuous man in a failed society like Somalia or on the troubled streets of Baltimore. Think of the great heroes of the American frontier era and their failure to adapt to the societies they had created – their virtues simply weren't valued when society had transitioned from survivalist to urban. Similarly, a virtuous man in, say, the open-world survival game *S.T.A.L.K.E.R.* (GSC Game World, 2007–09) is the protagonist who sticks to his word, disposes of aggressive men and creatures, but doesn't harm others. The Stalker who kills a man for a can of beans couldn't be called virtuous or a hero.

Despite that, Hobbs does think that at least one of Garriott's cardinal virtues seems to be true of all societies: courage.

> 'Virtues have arisen because societies needed certain qualities. Some of those, like courage and some form of justice, have been universal. They've defined it differently, but I can't think of a single society that hasn't esteemed courage. Other virtues come and go out of fashion. Christian virtues of modesty and humility were not praised by Aristotle, who regarded modesty as lying! To him, you were just being inaccurate about your own worth. If you were a Marxist, you might not value generosity, because you might see it as an indication of inequitable distributions of the world's resources.'

But courage, as Garriott identified, does seem to carry across all societies.

The flaws of virtue

It's worth noting that Garriott never contends that, merely because the individual is virtuous, their actions or their results are always ultimately good. The Avatar's actions throughout the series often are temporary solutions, leaving the world worse off in many ways than it was before. For example, the discovery of the virtues in *Ultima IV* leads to a conflict with an absolutist interpretation of them in *Ultima V*, and a war with the Gargoyles in *Ultima VI*. Each time the world changes, the hero has to reappraise his moral system, to check that his personal ethos still fits with his concept of virtue.

At least the big advantage of virtue theories is that they're meant to *sound* human. Whereas utilitarianism or deontologism can produce instinctively wrong statements (such as 'euthanise the miserable' or 'always obey your superiors'), it's hard to come up with a virtue theory that throws up *obvious* monsters. Virtuous people by definition act like good people. You can tell the Avatar is the Avatar because they act like the Avatar should act.

That does make virtue theories somewhat circular – the good thing is what the good person does and the good person is the one who does the good thing, and we know both of these because we were brought up to recognise the good. 'It doesn't give you very precise normative rules on how to behave in the way that Kant or Christian ethics does,' says Hobbs, 'but that's not entirely fair. The more a virtue theory goes into the life of a virtuous person, the more it imagines that narrative, the more precise guidance it gives.'

Another problem is that not everyone can be virtuous. That's a key point about the virtuous life, an unusual concept the ancient Greeks called *akrasia*, most commonly translated as '**moral incontinence**'. It simply means that not everyone does the right thing, even if they know what it is. We know we shouldn't litter, because the world will be worse if everyone litters, but sometimes we do. We know we shouldn't eat cheese, because we need to lose weight, but we still do. The Avatar's friend Dupre couldn't be the Avatar because he drinks to excess.

The true virtuous man

Unlike Garriott's Avatar, who struggles (under our control) with moral choice, the truly virtuous person has none of these concerns; they look at the cheese and the temptation to eat it doesn't even cross their mind. Most people aren't that mentally coherent or simple – the virtuous person doesn't have to be a clever person so one could argue that an ape or automaton could fit the model of virtue perfectly well. This is the most uncomfortable part of these moral heroes – that in their infallibility they don't seem believably human.

Could we argue, then, that Mario and his kind, the linear unthinking heroes whose actions always result in the best Panglossian* outcome, who never have a choice but to be good, are the perfect virtuous characters? After all, the point about being virtuous is that you do the right thing instinctively – the only thought involved is in thinking of the way to do the right thing, not whether the thing is right itself.

A final criticism of virtue theory is that being a consistently good person is conservative, fitting just the civilisation it's in. The society-oriented nature of virtue theories can make virtue heroes seem extremely subjective, their virtue only applicable in particular narrow times, locales and societies. Says Hobbs:

> 'Is it conservative? That can be posed against any ethical theory that makes role models central to it. How do you get praise? Do the things that your society already admires, emulate the heroes your society already esteems. There's a replication of heroes going on – an inbuilt tendency to replicate. In more reflective hands, it doesn't have to – for example, in Plato's hands, because he rips Athenian society to shreds and starts again.'

* Otherwise known as 'Leibnizian optimism'. Dr Pangloss was a character in Voltaire's novel *Candide* who professed, despite the endless horrors the characters are subjected to, that this is 'the best of all possible worlds' and that 'all is for the best', parodying the philosopher Leibniz, who said that despite its imperfections, this is the best of all possible worlds, because it was created by a perfect God, who must only create perfect things. This theory has more holes in it than the Jumblies' boat . . . but that's for another time.

Similarly, Garriott's Avatar has to build up from scratch in *Ultima IV*, and finds himself having to adjust his behaviour throughout the series.

Even within this subjective societal perspective, a virtuous person's good actions don't always have to result in good outcomes – after all, we wouldn't dare argue that all ethical systems are internally logically consistent or that all ethical actors are omniscient. Hobbs explains:

> 'You could have a virtuous person who was focused on intention rather than results. None of the ancient Greek virtue ethicists would fall into that – they require a certain level of competence. You couldn't be virtuous if you kept messing up – you'd lack the virtues of theoretical and practical wisdom. For both Plato and Aristotle, all virtues are connected – you can't really have one virtue without having them all, which is why they have the notion of a virtuous human. One way of looking at the Aristotelian or Platonic virtues is that they all involve understanding the human good, but in different spheres of action. In dangerous situations, your understanding of the human good manifests as courage; if you have to distribute scant resources, it manifests as justice.'

In the end, Garriott's attempt to create a compelling mechanic for his games, and to pre-empt any accusations of immorality, resulted in a fascinating insight into what it is to be a good person. Despite the problems with the theory of virtue ethics – its potential circularity, its conservatism and its limited applicability to certain societies – it's compelling in its simplicity. Look, here is the good man – the avatar – and look, he does the good acts, which we should copy.

Yet on a wider scale, the theory says little specific about how to live our lives, save for the vaguely universal virtues of courage and justice. There isn't a moral prescription here, more just a cultural conformity to maintain a society. And it says nothing about the people outside our society – outside the Fellowship, say. It is more of a framework for a moral ethos than an ethos itself, as *Ultima's* endless versions show.

Duty, virtue and . . .

Some philosophers argue that duty and virtues ethics work best hand-in-hand – it seems more human to say that, if you're avoiding judging people on the unpredictable consequences of their actions, then taking into account both the character of the actor and their intentions makes sense. You can say that being a virtuous person would help you know your duties better and perform them better – and that being a dutiful person would help you carry out virtuous actions in time-sensitive situations, without worrying too much about the consequences.

Yet other philosophers even require something consequentialist as well, so that all three elements matter: the action we take, the actor taking it and the consequence of that action. Before we can talk more extensively about that, however, we should look at our third big ethical theory, the one that's still most dominant today, and one that's explicitly consequentialist – utilitarianism.

Limbo, happily.

....

Maria: Anyway, those princes. Aren't they blissful? Prince Orange is a total dish.

Luisa: Isn't he the Prince *of* Orange? I always preferred Princess Plum. Sigh. Anyway, they're royalty. They're not interested in a pair of plumbers from the Lower East Side. Not even if we rescued them from that giant lizard.

Maria: Why not? Why shouldn't they be happy with us? Why shouldn't we all be happy?

Luisa: Oh yes, that's true – we should all be happy. That seems like something we can all agree is a good thing – forget about being a hero, or following rules.

Maria: Yes, I was a little confused about that. Why would anyone think the good thing to do was following orders or doing things out of good intentions?

Luisa: The problem now is how do we decide who or what gets to be happy? People, animals . . . vegetables?

Maria: Is this about the mushroom again? Look, I said—

Luisa: Well, yes. Mushrooms have feelings too, it turns out. Maybe their happiness counts for something.

Maria: Well, I don't see how you could add my happiness to yours. They're entirely different things.

Luisa: And my happiness is more valuable because I prefer higher things – fine art, wine, pasta, Princess Plum . . .

Maria: Snob. Let's assume your happiness is more valuable than mine. Even so, how are we going to work it out? Let's assume I want to eat a mushroom and you don't want me to. How can we calculate anything there?

Luisa: Well, ignoring the mushroom's feelings for the moment, I guess we just . . . I guess. I guess we do our best?

Maria: That doesn't feel much better than being a hero or following rules, really. Hmm.

Luisa: Look, there are some circumstances where we can't decide on how to maximise happiness, but generally we can. We can look at statistics and trends and personal preferences and—
Maria: —just not on the spur of the moment.
Luisa: Look, this is getting rather academic. Let's move on.

CHAPTER EIGHT

On utilitarianism: BioWare's baddies

....

'Let no one be slow to seek wisdom when he is young nor weary in the search of it when he has grown old. For no age is too early or too late for the health of the soul. And to say that the season for studying philosophy has not yet come, or that it is past and gone, is like saying that the season for happiness is not yet or that it is now no more.'[*]

Epicurus (341–270 BC)

'. . . men grow old because they stop playing, and not conversely, for play is, at bottom, growth, and at the top of the intellectual scale it is the eternal type of research from sheer love of truth.'[†]

G. Stanley Hall (1846–1924)

You're playing as Commander Shepard in *Mass Effect 2: Arrival* (BioWare, 2011). The commander happens across a faster-than-light travel relay station on the edge of the galaxy. Sadly, she (or, if the player wants, he) soon discovers that the genocidal Reapers – super-intelligent bio-organic robots – plan to use it to destroy all life in the galaxy.

The only way to delay this invasion and buy time for the people of the galaxy to prepare is to destroy the relay itself – but to do so involves the destruction of a nearby planet and the near-complete genocide of its inhabitants, a race called the Batarians. The player is presented with no choice in this matter, though they are able to

[*] Epicurus, *Letter to Menoeceus*.
[†] *Adolescence: Its Psychology and Its Relations to Physiology, Anthropology, Sociology, Sex, Crime, Religion and Education* (1904).

attempt contact with the planet to order an evacuation, if they wish. There is only one way of solving this problem, and you have to push the button. When the dust clears, three hundred thousand lives have been lost to save trillions.

This is philosophy in action. **And the philosophy is utilitarianism.**

All sections of philosophy bleed somewhat into each other. In this case, the most important questions of ethics slip into politics, as they should (see Chapter 9). Politics is the realm of shaping lives according to a creed, but before we can act upon it, we first have to answer the ethical question: How should we live our lives?

In Chapter 7 we encountered two ancient ethical theories:

1 **Virtue ethics** We should live our lives by being the best people we can, to have the best lives we can.
2 **Duty ethics** We should always act correctly, because it's by our actions that we're judged.

Yet both seemed weak in the end, focusing too strongly on a society's already-established morality.

Utilitarianism is a form of consequentialism* that gives what appears the simplest answer to the question of how we should live our lives: we should be as happy as possible. More specifically, we should live for the greatest happiness of the greatest number. (Utility is often taken as a near synonym for happiness, though we'll get deeper into that later.) Yet working out what that statement actually means can get complicated beyond all reason, to the point where it becomes difficult to act on. Utilitarianism is the most obviously right, practical philosophy around, but that doesn't make it easy.

That's because it's also a philosophy that can throw up seemingly evil or impossible decisions. While the choice for Commander Shepard described above seems horrible, at least it's relatively easy: choosing between the loss of some life and all life. But if the numbers were balanced, would it be so easy? If Shepard had to kill every last

* Consequentialism is a morality that judges actions entirely by their consequences.

person personally? If she (or he) had to plunge half the galaxy into lifelong poverty to save the rest? If she had to torture a hundred men to save a thousand? If she had to get elected first and had to lie about her intentions in order to get elected? The question of what constitutes the happiest outcome gets harder and harder as the question gets closer to a real situation.

EPICURUS AND *HARVEST MOON*

The origins of utilitarianism lie in antiquity. The primary concern of the fathers of ancient Greek philosophy, after all, was happiness. Their key concept of happiness was *eudaimonia*, which roughly translates as the 'life lived with a happy spirit' or more clearly 'human flourishing'. They mostly differed about what that life might be: Plato (through the mouthpiece of Socrates) and the Stoics thought that being perfectly virtuous was necessary for *eudaimonia*; Aristotle thought it involved virtuous activity but not perfection. They generally agreed, however, that being virtuous was key to having the happiest, best life.

But our story of utilitarianism starts with Epicurus, in Athens in the fourth century BC. Epicurus rejected Plato's otherworldly concept of the good and instead posited a philosophy called hedonism, from the ancient Greek *hēdonē*, meaning 'pleasure'. It argued that the natural measure of moral value is of how much pleasure an action creates for the individual. Beyond that, the individual should adhere to the rules of his society, but otherwise seek to maximise his pleasure.

This doesn't, however, mean Epicurus was arguing we should spend our days in an orgiastic frenzy. He famously conceived of the happy life as one involving self-sufficiency, self-study and friendship, and said that he got the most pleasure from eating barley cakes and drinking water (for more on virtue ethics see Chapter 7). As he said:

'It is impossible to live a pleasant life without living wisely and honorably and justly, and it is impossible to live wisely and honorably and justly without living pleasantly.'*

* Epicurus, *Principal Doctrines*. Translated by Robert Drew Hicks.

The bucolic Nintendo idyll

Instead, Epicurus' world seems rather like *Harvest Moon* (Amccus, 1996), *Animal Crossing* (Nintendo, 2001) or *Stardew Valley* (ConcernedApe, 2016). In these games, the player's character has a simple life in a small town. You know everyone and manage to keep house and home together with simple actions that allow you to be self-sufficient. This frees your time up for your friends (which, as in Epicurus' vision, includes women and all social classes), and for those activities that give you the most pleasure, physical or mental. In this world, you are free from worrying and suffering, and are aware of that. In these games, there's no chance of death or illness, which Epicurus thinks are the major reasons for sadness in life, and politics is alien and undesirable. No wonder these games are so popular!

Utilitarianism seems even simpler than this ancient theory of a happy life. It is consequentialist – that is, its adherents believe actions only matter if they result in a certain end, in this case increased happiness. The theory doesn't initially say anything about the character of the action, about whose happiness counts or about how happiness can be measured. It just puts it out there, like the aptly named English virtue ethicist John Gay did in 1731:

'Happiness, private happiness, is the proper or ultimate end of all our actions . . .'*

Or as the Scottish philosopher David Hume said in 1751:

'In all determinations of morality, this circumstance of public utility is ever principally in view; and wherever disputes arise, either in philosophy or common life, concerning the bounds of duty, the question cannot, by any means, be decided with greater certainty, than by ascertaining, on any side, the true interests of mankind.'†

---

* *Dissertation concerning the Fundamental Principle of Virtue or Morality*, 1731.
† David Hume, *An Enquiry Concerning the Principles of Morals* (1751).

To reiterate, utility is a near-synonym for happiness.* As the nine-teenth-century English philosopher John Stuart Mill defined it:

> 'The creed which accepts as the foundation of morals, Utility, or the Greatest-Happiness Principle, holds that actions are right in proportion as they tend to promote happiness, wrong as they tend to produce the reverse of happiness.'†

TODAY'S HEROES, TOMORROW'S VILLAINS

There are examples galore of utilitarianism in video games – but most of it either comes from a sceptical viewpoint or pushes utilitarianism to villainous extremes. It's notable that many villains and antiheroes are implicitly utilitarians – from *Mass Effect*'s (BioWare, 2007–12) Illusive Man and Catalyst to the hegemonising Qun in *Dragon Age: Origins* (BioWare, 2009) and John Henry Eden in *Fallout 3* (Bethesda, 2008). They're often the most sympathetic of villains because they are attempting to make the universe a happier, better place. It just so happens that their calculations look inhuman to the rest of us.

RPGs are really the peak of this trend. In *System Shock 2* (Irrational Games and Looking Glass Studios, 1999), the main antagonists were The Many – a gestalt post-human consciousness accidentally created by series villain SHODAN. They (or it) absorb humans into their group mind because it will make these humans more capable and mostly happier. They ask the player:

> 'What is a drop of rain, compared to the storm? What is a thought, compared to a mind? Our unity is full of wonder,

---

* It's worth noting that utilitarianism differs from hedonism. Hedonism is about maximising the individual's happiness, where utilitarianism is about society's. Hedonism can feed into a utilitarian solution, but it doesn't necessarily – and one selfish hedonist in charge could make all our utilitarian maths go awry.

† John Stuart Mill, *Utilitarianism* (1863).

which your tiny individualism cannot even conceive . . . Is your vision so small that you cannot see the value of our way?'*

Mass Effect's Reapers have a similar purpose. In the ending to *Mass Effect 3*, Commander Shepard discovers that the galaxy has experienced several cycles of war between organic life and synthetic life, each of which had threatened to wipe out all life, completely. The ancient race of Leviathans created an AI called the Catalyst to solve the problem. This AI made a totalitarian utilitarian decision to build bio-organic machines (the Reapers) to cull all life, so that it could grow back cyclically, without ever being wiped out. As the Catalyst says:

> 'Organics create synthetics to improve their own existence, but those improvements have limits. To exceed those limits, synthetics must be allowed to evolve. They must by definition surpass their creators. The result is conflict, destruction, chaos. It is inevitable. Reapers harvest all life, organic and synthetic, preserving them before they are forever lost to this conflict.'†

Thus the Reapers, which appear to be the nemesis of the galaxy's races, are in fact the stored versions of all the preceding organic and synthetic races.

In *Fallout* (Interplay Entertainment, 1997), a villain called the Master is spreading a Forced Evolutionary Virus that's already infected and heavily mutated him. The virus turns a fraction of radiation-free humans into advanced Super Mutants, which are better suited for surviving in post-apocalyptic America, while other subjects die or become otherwise mutated. But the Super Mutants are not only better suited for the irradiated world – they're also identical creatures with an identical purpose, a change that the Master believes will unify them for global peace (something he enforces by killing or sterilising any non-mutants).

In *Fallout: New Vegas* (Obsidian Entertainment, 2010), the gentler Mr House has a plan for healing the wasteland that America

---

* *System Shock 2*, Irrational Games/Looking Glass Studios (Electronic Arts, 1999).

† *Mass Effect 3*, BioWare (Electronic Arts, 2012)

has become and rebuilding human technology. Sadly, it requires him using force on all the current survivors to achieve it, using his army of Securitrons, while getting the other factions to fight to the death.

In *Arcanum: Of Steamworks and Magick Obscura* (Troika Games, 2001), the villain Kerghan is an ancient wizard who has visited the realm of the dead and found it to be both peaceful and eternally happy. Quite reasonably, he takes it upon himself to kill everyone else to make them happy.

Even GlaDOS in *Portal* (Valve Corporation, 2007) claims that her endless, sadistic testing system is for the greater good of any surviving humans – though it's quite likely she's killed all of them in the process of working out how to make their lives better.

These villainous utilitarians in games all share some traits: they're ridiculously intelligent, well intentioned and incredibly powerful. And thoroughly misguided. For example, though the Master's Super Mutants are intelligent and better suited to survival in the wasteland, the player is able to discover that they're also sterile. This means that they can't eliminate the normal humans, because they need them to make more Super Mutants in the long run. When this discovery is pointed out to the Master he takes it very badly.

Yet, most of the villains' problems stem from the apparent simplicity of utilitarianism. One of its nineteenth-century creators, English philosopher Jeremy Bentham, said that: 'it is the greatest happiness of the greatest number that is the measure of right and wrong' which is the fundamental axiom of utilitarianism. He called this the 'greatest happiness principle'.* However, as we said earlier, this is extremely lacking in specifics – while the principle seems intuitive, how to implement it is not. To illustrate that, let's look at an explicitly utilitarian game: *BioShock 2* (2K Marin, 2010).

TWO VARIETIES OF SELF-INTEREST

The first *BioShock* (2K Boston and 2K Australia, 2007) balanced two outlooks. The first was the narcissistic pragmatism of the gangster

* *A Fragment on Government* (1776)

known as Frank Fontaine.* This anonymous thug pretended to be both Fontaine (having killed the real Fontaine before reaching Rapture) and the revolutionary leader Atlas (who never really existed) to take control of Rapture. His actions are devoid of ethical considerations and are targeted at seizing control of the city, for his own benefit.

Second, and most importantly, you had the **Objectivism** of Andrew Ryan, the founder of Rapture, the underwater city where *BioShock* is set. This philosophy was based, as Ryan's anagrammatic name might imply, on the writings of an American-Russian philosopher with the pen-name 'Ayn Rand' (real name Alisa Zinov'yevna Rosenbaum).

Rand was a once-wealthy refugee from Communist Russia who arrived in the United States in the 1920s, and espoused her philosophy in novels such as *Atlas Shrugged*, *The Fountainhead* and *Anthem*. Rand's simple contention was that the best morality for everyone was rational self-interest. She was a pure meritocrat who believed that humans consisted of great men and 'parasites', and that the great men owed the rest of society nothing – and that if they couldn't help themselves, they deserved nothing. As she writes in *The Fountainhead*:

'I came here to say that I do not recognize anyone's right to one minute of my life. Nor to any part of my energy. Nor to any achievement of mine. No matter who makes the claim, how large their number or how great their need.'†

Rand, fundamentally, is anti-socialist.

---

* What we colloquially call pragmatism here is often called by different names around the English-language world; here we mean Realpolitik, a political theory based primarily on practical considerations. Pragmatism itself is a much-confused word, often taken to mean 'centrism' or 'conservatism' – a political viewpoint that accepts society as it is, with middling equality and middling hierarchy. It also differs from American Pragmatism, which is a philosophical movement that judges thoughts and philosophical topics in terms of their practical uses and not their truth.
† Ayn Rand, *The Fountainhead* (1943).

In novels like *The Fountainhead*, Rand attempted to justify her philosophy through stories of great men held back and weakened by the wider public, who would steal their inventions or restrain their creativity with laws and taxation. Without these great men and women, Rand argues, society would collapse back to the Stone Age – and, indeed, that is what happens in her most famous work, *Atlas Shrugged*. This position is notably similar to that of the many libertarian politicians in America (unsurprisingly given the penetration of Ayn Rand's ideas into the Republican movement).

Objectivism in BioShock

As *BioShock 2*'s Creative Director Jordan Thomas points out, Objectivism –

'. . . still animates a lot of people who might not admit to it in public. I think it has such a core simplicity and it goes so obviously against what you've been told by your parents. A young twenty-something who's in a career climbing mode can use it as an organising principle, erroneously I think, to sort of cut away all parts of their life which do not serve their immediate interests. It is liberating for that kind of mind – and still a very dangerous drug, really.

'I read *Atlas Shrugged* at the tail end of *BioShock* and finished it during *BioShock 2*, just to build a baseline against which to compare some opposing philosophies. The thing that appealed to me the most about it was as a kind of grotesque parable, a mythology from a culture that scares me, that I consider kind of antique. As I mentioned, I think the idea that it helps you cast yourself as a liberator, as a person who is dispelling illusions held by others, is so potent and sort of an opiate unto itself. I could see it changing lives while I read it, although mine was not one of them . . . Rand talks like a super-villain. I enjoyed the overlap between what I saw to be pulp archetypes, and actual speeches given by this supposed book of philosophy.'

In *BioShock*, Ryan follows Rand in all things. He builds his underwater city Rapture to set the powerful men free and invites all the greatest and best people in the world to move there. (The surface world . . . doesn't really notice). And, by gum, he's got some good lines to motivate you:

> 'Is a man not entitled to the sweat of his brow?
>> "No," says the man in Washington, "it belongs to the poor."
>> "No," says the man in the Vatican, "it belongs to God."
>> "No," says the man in Moscow, "it belongs to everyone."
>> 'I rejected those answers; instead, I chose something different. I chose the impossible. I chose . . . Rapture. A city where the artist would not fear the censor; where the scientist would not be bound by petty morality; where the great would not be constrained by the small! And with the sweat of your brow, Rapture can become your city as well.'*

It doesn't really work out for Rapture, despite some amazing scientific advances, but it gives us a good highlight reel of Randian Objectivism. Meanwhile, the population of the city basically end up insane, mutated and murderous monsters, ruled by Andrew Ryan with an iron fist. The player's role in the first *BioShock* is to remove Ryan from the rule of Rapture.†

RAPTURE AND HAPPINESS

By the time of *BioShock 2*, the series had lost its lead writer and creative director Ken Levine‡, who moved on to *BioShock Infinite*§ (Irrational Games, 2013). He was replaced as creative director by Jordan Thomas, lead designer on the superb *Thief: Deadly Shadows*

---

* *BioShock*, Irrational Games/2K Australia (2KGames, 2007)
† To read more about *BioShock*, see Chapter 6.
‡ Levine told Eurogamer that 'The reason we didn't do *BioShock 2* is because . . . The time frame that game had, and the company understandably wanted another game in Rapture . . . But we felt we had said what we wanted to say about Rapture, about those kind of environments and that kind of feel.' Despite that, he went back to Rapture in the expansion packs to his 2013 sequel *BioShock Infinite*.
§ See Chapter 5.

(Ion Storm Austin, 2004), creator of the Fort Frolic entertainment area in *BioShock*, and later designer of *The Magic Circle* (Question, 2016), a satire on big-budget video games. In search of a concept for *BioShock 2*, to succeed Ryan's Objectivism as a motivating factor, Thomas settled on utilitarianism. As Thomas told us:,

> 'It started that way because I was originally very inspired by Mill as a young man. In the same way that Ken talks about having read Rand early, in that classic sort of comic-book, over-the-top, young, ambitious, often male – not in every case but often male – he found himself vulnerable and taken up by those ideas. He didn't full-time implement them in his life or anything like that, but he has talked about how they were appealing at a certain point. Same thing. Utilitarianism, for a while I was like, "This guy figured it out and the world whipped on it." '

Yet age tempered the utilitarian fires of Thomas' youth.

> 'I think I was thirty when *BioShock 2* started, give or take, and I had seen I guess a little more of the world, and I had seen what could potentially be the flaws in that logic, particularly when you try to apply it over the broadest possible scale. I started with Mill, but I added some Singer. I added some Pearce and so forth, looking for some additional dimensionality. Dawkins, crucially, was the last and biggest change to her, that to try and have her [Lamb's] philosophy bridge it due to genetics, I needed ideas that were really not born until the seventies.'

Thomas inserted this totalitarian utilitarianism into Rapture, exemplified by Dr Sofia Lamb, a classic utilitarian in the Benthamite model. (We'll come back to those writers Thomas cited – John Stuart Mill, Peter Singer, David Pearce and Richard Dawkins – later.)

Thomas followed Levine, in trying to concentrate the core modern utilitarian philosophy into an accessible format for his players.

> 'I felt pressure to offer a similarly concentrated kind of high-lights view of utilitarianism because we had grenades going

off left and right around the players. If they were going to grasp any of it, it needed to show the obvious and most interesting contours of the iceberg and leave the rest for the people who wanted to do Wikipedia diving afterwards.'

The philosophy of triage

So in *BioShock 2* the deceased Ryan has been replaced by a new ruler, Dr Sofia Lamb, who has stabilised some areas of the city under her rule, while she institutes her new philosophy. Lamb is an Oxford graduate with a speciality in clinical psychiatry, brought up to believe completely in utilitarianism*, as she says:

> 'My father was a physician. He raised me not to echo him, but to model the world as it ought to be. I was to teach a simple moral calculus, each choice as though the world must bear it, each life or death for the common good. He called it the "triage imperative", and would laugh without smiling.'[†]

'Triage' is a medical term that means to treat patients in the order of the severity of their injuries. In this context it seems to mean making every choice in order that the worst-off benefit.

The early Lamb gets the world

It's worth noting that in the backstory to the game we can identify two Sofia Lambs. There is what we'll call the 'Early Lamb' of that previous quote. She's a traditional utilitarian, who shares the beliefs of the libertarian Ryan that liberty and equality are foundation stones of a good society, but disagrees with his individualism, which she regards as anti-societal. In the prehistory of the original *BioShock*, she has public debates with Andrew Ryan about which of their philosophies is correct – and the populace decides she wins, for which Ryan locks her away.

---

* This is a deliberate parallel with the life of John Stuart Mill, the pre-eminent utilitarian, who was brought up by his father and Jeremy Bentham with the specific intention of carrying on the cause of utilitarianism. We'll get to him later.

† *BioShock 2*, 2K Marin (2K Games, 2010)

The earlier Lamb is characterised by these quotes:

'What is good? Only one definition endures. Good is pleasure in the absence of suffering. What then is the greater good? To calculate pleasure or suffering in the majority, we must account for the dimension of time. Each act must be measured not merely within the moment, but against all causality. The greater good, therefore, equates to total pleasure over time.'[*]

This is a clearly utilitarian statement. Indeed, it is a more clear utilitarian statement than most philosophers have made. And, interestingly, it deals with the core problem of utilitarianism – how to sum up happiness.

In his 1780 book *An Introduction to the Principles of Morals and Legislation*, Bentham identified pleasure and the absence of pain as the key methods of measuring on an action-by-action basis, tracking the intensity, duration, certainty and extent, amongst other things, to come up with a value for the action. This value was called the utility of the action, and this is the sole determinant of its moral worth. For him, the good was whatever brought the greatest happiness to the greatest number of people:

'Priestley[†] was the first (unless it was Beccaria[‡]) who taught my lips to pronounce this sacred truth — that the greatest happiness of the greatest number is the foundation of morals and legislation.'[§]

[*] *BioShock 2*, 2K Marin (2K Games, 2010)
[†] Joseph Priestley (1733–1804) was an English priest, political theorist and scientist, normally credited with the discovery of oxygen.
[‡] Cesare Beccaria (1738–94) was an Italian criminologist, legal specialist, philosopher and politician, and a founder of modern criminal theory. It seems that nobody had just one job in those days.
[§] Extracts from Bentham's 'Commonplace Book', in *Collected Works 10* (1843).

Problems with utilitarianism

There are obvious imperfections with this, prompting many questions. Is it possible to sum up happiness? Is every moment of happiness equal? What about the maintenance of other values? Do liberty, individualism, equality, lifespan and other values have any worth whatsoever beyond their function in some utilitarian equation? And whose happiness counts – just humans, or animals too, or even plants? 'Lamb doesn't even get into the animal sphere, like Peter Singer does,' says Thomas. 'It gets really confusing when you start to mix and match the atomic unit of suffering between two species.'

The biggest of these problems is that of summation: how do you add up happiness? Thomas also felt that there might be disagreement about these calculations, as Lamb demonstrated.

> 'The things I was interested in with Lamb were, first, that she claimed to be able to quantify suffering. To say that you are an advocate of the greater good means that you are also the arbitrator of what good means. She did, for her own view. She absolutely did maximize pleasure and minimize pain, she thought. But for many other people who saw that pleasure or pain differently, she was taking away their will to make decisions on their own.'

A major criticism from Bentham's day to now has been that, taken like this, the most bestial pleasures (sex, food, basking in the sun, video games*, etc.) are on a par with seemingly elevated pleasures (literature, music, art, video games, etc.). By this measure, the idiotic Epsilons in *Brave New World* are as happy as the elevated Alphas. Bentham seemed explicitly to accept this:

> 'There is no taste which deserves the epithet good, unless it be the taste for such employments which, to the pleasure actually produced by them, conjoin some contingent or future utility: there is no taste which deserves to be characterized as bad,

* This is a joke (see Chapter 11).

unless it be a taste for some occupation which has mischievous tendency."*

Moreover, Bentham felt that this measure of utility should be extended beyond what we might consider normal moral subjects: i.e. beyond humans.

'The day may come when the rest of the animal creation may acquire those rights which never could have been withholden from them but by the hand of tyranny. The French have already discovered that the blackness of the skin is no reason why a human being should be abandoned without redress to the caprice of a tormentor. It may one day come to be recognized that the number of legs, the villosity† of the skin, or the termination of the os sacrum‡ are reasons equally insufficient for abandoning a sensitive being to the same fate.

'What else is it that should trace the insuperable line? Is it the faculty of reason, or perhaps the faculty of discourse? But a full-grown horse or dog is beyond comparison a more rational, as well as a more conversable animal, than an infant of a day or a week or even a month, old. But suppose they were otherwise, what would it avail? The question is not Can they reason?, nor Can they talk?, but Can they suffer?'§

For Bentham, then, the avoidance of pain for all creatures is key.

Mill and the quality of happiness

John Stuart Mill was Bentham's chosen successor. He's the person Sofia Lamb is explicitly based on. Mill was brought up by his father James Mill and by Bentham (as a second parent) to be a genius intellect and a perfectly moral avatar for their philosophical ideas, to

* *Théorie des peines et des récompenses* (1811).
† Hairiness.
‡ The bottom of the spine, i.e. where a tail would grow from.
§ *An Introduction to the Principles of Morals and Legislation* (1789).

create a just society. He had an education that so crammed him with information that he was reading ancient Greek at the age of three and wrote a poetic continuation of the *Iliad* at the age of eight.

Despite that (or perhaps because of it), the combination of a nervous breakdown at the age of twenty, the poetry of Wordsworth and the brilliant character of his wife Harriet Taylor combined to let him shake off his guardians' dominance of his thought. He embarked on an exemplary utilitarian life, spreading democracy in his country, and working for utility, equality and emancipation wherever he went.

Despite agreeing with Bentham on much, Mill felt that different pleasures had different gradations of value. He denied that these pleasures are merely circumstantially advantageous (due to societal norms perhaps), but instead argues that they're inherently better, and that all competent judges would agree:

> 'A being of higher faculties requires more to make him happy, is capable probably of more acute suffering, and is certainly accessible to it at more points, than one of an inferior type; but in spite of these liabilities, he can never really wish to sink into what he feels to be a lower grade of existence . . . It is better to be a human being dissatisfied than a pig satisfied; better to be Socrates dissatisfied than a fool satisfied. And if the fool, or the pig, are of a different opinion, it is because they only know their own side of the question . . .'*

In positing it, Mill introduces a parallel value system alongside utility, one that seems to rely on an ill-defined 'being of higher faculties'. Mill argued that these spiritual, cultural and intellectual pleasures are of greater value than the merely physical pleasures, as judged by a competent judge. And a competent judge is anyone who has experienced both the lower and higher pleasures.

It's not an unusual thought. We've all been brought up to believe that certain pleasures are intrinsically more valuable than others: oil painting and wine being superior to video games and burgers, say.

* John Stuart Mill, *Utilitarianism* (1861).

And so have our favourite game characters. In *Phoenix Wright: Ace Attorney* (Capcom, 2001), snobbish lawyer Miles Edgeworth has a secret love of a low-brow kids' TV show called *The Steel Samurai*, going so far as to buy an expensive miniature of the titular character. In *Dragon Age: Inquisition* (BioWare, 2014), it emerges that the badass noble and Seeker Cassandra Pentaghast is embarrassed to admit she loves reading the dwarf Varric's romance books (which he himself thinks are absolutely awful).

And in *Mass Effect 2*, you can find a secret dossier on the synthetic Geth sniper called Legion, which was created solely to preserve its species. This dossier shows that this apparently serious Geth spends a lot of processing time playing video games – ranging from playing as a Level 612 Ardat-Yakshi Necromancer in *Galaxy of Fantasy*, an in-universe MMO with over eleven billion players, to being a max-scoring sniper in *Code of Honor: Medal of Duty*.

Pigs in mud

Though we may applaud his statements about higher pleasures, Mill doesn't actually justify this distinction, except by reference to our prejudices – and those are never very good guides to the truth. This is an obvious stretch, this search for inherently higher values, and one that much-maligned popular culture seems to provide the lie to. It's perfectly plausible to imagine someone valuing *Call of Duty* (Infinity Ward, Treyarch and Sledgehammer Games, 2003–) over *Papers Please* (3909 LLC, 2013), or *Super Mario Galaxy* (Nintendo, 2007) over *Gone Home* (The Fullbright Company, 2013), and it's hard to point to an objective truth, when these are items of our own creation. Moreover, our oft-denigrated video games are happiness-creators *par excellence*. Because whatever happiness or utility is, video games have a very good claim to being the form of media that maximise it easily, while minimising pain.*

By contrast, the Lamb we encounter in *BioShock 2* didn't share Mill's constraints or interests. Where Mill went on to write the more

---

* Studies seem to show that video games generally are able to promote dopamine and other brain chemicals easily, while also being able to distract players from ongoing pain.

political book *On Liberty*, explicitly defending the individual's rights against the state's interference, the Lamb we encounter had no such qualms . . .

THE FOOL, THE PIG, THE LION AND THE LAMB

In *BioShock 2* itself, the player is confronting not the early idealistic Lamb, who may have agreed with Mill, but the Late Lamb – the same individual, but with all those moral constraints and higher values stripped away. To Mill, she would be abhorrent. Thomas explains:

> '*Jekyll and Hyde* is my favourite story of all time. You have this Jekyll figure who is trying in vain to be a full-time moral agent. The problem with all attempts to adopt philosophy into a practical life, is that Jekyll says, "Okay, how can I be the best, how can I cause the least pain, how can I make the world maximally better for my passing?" Then you have Hyde. Hyde is a creature of the now, is a creature of actual practical everyday concerns, wants, drives, so forth. Without really intending to be evil whatsoever, he just has to serve the self, almost automatically. The second that Jekyll wakes up and measures everything Hyde's been up to, it's like, "Oh, good Lord." None of this is in accordance with the plan, if you measure from an external I. These things were evil-producing or suffering-producing, pick your poison. I still had to do something with the limited time I have, you have to make a split-second decision in a lot of cases.'

'Similarly, [Lamb] eventually became so fed up with trying to teach people to adopt her philosophy that she adopted a kind of proto-Dawkins view.' This is a thought that Thomas has taken from Richard Dawkins – that our selfish genes are working against true happiness and collectivism. 'Lamb would say that that voice all the way from the gene's-eye view up to the sentient collection thereof is telling you, suddenly and at all times, that you are the protagonist. If you buy your own hype, if you listen to that voice too often, it is very easy when you start to succeed a little, to say, "Yes, I was entitled to this and more" and the "and more" is the terrifying component there.' That 'and more', says Thomas, is the core of Rand's objectivist project.

> 'With the *BioShock* series ... Whether you love or hate the idea that any given game in this series presents, maybe the most obvious one that sort of connects them thematically is that philosophy sounds all well and good until you add the slightest bit of pressure. Then suddenly the atavistic impulse, the animal, takes over and does so so swiftly and so decisively that chaos ensues.'

Defeating dead Ryan

To Lamb that means to defeat Ryan – even when he's dead – she needs to go further than is possible in modern science. Thomas continues:

> 'Lamb was trying to just pull Hyde completely out of the mix. Her potion was the opposite, it was to take all of us, the Hyde figures, and turn us into full-time Jekylls ... She believed that the self-interested impulse began at the genetic level, so she reduced pleasure and pain down to what a gene wants, and then tried to essentially solve us from the ground up. She went down to, "Okay, if utopia is so commonly discussed as a place in which we will eventually get to live, but we ourselves are having original sin, which at the genetic level is saying, 'What's in this for me?', I'm going to solve that. I'm going to make a people who deserve to exist in this city without the self."'

Lamb's plan was to remove the self – to remove the need for liberty by cutting out the selfish impulse. Thomas explains:

> 'She says, "I'm going to build the first person who inherently, at the genetic level, wishes to promote pleasure and reduce pain over the widest possible surface area, has no inherent bias toward the self whatsoever." She was sacrificing her own daughter to that god of utility. So the way to do that is remove

the inherent bias toward the self, that Hyde figure, the whispers from the gene.'

Lamb's plan is to use her daughter to create a perfect utilitarian, by imbuing her with the thoughts and memories of everyone in Rapture.

In *BioShock 2*'s storyline, Sofia Lamb has seen her followers experimented on and persecuted by Ryan when his objectivist philosophy failed. She's so impressed and horrified by Ryan's brainwashing attempts on her allies that she attempts to co-opt and replicate these techniques, in the spirit of general happiness. This is her totalitarian utilitarianism, which abandons much of the respect for the individual that Mill and Bentham retained, and introduces a strange religiosity and collectivism. She says:

> 'Each of us has a moral duty to increase the common joy, and ease the common pain. Alone, we are nothing, mere engines of self-interest. Together, we are the Family, and through unity, we transcend the self.
>
> 'Is the Rapture Family religious, or secular? The question is irrelevant. Observe instead our mutualism. Beneath the myth, God is just a name for our moral duty to others. It is that impulse which unites the collective.'*†

---

* *BioShock 2*, 2K Marin (2K Games, 2010)

† As a sidenote, it's odd to compare the overtly religious overtones of the villains in *BioShock 2* and *BioShock Infinite*. Comstock's elevation to the status of prophet is understandable, given the conservative Christian society he begins – but as Thomas says, the way that Lamb's society morphs into a cult isn't unfamiliar either: 'Like a lot of the people who became great leaders of various communistic schools of thought, there is an inherent hypocrisy. The teacher, the person who keeps the most knowledge, ends up being elevated above them by default, and Lamb would say, "That was never my intent", but it always ends up happening. The sort of Messiah . . . she ends up co-opting religion, because it gets essentially thrust onto her, because as the person who spends the most time thinking about the moral ideas, there is an inherent cloud. You can't actually remove all stratification from human groups.'

The quantum of suffering

Though this sounds strange, philosophers like Peter Singer and David Pearce seem to have said similar things: that we should eliminate suffering of all sorts, for both man and the wider animal kingdom, at almost any cost.

Singer has argued that the right to life is a concomitant of a being's capacity to feel pleasure and pain – which shapes the preferences you have – and which means he's pro-euthanasia in cases where people can't have preferences and hence can't consent, including abortion. Thomas sees Lamb as following Singer in this, questioning 'whether the capacity to feel pleasure at all needs to be entered into the calculus, because he has been accused of saying, "Hey, people should be able to euthanize their severely disabled infants, because they're going to have a life of suffering." But then you're comparing it to no stimulus whatsoever. You're comparing to the implicit suffering of not having lived. Who gets to be the judge of that? Lambs and Ryans always answer, "Me. I've thought about it longer than you have."'

Indeed, the humanist Pearce has argued that engineering of human happiness like Lamb's may be in our near future:

'I probably sound a naive optimist. I anticipate a future of paradise engineering. One species of recursively self-improving organic robot is poised to master its own genetic source code and bootstrap its way to full-spectrum superintelligence. The biology of suffering, aging and disease will shortly pass into history. A future discipline of compassionate biology will replace conservation biology. Our descendants will be animated by gradients of genetically preprogrammed bliss orders of magnitude richer than anything physiologically accessible today. A few centuries hence, no experience below "hedonic zero" will pollute our forward light-cone.'*

In the light of thoughts like that, Lamb's goal isn't beyond the pale of modern philosophy, though her methods are more suspect. 'We're

* Pearce, David, 'Is Humanity Accelerating Towards . . . Apocalyse? Or Utopia?' (IEET, June 2012)

already into deep pulp here,' says Thomas. 'But it was a thought experiment that made sense for a game called *BioShock*, a franchise about genes. [Lamb] takes the ultimate representation of the traditional genetic investment, which is your child, the thing that you are the most biased about, and sacrifices it to become this utopia.' And it was a sacrifice, given the failure of her previous experiments.

Indeed, given Rapture's collapse into chaos and horror after Ryan's death, Lamb has a lot of high-quality material to pour into the experiment. Thomas continues:

> 'Because Rapture is decaying around her, she decides to use the constituent minds, these great thinkers, writers, artists, athletes, musicians and so forth, and put them all into these various test subjects and then eventually her own daughter. The player ends up rescuing Elinor from that fate ultimately, and if anything sort of provides a very strong counter-example, that whatever individualistic tendency you show, she mimics. You end up being a little more of a Rand figure by default in contrast to Lamb.'

LIBERTY, EQUALITY AND THE MANY

Bentham would not have recognised his utilitarianism in Lamb's society – because much classical utilitarianism also took explicit account of other elements of value in society, such as liberty and equality. 'Liberty' is the concept that a person is free in their actions – either in the sense that they're free from external constraint (what the Russian-British philosopher Isaiah Berlin called **'negative' freedom**) or free from internal constraints (what Berlin called **'positive' freedom**, which seems to be a form of self-mastery).

Lamb's society has disposed of liberty, descending into a murderous mockery; people are turned into tools to be used to maximise happiness. Equality only happens by the by, and she herself is raised into something of a Messiah, as a side effect. Respect for the conscious individual's rights, which even Singer argues for, has vanished.

Learning from Ryan, Lamb's solution to most obstacles and obstructive people is to remove them – not peaceably, by re-education, but forcibly, with violence. Says Thomas:

'From every practical point of view, from anybody who has any kind of common sense, it looks horrific. But there's a kind of logic to it as well. Her thinking was, well, if you remove the people to look on in horror, this will simply make the world a better place for all involved because they will agree it was necessary . . . Did you create more suffering by taking away my ability to perceive it? That gets meta as hell in a hurry. Those are the kinds of questions that people who criticise Lamb and Rapture were asking.'

Bentham ran up against similar problems. He denied natural rights, instead seeing freedom from constraint as something conducive to utilitarianism. Indeed, Bentham was instrumental in the design of the panopticon – a special glass prison built in a circle around a central guard tower so as to totally eliminate the prisoner's privacy. Mill was keener than Bentham to retain other rights in his utilitarianism, and hence wrote two books explicitly about those subjects: *On Liberty* and *The Subjection of Women*.

THE VEIL OF IGNORANCE

But Lamb's reduction of everyone to equality, by pruning her opponents and by making a perfect utilitarian out of her daughter, was originally much more totalitarian. Thomas again:

'Prior to the daughter-sacrificing theme, there was a plot which involved Lamb trying to connect everyone so that empathy would be equal and literally you could walk a mile in my shoes in an instant, so that every decision you would make there onward would be informed by that knowledge of how I would suffer or benefit from your decision. We didn't end up going that way because we wanted it to be set in a utilitarian utopia.'

That feels much like the American philosopher John Rawls' investigations into what he called the 'Original Position'. This was a thought experiment where a group of people must reach agreement about the kind of structure they want for a society. However, each person must make the decision from behind a 'veil of ignorance' – where they lack knowledge of the details of the position they'd occupy in that society. Without knowledge of their intelligence, wealth, skills, education, religion, gender, race, age and so on, when the individuals rationally pursue their advantage in society, we would avoid unjust proposals, Rawls argues.

Lucas Pope thinks that his game *Papers Please* (see Chapter 9), in which you play as a border guard, is a step that way – to providing players with empathy for people they're not.

'Immigration inspectors are not a respected class of people anywhere almost, and a lot of people tell me they have a better understanding of what it means to . . . Of how these are not the bad guys, basically. They're not evil. They're not out to just screw me, personally.

'I think there's some potential there, especially with VR. I think there's a lot of potential for kind of building empathy and understanding other people's perspectives. Just close your eyes and imagine you're that person. Throw away all of your preconceptions and all of your wants and desires and imagine, "That's me. What would I feel? How would I think?" You know? And maybe I can only do that because I have a positive outlook, that I even care to try to get inside someone's head."

Rawl's 'original position' seeks to persuade us to that position but for all people, to help us make the right choice for all people, rather than just for us.

BIG DATA AND UTILITARIANISM

Perhaps utility, like economics, is just waiting for sufficiently advanced computational machines. After all, we have just entered an age of big data, where humans are finally able to use computer systems to extract unforeseen correlations, patterns and associations, alongside biometric systems that could conceivably be developed to measure a range of elements of wellbeing. And with the advent of more complex artificial intelligences, it's plausible that should a measure of utility be established, it could be tracked.

On an individual level, what are the practical upshots of all these criticisms of utilitarianism? Yes, it may be impossible to sum utility effectively – even the real Mill and the fictional Lamb, both brought up from birth to be perfect utilitarians, found it hard to sum utility effectively, and Mill later abandoned Bentham's calculator. Yet Mill's life seems a testament to the effectiveness of the utilitarian education he received. From the perspective of history few other men have achieved so much for the greater good as he did, in his work to extend the rights of men and women. He may not have been able to sum utility in mathematical formulae that gave an objective viewpoint, but he certainly behaved well enough that we could argue that a utilitarian perspective generally improves the lives of many.

For us, more limited in our conception and intellect, perhaps the best bet is to behave like Epicurus, Commander Shepard and the early Lamb – doing those things from moment to moment that are certain to improve local happiness, given that you're not able to predict the impossible mathematics sufficiently, and perhaps following general rules for wider behaviour where we can generally agree on them.

Limbo, anarchy.

Maria: Hmm. That chapter's left me a little lost. I'm not sure where we go from here. This way?

Luisa: No, this way. It's, uh, more frabjous, positively slithey.

Maria: (*squinting*) It looks pretty mimsy to me. Come now, we can't argue. Can't we come to some agreement?

Luisa: Well, how about we vote on it.

Maria: There's two of us! That makes no sense, unless we already agree. We need something stronger.

Luisa: Well, how about we agree to take turns being leader? I'll go first.

Maria: Okay.

Luisa: So we'll go this way.

Maria: . . .

Maria: Well, we went this way. It's still a bleak, endless expanse.

Luisa: Hey, I don't think I stopped being leader. Let's keep going.

Maria: . . .

Maria: When do I get to be leader?

Luisa: When the leader says so.

Maria: I'm never going to be leader am I?

Luisa: . . . No.

Maria: What about equality? Liberty? Sorority?

Luisa: They all sound like excellent hobbies. I don't mind what you do with your free time, as long as you do what I say in the rest of your time. Which is all the time.

Maria: Is this your way of making a point about political institutions and game theory?

Luisa: Quiet, pleb. Now we go this way. And no snacking on mushrooms en route.

CHAPTER NINE

On politics: from autocracy to democracy (and back again)

....

'Theoretically I believe in democracy, as most people do. I believe in democracy with an engaged, educated and informed electorate – but, of course, that's where it all goes tits up.'

Cliff Harris (creator of the *Democracy* game series)

'Strange game. The only winning move is not to play. How about a nice game of chess?'

Joshua in *WarGames* (written by Lawrence Lasker and Walter F. Parkes)

You're sitting in your booth. It's crowded with the paraphernalia of your job – stamps, guidebooks, pictures of significant people – and is a nightmare to keep tidy. Every few minutes, someone else walks up to your counter, and presents their passport. It's your job to check the paperwork against the reams of official documentation and against their face, and see if you should let them into the country or not. A simple job, surely?

Yet it feels like every day the government changes the rules. You're so busy trying to keep up with the new regulations, so concerned with keeping your family alive (and they are regularly ill, starving or cold) and so desperate to keep your job that you don't often have time to notice the desperation in the faces of those you turn away. And every day you turn away more and more.

Then one day a husband and wife walk up. He has the right papers, she has . . . nothing. He pleads with you – he's a dissident from his country. If she goes back, she'll be killed. You have a horrible ethical decision to make. If you're caught letting her through, who knows what will happen to you? And if you disappear, what will happen to your family?

That's not a story from North Korea or Soviet Russia, but from *Papers Please* (3909 LLC, 2013), a game by Lucas Pope. Your role is to be a border guard for the fictional country of Arstotzka, checking passports and deciding who to let in. Sometimes that person runs past your counter and is machine-gunned down. Rarely, they attempt to throw a bomb. Most of the time they just look worn out and sad, whether you turn them away or let them in.

Though from the player's perspective *Papers Please* is mostly a game about ethical choices and survival, it's also a totalitarian regime simulator. You're role-playing someone having to live in a country that sets extremely tight rules on behaviour, amidst similarly hostile neighbours. You may love that country – you may accept that the rules are necessary to maintain whatever it is that you value (national integrity, the safety of its citizens, the continuation of its political philosophy), or you might just care more about your family than political dissidents, whether external or internal. Whatever the reason, you have to sit in that booth and weigh the lives and happiness of the people passing in front of you against yours, your family's and your fellow's.

That's how the society of Arstotzka works. But it isn't the only way a government *can* work. There are democracies, dictatorships, elective oligarchies, aristocracies, benevolent despots, anarchies . . . the human mind never seems to cease generating institutions to twist societal management into new forms. So which way should a society be run? What does a fair society look like? Politics, after all, is the implementation of ethics (and we've already thought long and hard about our ethical ideals in Chapters 7 and 8).

SimCity and hidden bias

Games, as always, let you choose and experiment. A game like *SimCity* (Maxis, 1989) lets you run certain functions in a small city. You have the limited powers of a city mayor, to zone and set tax, and build large public institutions. Though there are hard limits on what you can do, you can decide to construct public buildings, put the cheap housing by the beautiful river, tax the rich more, minimise policing, and so on. Essentially, you can implement your political philosophy through legislation.

But, as *Democracy* (Positech Games, 2005) creator Cliff Harris says, generally 'games run away from politics. They have a very HBO version of politics, in that they want an angle. Nobody does a game about politics that isn't saying something and making its bias really obvious.' (Nobody apart from the creator of *Papers Please*, Lucas Pope, apparently.)

Yet, core to many apparently non-political games are design decisions, mostly hidden, which have political – and hence ethical – assumptions. For example, the *SimCity* (Maxis, 2013) remake led players down a particular political path, though it never made that explicit. Players can vary the tax rate for different sectors of society, which has an impact on the happiness of each class.* Behind the scenes, the ideal situation is that you tax the wealthy 10 per cent, the middle class 11 per cent and the poor 12 per cent – that is, the game's systems have inherent prejudices that favour a lower tax on the rich[†] and higher on the poor. You can still buck them, but it'll be much harder to keep that city on an even keel. The game is encouraging you, deliberately or not, to take a path associated with libertarian economics.

So it's worth asking what we actually believe. Is it right to tax different people differently? Is it wrong to only care about the people of Arstotzka and not those who live in the neighbouring states of Obristan or Kolechia? How far should the rights of individuals in any of these countries be restricted to maintain equality? What should be considered a crime? Should we work with the underlying structures of society or work against them? Who should rule and in favour of whom? These wildly diverse questions are all put under the title of '**political philosophy**' – something we could characterise as ethics applied to society. And, surprisingly, games are pretty good at offering answers.

---

* http://www.simcityplanningguide.com/2013/11/ideal-tax-rates.html
† It's unknown how much these prejudices reflect those of the original game's creator Will Wright, but we do know that he donated over $120,000 to the United States Republican party between 2006 and 2016, according to www.politicalmoneyline.com.

Who should rule?

Pope's *Papers Please* obviously isn't how we imagine the operation of our own nation's politics. We don't live in fear of a shadowy oligarchy that criminalises a different way of living every day and maintains control through brutality and fear. That's because most of us today live in representative democracies.

Democracy is a form of government that spread over the world mainly during the twentieth century. It's a governmental system that lets the vast majority of people decide who should run the country on their behalf (hence the name, from the Greek *demos* meaning people and *kratos* meaning power.[*]) It's typically contrasted with oligarchy (from *oligoi* meaning few) and autocracy (from *auto* meaning self), respectively the rule of few and the rule of one.

Yet, the modern form isn't direct democracy, as it was when it was established in ancient Athens – the people aren't directly involved in government themselves, deciding on laws. Instead, the modern form of democracy has representatives typically selected by a party system – normally a political party with a particular ethical stance and set of beliefs. These candidates go through an electoral system that constrains who can run and how their votes are translated into political representation and institutional control. This is crucial, because it means that the group of people who end up as representatives and/or running the country can be very different from the various groups that elected or selected them.

And the electorate isn't actually all the people. Every democracy in the world has a restricted 'franchise' – a set of rules about voting that typically exclude the young, the mentally-disabled, sometimes criminals and in certain countries certain classes (like the members of the House of Lords in the UK). These are mostly restrictions of capability and some people think the franchise should be further restricted, on the basis of capability.

For example, earlier we mentioned Cliff Harris, a developer who has made a popular series of strategy games called *Democracy*. We

* And, yes, that is where the Spartan warrior Kratos from the *God of War* series gets his name.

tend to think that democracy is an obviously fair governmental system – but Harris is keen we check that assumption.

'Theoretically I believe in democracy, as most people do. I believe in democracy with an engaged and educated and informed electorate, but of course that's where it all goes tits up. I'm one of those people that openly muses that maybe there should be a questionnaire when you go to vote to, like, weed out people who are just voting for the guy with the beard. I can understand to some extent, shockingly, the *Daily Mail*-esque opinion that people on benefits shouldn't be able to vote. I wouldn't go along with that, but I can see that there's some logic there. Should prisoners be able to vote? If you're mentally ill do you have a vote? And then how do you define "mentally ill"?'

Nor is the popular vote necessarily accurately translated into laws, or indeed, into representation. The presidential election of the United States of America is supposedly a directly democratic vote, to elect a single person. Yet on five occasions in two centuries, the winner of the popular vote has not become president thanks to the strange electoral system. Most notably, in the 2016 election, the Democratic candidate Hillary Clinton won 1.6 million more votes than the Republican candidate Donald Trump, constituting 1.3 per cent of the vote.*

The resistible rise of democracy

Nor has democracy been a dominant force, historically. Across the sweep of history, democracy has almost always lost out to other forms of government. According to the Polity IV historical survey, up until the early nineteenth century there were no democracies in the world. Their numbers gradually rose until the 1920s to around twenty, and fell to below ten again during the Second World War. With the decolonisation movements of the 1940s and '50s, the

---

* Data correct as of November 2016, source: '2016 National Popular Vote Tracker', *The Cooke Political Report*.

number of countries in the world increased substantially, and with it the number of democracies. Yet it was only in 1989 that the number of democracies exceeded the number of autocracies, and only in the 2000s that they reached an absolute majority over other forms of government.* Yes, democracy as a dominant political force – one that represents the majority of the world's people – is less than twenty years old. Despite that, democracy has been a political system for more than two millennia, since it was created in ancient Athens in the fifth century BC. But ever since then it's been the subject of dispute.

The foundational text of many philosophical traditions is *The Republic* by Plato (428–348 BC). It's also a foundational text for democratic thought, given that it's entirely about the foundation of a perfectly just state. This book identified five forms of government, in decreasing order of desirability: Aristocracy, Timocracy, Oligarchy, Democracy and Tyranny. In Plato's view, democracy was the second-worst political system for a city-state, after tyranny (the rule of one person).

That's notable, because democracy was a relatively new form of government then – the Athenians had established it for the first time around fifty years before Plato's time. It had replaced an aristocratic system and was significant in that it allowed ordinary Athenians to directly participate in democracy, from voting in a general assembly on the issues of the day to being randomly selected to be jurors or legislators. There were no 'representatives of the people'; instead the people themselves were directly involved. It was this democratic environment that allowed for the first freedom of expression, being no longer under the constant authoritarian scrutiny of kings and aristocrats – and hence, perhaps, why Athens was such a gathering point for philosophers.

It's worth noting though that, as Harris implied earlier, 'ordinary Athenians' in this context is something of a misnomer. It didn't mean women, who had very limited public rights; it didn't mean slaves or even freed slaves; it didn't mean debtors (and debt was

---

* Max Roser, 'Democracy' (2016). Published online at OurWorldInData. org. Retrieved from: https://ourworldindata.org/democracy/

inheritable); it didn't mean foreigners like Aristotle, no matter how long they had lived there; it only meant citizens. And to be a citizen was to be an adult, to have completed your military training and to own land. All told, maybe just 10–20 per cent of the population had the right to vote in this, the original form of democracy. By contrast, just under 70 per cent of the population of the modern United Kingdom of Great Britain and the United States is eligible to vote, including women, the young, debtors* and immigrants.†‡

That huge increase in participation didn't just happen. It's not just a reflection of better record keeping. It's a reflection of 2500 years of striving for equal rights, liberties and personal freedoms – and that's all part of the story of political philosophy too. Before we can talk more about democracy – and why we ascribe it such value, whatever its faults – we have to look more closely at the forms of government it displaced.

THE PHILOSOPHER-RULERS

As we said earlier, Lucas Pope's *Papers Please* is an example of **autocracy** or **oligarchy**: the rule of a small set of unaccountable people, or perhaps just one person. This isn't necessarily a system that's totalitarian§ or malevolent – though in this case it seems to be to us. Pope explained his vision to us over a crackly line from Japan.

* Which is everyone, nowadays, after all, thanks to the general expansion of cheap credit.
† Source: UK Office of National Statistics.
https://www.ons.gov.uk/peoplepopulationandcommunity/elections/electoralregistration/bulletins/electoralstatisticsforuk/2015
‡ http://www.statisticbrain.com/voting-statistics/
§ Where an authoritarian government suppresses political expression, totalitarianism is one step further. This is where the government exercises absolute control over all aspects of life, from education to morals to citizens' private lives. This is the way Earth is run under both *Half-Life 2*'s Combine government or *XCOM 2*'s Advent government – though totalitarian governments in history and the current day tend to mostly refrain from wholesale elimination of their populace.

"My own feelings on politics are . . . I don't strongly believe that any system is right. I think they're all just systems that, except for a straight up dictatorship, are trying to help but have flaws in the system somewhere. Nothing is perfect. We're seeing now[*] that democracy can get pretty screwed up, or a republic can get pretty screwed up. I'm not, like, putting anything forward to say it's better. I'm just trying to use interactive media, use a game, to show how people are not evil.

'I intentionally haven't studied politics, because my general feeling about politics is it's just a polarising thing where you latch on to what you latch on to and you've got to fight for it forever. It's hard to keep an open mind when you're thinking very strongly about politics. Typically, political games start with an issue, and then they present the issue and set up how you should look at the issue and their side of it, and why they're right and everyone else is wrong. I hesitate to call *Papers Please* a political game, but what I kind of wanted to do is I wanted to look at a more generalised look at politics and the philosophy of "I'm right and they're wrong". How politics works, where you kind of get invested in your side and it's really hard to see from the other person's position why they think that way or why they're different than you.'

To inculcate that empathy, Pope puts the player in a situation where you can see the other side and understand why someone might behave the way that they do – the position of a border guard in a totalitarian state. 'With Arstotzka, the government for me was a generic communist bureaucracy, mostly incompetent but very strict. In America, we all have this popular image from the 80s of the whole Red Scare thing, so that's what I built it out of. But it was nothing very specific and nothing I wouldn't be able to nail down . . .' And, playing as the border guard, you can understand their motivations. 'It's not because they're an evil person, it's not because they're dumb. It's just that they're different people, their situation is different . . .'

* The 2016 Presidential election.

262

Pope thinks games and interactive media like *Papers Please* are the perfect medium for raising these questions and creating empathy.

'I felt it was really important not to say that communism is bad or bureaucracy is bad or stringent borders are bad. I wanted to say, "Well, stringent borders can be bad, but there's a reason people believe they need a very tight order", and when you just dismiss the idea that you need to control your borders and say that the people who want to control their borders are racist or xenophobic or something, you're missing what's really happening. I mean, they're people just like us and they believe this thing for a reason. I kind of wanted to show in the game those things in a more interactive context.

'We look at Putin and say, "That's terrible", but if you ask a Russian, they'll say, "You know what? We kind of like him. He's not so bad. He helped this country a lot. We were in a really bad shape before and now we're not, so he's got to get some credit." In *Papers Please*, it's a maybe fascist or communist government, a socialist government, but I also wanted to highlight that it's a government made of people and a bureaucracy is kind of the bad head of the thing made of lots of people, but it's not always with bad intention. It's just kind of how it drifts into this bad place, but they're making rules and they're trying to set standards that they think will help people.

'I tried to use different events in the game to show, "Well, these crazy rules that this government is imposing on you, they're there for a reason and maybe they're not so crazy" or, "These rebels who are fighting you, they're fighting for something important, and both sides are right, so what do you do?" And that's how life is. I wanted players to be faced with that problem where they don't really know what's going on. They don't know who's right or wrong, but everybody seems kind of right or everybody seems kind of wrong. It's a very vague, nebulous thing that I think is a big part of politics.'

THE REPUBLIC

Arstotzka might seem a long way from ancient Athens. But both places were ruled by a small élite, ostensibly in favour of the population. This political set-up is called **benevolent oligarchy**. Today, oligarchy is synonymous with aristocracy – the inherited rule of the rich – and élite corruption. So it's strange to modern eyes that Plato argues in *The Republic* in favour of a form of oligarchy.

Plato's major concern in this book is justice: that everyone gets what they deserve from everyone else, and that they all perform to the best of their capabilities, for the best possible life. Plato thought that a person was split into three competing drives (roughly, intellectual drives came from the brain, spiritual from the heart and materialistic from the gut), which reflected the way that society is split into three separate classes, each of whom was dominated by one of those drives. And the one class that should rule the others is . . . the philosophers, dominated by their brains.

Oddly enough, there aren't very many games that talk about aristocracy in a praiseworthy fashion. We are, after all, a liberal democratic society, and we have taken certain values on board almost entirely, reflected in our popular media; one of those seems to be that aristocrats are inherently decadent and evil. For example, the *Dragon Age* and *The Witcher* series do have aristocrats running their states, but they're mostly as brutal, brutish and cynical as everyone else in those low fantasy worlds.

For Plato, though, this ruling class is different. He believed that all children in his society should be brought up in common, without knowing who their parents were, to avoid favouritism in society. His aristocrats should be picked from the best children and educated differently, leaving behind the third class of merchants and workers (who were best suited to growing produce and manufacturing goods).

A second selection process separated out the soldiers from the ruling class, and trained the soldiers for war and policing. The soldiers' job was to enforce the policies of the philosopher-rulers, inside and outside the city-state. Neither Plato's soldiers nor his philosopher-rulers were allowed to own property, to avoid conflicts of interests in their rulings.

Philosopher kings . . . and queens

After all that winnowing, all we're left with is the rulers themselves. Having been educated by philosophers, Plato has the rulers become selfless and intellectually rigorous, through their access to perfect knowledge.* They rule the state even-handedly and wisely, because only they know what the best way to live is for everyone. These rare beasts could be any gender – though Plato believed that women were mostly inferior to men, he didn't think it was outside the realm of possibility that some women could have superior capacities:

> '. . . the natural capacities are distributed alike among both creatures, and women naturally share in all pursuits and men in all . . . Women and men have the same nature in respect to the guardianship of the state, save insofar as the one is weaker and the other is stronger . . . Women of this kind, then, must be selected to cohabit with men of this kind and to serve with them as guardians since they are capable of it and akin by nature.'†

Plato's system does have some appeal – especially to philosophers, who get to be kings. It's essentially a modern technical education scheme, with very early selection and separation of pupils. It also demonstrates the beginnings of modern thought on governmental forms, justice, psychology, metaphysics and much more. It even has a strand of feminism, considering Plato thought women were capable of being both soldiers and philosopher-kings.

On the other hand, Plato's philosophy did have some nasty, totalitarian elements, including lying to the population on a regular basis (such as fixing a supposedly random marital lottery to produce eugenic results) and making up myths about the origins of the state.

---

* Plato's concept of the good is an entirely separate topic, touching on transcendentalism, where sufficiently studied philosophers would get access to primal concepts of ideas, like the good. Basically, you should buy *The Republic*. It's not only one of the first philosophy books, but also one of the easiest to read.
† *The Republic*, Book 5.

It was also the inspiration to Giovanni Gentile, the Italian philosopher who created fascism and totalitarianism. But for a starting place, it's pretty impressive.

MONARCHY AND *CRUSADER KINGS*

Between Plato and the next significant advances in political thought was a gap of roughly two thousand years. It's worth focusing on this because, as we emphasised earlier, democracy has only really become the dominant political system in the last century. What continued to dominate world politics during this period was generally **autocracy**: the rule of king, despots, chiefs or tyrants.

So the various historical strategy series made by Paradox Interactive are a better representation than Harris' *Democracy* of the patterns of political philosophy over time. In games such as *Crusader Kings II* (Paradox Development Studio, 2012) or *Europa Universalis IV* (Paradox Development Studio, 2013), you take on the role of a leader in a historical state. Unlike similar strategy games, you may well not be the ultimate ruler – you're bound by treaties and you're more likely to be a vassal to a more powerful nobleman or king, than independent yourself.

Johan Andersson is the head of development at Paradox.

'We always try to model all the major government forms that existed in the era covered by the particular game. For example, *Europa Universalis: Rome* (Paradox Development Studio, 2008) had five types of Republic, Roman-style Dictatorships, the Roman Principate, Theocracy, three forms of Monarchy, and four types of tribal rule; all with unique mechanics.

'Sometimes a particular form of government does not suit the core mechanics of a game though. For example, in *Crusader Kings II* you cannot play as a Theocracy because it's a game about dynasties and hereditary realms.'

That said, whatever your role, you're the ultimate source of authority in your small state – though your actions might be heavily constrained by what your people and your neighbours accept as legitimate behaviour.

For example, in Paradox games, declaring war without a reason, without a so-called *casus belli*, is still seen as behaviour bad enough to put you beyond the pale of diplomacy. Even the Nazi regime couldn't invade Poland in 1939 without faking up several border events (such as the Gleiwitz incident, where they forced concentration camp detainees dressed as Polish soldiers to attack a German radio tower).

Look at *Call of Duty: Modern Warfare 2* (Infinity Ward, 2009). Here, both the US and Russian armies are secretly itching to go to war, but have no justification and their governments are understandably opposed. The two militaries collaborate to place an undercover CIA agent into the cell of the Russian terrorist Vladimir Makarov, who then commits a massacre in a Moscow airport (the infamous 'No Russian' level) and dumps the agent's body there to frame the Americans. This provides an internationally acceptable pretext for war.

As Andersson implies, the authority of a leader was justified in various ways at different times. Most states were religious so tended to work with a version of the Divine Right of Kings – that kings were appointed by a God (the main god in monotheistic cultures, one of the leading gods in polytheistic cultures) to rule over their people. In the modern Western culture of diversity, atheism and multiple religious strands that may seem hard to justify, but in those days of religious hegemony it was a pretty convincing argument.

Take another look at Comstock's miraculous city of Columbia in *BioShock Infinite* (Irrational Games, 2013). Comstock rules this city, not with an iron fist, but because the ruling majority of the population are nativist, evangelical Christians. This is a classic theocracy, as the population believe that Comstock is a prophet appointed by God to lead the true America.

In the Judeo-Christian tradition, kings were the 'Lord's anointed' following the prophet Samuel's blessing of Saul and David as kings over Israel. Similarly, Islamic rulers could appeal to their descent from Muhammad or one of his uncles. Aside from this religious form, the ruler's authority might instead be justified by benevolent despotism (Joseph II of Austria, for example), familial glory (as pushed by Louis XIV), or even a view of the state as the personal property of the monarch (for example, the Congo as private holdings of Leopold II of Belgium).

Each of these justifications would also, of course, necessitate a different ostensible goal for the state. Andersson explains:

> 'A lot of our players actually don't play to "win", but rather set specific goals for themselves that they then try to achieve, or just role-play a barbarian reaver, a benevolent head of the family or a ruthless tyrant. The role-players are especially common in *Crusader Kings*. We try to cater to many different types of player, and it's reflected in how we program the AI as well; it does not always play to win, but also to act "in character". After all, the computer opposition is only there for the player's enjoyment.'

Machiavelli and consequentialism

Ultimately though, whatever the justification for your rule, the key thing about this era was that you were expected to be a good king – which is why the teachings of Niccolò di Bernardo dei Machiavelli (1469–1527) were so scandalous. Normally known just as Machiavelli, he was a bureaucrat in medieval Florence, who was expelled from the city for opposing the powerful Medici family. In exile, he wrote widely, mainly focusing on plays, but also writing historical analysis and political advice. It is the latter work, specifically his book *The Prince* (1513), that has won him lasting fame – and notoriety.

Like Plato's interlocutor Thrasymachus in *The Republic*, Machiavelli advises an approach to the law that's often called **'consequentialist'**.* That means, though it's unlikely that he ever said it, his political philosophy is all about 'the end justifies the means' – or as a gamer might put it, Machiavelli advised playing to win. The traditional teachings of courtly behaviour sometimes read like they're out of a Disney cartoon, designed to build fairy-tale princes.

* See Chapter 8.

But instead Machiavelli advises new leaders that they should separate off their public and private morality; 'look like the innocent flower/ but be the serpent beneath it' as Shakespeare puts it, likely influenced by Machiavelli.

It's worth noting that Machiavelli never advised evil for evil's sake – but more that, for achieving a prince's aims, whatever they may be, evil acts are sometimes necessary. That's something games understand very well. Think of how, in *The Witcher 3*, Geralt and Yennefer will do anything to get their adoptive daughter Ciri back – whether that means destroying ancient artefacts and desecrating sacred shrines in Yennefer's case or Geralt eliminating every last rare species and butchering his way across three continents.

The difference is that Machiavelli advised that you should do these terrible, evil things that conduce to your aim – but that you should also maintain your public image while doing so – that you should fight your fights legally and diplomatically wherever possibly, but be prepared for war at all times. As he said:

> 'How laudable it is for a prince to keep good faith and live with integrity, and not with astuteness, every one knows. Still the experience of our times shows those princes to have done great things who have had little regard for good faith, and have been able by astuteness to confuse men's brains, and who have ultimately overcome those who have made loyalty their foundation. You must know, then, that there are two methods of fighting, the one by law, the other by force: the first method is that of men, the second of beasts; but as the first method is often insufficient, one must have recourse to the second. It is therefore necessary to know well how to use both the beast and the man.'[*]

Ideally, he says, '. . . one ought to be both feared and loved, but as it is difficult for the two to go together, it is much safer to be feared than loved, if one of the two has to be wanting'.[†]

---

[*] Niccolò Machiavelli, *Il Principe* (1505), Chapter 18.
[†] Ibid, Chapter 17.

Indeed, despite the various rights we've accrued over the millennia, it's arguable that Machiavelli's thought processes are still at the fore. Though our leaders use the language of ethics, their actions often seem to follow the path of realpolitik as advised by Machiavelli.

THE STATE OF NATURE, THE SOCIAL CONTRACT AND . . . RUST?

We can see from these games how these rulers really weren't ruling with their people's consent, but more some higher authority's consent. And some, taking Machiavelli's advice, were only faking morality and faith. When the seventeenth century rolled around, an increasingly educated and stable middle class, perhaps self-educated from books from the new printing presses, began to question the legitimacy of its rulers. Several philosophers argued against Divine Right, particularly given the religious upheavals of the Reformation. Many followed Plato's *Crito** instead of *The Republic*, arguing that we must look to something called '**the state of nature**' for the legitimisation of government.

This theory started from the Dutch jurist Hugo de Groot (1583–1645), commonly called Grotius. He argued that humans had natural rights, including the right to preserve ourselves and punish any breach of that right that we witnessed – and that, crucially, we'd have those rights irrespective if there was a god or not.

This was developed later in the same century by the English philosopher Thomas Hobbes (1588–1679). Hobbes had lived through the English Civil War, where the king had attempted to assert his Divine Right and supremacy over his people, represented by the English parliament, and had been judicially beheaded for his pains. The two wars the king had provoked had divided the country and ruined it, leaving it looking like something out of *Game of Thrones*.

So Hobbes followed Grotius, and argued that people had a right to protect themselves against the sorts of monarchs that Machiavelli

* Plato's *Crito* is set the day before Socrates' execution and is a dialogue between Socrates and his rich friend Crito, who has arranged to smuggle him out of the city. We talk about it more below.

had advocated. He proposed that, in the state of nature, there is anarchy and misery – that life is 'solitary, poor, nasty, brutish and short'* – and that the fear of death and of each other passionately motivates the people to improve their situation, which impels them towards a new idea – a 'social contract'.

Nasty, brutish and short

The Hobbesian state of nature has come to the forefront in games relatively recently, in the newly popular genre of multiplayer survival games. These started with the *Arma 2* (Bohemia Interactive, 2009) mod† *DayZ* (2013), and soon proliferated with games like *Ark: Survival Evolved* (Studio Wildcard, early access), *7 Days to Die* (The Fun Pimps, early access) and *The Forest* (Endnight Games Ltd, early access).

Rust (Facepunch Studios‡, early access) is a classic and hugely popular example of the genre. Players start in a random place in this world, naked and without any possessions save for a large rock. Then their task is to survive by gathering resources, like food or wood for shelter.

Normally, a new player will be killed fairly soon. Not by the game's hostile wildlife or by starvation or thirst or cold, but by another player. Mostly players kill each other in pursuit of any resources they may have gathered. Sometimes players just kill each other because they can or to remove competition for recurring local resources. Life in *Rust* really is nasty, brutish and short.

Other survival simulators are equally brutal. *DayZ*, the original simulator of this type, spawns new players with little equipment, meaning they should be of little interest to established players. Sometimes, though, well-armed established players enslave new

---

* Thomas Hobbes, *Leviathan* (1651), The First Part, Chapter 13.
† 'Mod' is short for 'modification' and is a user-made alteration to a video game (almost always on PC). Since at least the days of *DOOM*, teams of fans have grouped up to alter games, improve them, fix bugs or even create entirely new games from them. The latter type of mod has led to famous and hugely popular games like *Counter-Strike*, *DOTA* and *Team Fortress 2*.
‡ Better known for their first project, *Garry's Mod* (2004).

players – using them to carry items, as bait for zombies, or as mobile blood banks (using the in-game transfusion kit, assuming they have the right blood type). Or they'll just kill them, as most players in *DayZ* assume mutual hostility and kill any other player on sight.

By contrast, a player in *Rust* has less incentive to kill new players and more to co-operate, to build structures and for mutual benefit. But you can still kill your compatriots at will, if you're running low on resources. Even in a small tribe, this state of nature is just survival (and not particularly good survival at that). Something more is needed for human satisfaction, if not human happiness. Craig Pearson is a writer at its developer Facepunch:

> '*Rust* is a game that requires time and effort to "succeed" in. Servers currently last for a month, so when you hack to gain advantage, you can destroy days or even weeks of work. Hackers can see through walls, aimhack*, and see a huge amount of game data, like where resources are, if they're being watched by another player, or where things are buried. We've gotten pretty good at stopping things like jumping hacks and speed hacks, but the more invisible hacks are tougher to keep track of.'

And Pearson and his team can see that people really do want more than mere survival. Players bond together for mutual benefit. The developers can see that in the game by watching hackers, who are easily tracked, along with any players that associate with them. Each time there's a monthly reset of their in-game progress, these identifiable groups of players regroup quickly, often hacking to speed up their initial building and development.

> 'Because it's a risky proposition – if you're caught we ban the account – there are groups who don't hack, but who will have

---

* An 'aimhack' is a specialised software program that hacks into an online video game and allows the player to never miss a shot – often by automatically shooting in the head any hostile creature that comes within range. Users of such hacks are normally banned.

a known hacker play alongside them. If we find out that some-one has benefited from doing that, we'll server ban that group. What often happens is the whole group will move to another server, and the hacker will rejoin them with a new Steam account, and the cycle will repeat.'

Given the monthly server resets, these groups can't develop their society in the game – it definitely doesn't give enough time for social institutions to form. Similarly, in Hobbes' mooted state of nature, societies need something to tie them together, to prevent conflict. Hobbes argues that something is the rule of an authority – be it an individual or a group – that uses its power to ensure satisfaction or happiness are more achievable.

Unable to organise in a lasting way because of the server resets, people in *Rust* go to hackers for that power, says Pearson.

'Clans can "hire" a hacker to get the edge that a hack provides, but without the worry of being financially penalised by having their game banned. High-end *Rust* usually involves larger clans battling to destroy other bases, to claim land, weapons, resources, and more. Bases are player-built, so you don't know what you'll encounter, unless you have someone who can track people through walls, spot where the cupboard is [in *Rust*, a cupboard gives you control over a given building]. In a month long game you could easily dominate the server simply by taking down the bases of any other large clans, removing the threat and leaving the rest of the area free for you to exploit.'

In wider society, Hobbes argued that what the people would set up is a 'social contract' – an agreement between people or between a people and a monarch, where the people created a government to rule over them.

Plato, yet again
Plato's book *The Crito* featured one of the first mentions of a social contract. Here Socrates refuses to flee Athens, despite being

condemned to death for 'corrupting the youth'. In a moving scene, Socrates imagined the laws of Athens were talking to him:

> 'After having brought you into the world, and nurtured and educated you, and given you and every other citizen a share in every good that we had to give, we further proclaim and give the right to every Athenian, that if he does not like us when he has come of age and has seen the ways of the city, and made our acquaintance, he may go where he pleases and take his goods with him; and none of us laws will forbid him or inter-fere with him. Any of you who does not like us and the city, and who wants to go to a colony or to any other city, may go where he likes, and take his goods with him.
>
> 'But he who has experience of the manner in which we order justice and administer the State, and still remains, has entered into an implied contract that he will do as we command him. And he who disobeys us is, as we maintain, thrice wrong: first, because in disobeying us he is disobeying his parents; secondly, because we are the authors of his education; thirdly, because he has made an agreement with us that he will duly obey our commands; and he neither obeys them nor convinces us that our commands are wrong; and we do not rudely impose them, but give him the alternative of obeying or convincing us; that is what we offer, and he does neither.'*

So, Plato is arguing, because Socrates couldn't convince the state to change its laws but didn't leave, he implicitly accepted those laws. Now he's been condemned to death, the only moral thing to do is to carry through that acceptance.

However, Hobbes' version isn't coming from an existing society, like Socrates' Athens – he's assuming that, like *Rust*, we're in a state of nature, 'red in tooth and claw'. He wants his government – which he calls Leviathan, after a mythical monster – to protect the people and remove their fear. He argues that the people, in the state of nature, make a mutual agreement with one another, to transfer all

---

* *The Crito*, Plato (fifth century BC).

their power to a sovereign, who makes the law, and enforces this social contract with a monopoly of violence. It's an irrevocable deal.

In *Rust*, it would be like all the people on a server agreeing to give just one man all their weapons – or, perhaps, more reasonably, buying a game key and signing a licence agreement as part of the installation process that agreed to abide by the developer's terms and conditions in return for access to the game, and an understanding that the developer can alter or restrict their level of access at any time. The social contract in a video game is an actual contract: the End User Licence Agreement.

Justified revolution: John Locke and *Fable III*

The English philosopher John Locke (1632–1704) was a near contemporary of Hobbes, but disagreed with his characterisation of the social contract. He felt that the state of nature was more of an ideal state, like a co-operative farming game, such as *Harvest Moon* (Amccus, 1996) or *Stardew Valley* (ConcernedApe, 2016). Here people were naturally free and equal, and used their reason to understand what their purpose was in life. In this model, people chose to enter a political society via a social contract to avoid those occasions when the ideal state would degenerate into power struggles and theft – and hence to maintain their natural rights.

However, Locke argued that to give a ruler absolute authority would be an act of self-destruction on the part of the population:

> 'As if when men, quitting the state of Nature, entered into society, they agreed that all of them but one should be under the restraint of laws; but that he should still retain all the liberty of the state of Nature, increased with power, and made licentious by impunity. This is to think that men are so foolish that they take care to avoid what mischiefs may be done them by polecats or foxes, but are content, nay, think it safety, to be devoured by lions.'*

* *Second Treatise of Civil Government*, Chapter VII, sec. 93.

It's arguable that this difference of opinion on the fundamental nature of humanity, between Hobbe's solitary and bestial man and Locke's sociable and pacifistic man, persists today in the liberal and conservative political movements in many countries. (There are other ideologies, of course, such as socialism, Marxism and neoliberalism, which have displaced liberalism to a degree.)

So the liberal Locke felt that if that government went against their goods and rights, then the people have the right to tear up the rulebook – a justified revolution that would involve civil war and violence.

In *Fable III* (Lionhead Studios, 2010), we can see an example of a justified revolution. The player is the younger sibling of Logan, King of Albion. Mark Llabres Hill wrote *Fable III*, and explained that Fable's royal family had very shaky grounds for rule:

'The implication is that the Hero of *Fable II* (Lionhead Studios, 2008) went on to become King or Queen and a new monarchic line was set in motion, leading to the characters in *Fable III*. This suggests the legitimacy is indeed based on the heroic bloodline, which is a rather troubling way of coming to power. In *Fable* (Big Blue Box Studios, 2004), the bloodline was simply a way of explaining why certain people in Albion had superpowers. It didn't necessarily mean Heroes were all descended from the same line, but that there were genes that certain people had that gave them power. Essentially, they were a version of X-Men's mutants. This mutant parallel is even clearer in *Fable II*, set in a time when Heroes have been virtually wiped out for not being "normal". But by linking the bloodline with a monarchy, *Fable III* turns the concept into something uncomfortably crypto-fascist – an accusation levelled at many superhero comic books. As long as the player behaves morally, it remains "crypto", so to speak. It's even more troubling if the player chooses to be evil.'

The benevolent despot, revealed

As Hill says, this lack of legitimacy wouldn't matter so much if Logan was a heroic king, working for his people. Sadly, when the game starts, Logan is apparently a tyrannical king, choosing to push

Albion's industrial development at the cost of great popular suffering and discontent. Locke would say that he'd broken that social contract, to look after his people, and must be overthrown. When the player does assemble an army to overthrow him, however, you swiftly discover that he was always working in the people's interest, even if it was cruelly – a horde of demons is approaching and he needed a huge sum of military spending to defeat them. As the new monarch, you have to secretly fend off the horde and hence face the same impossible decisions as him, while maintaining a semblance of caring about your people. Says Hill:

> 'All these points are filtered through a different lens when you're making choices as a king or queen, because players are forced to make extreme decisions under the most difficult of circumstances and it's much harder to buy one's way out of the consequences. But perhaps equating the amount of money you have in your coffers with the number of lives you can save from an attack by shadowy demons didn't offer the most subtle expression of the difficulties of leadership.'

Hill is clear that *Fable III*'s political quandaries were more outgrowths of the moral quandaries players had faced in earlier games.

> 'The *Fable* games undermined these ethical foundations by allowing you to cheat your way back into people's good graces. Do enough silly dances in front of a character or shower him with gifts, and he'll eventually forgive you for murdering his family. Then again, the rich and the powerful often perform a more insidious version of this in real life, staying out of prison, remaining popular or even becoming presidents by virtue of their wealth and power.
>
> 'Even so, [*Fable III*] does offer a window into how politicians are forced to compromise their ideals in order to take power, keep power and then try to enact at least some of the policies they believe in. In the current climate, partisanship has reached such extremes that there doesn't seem to be any room for compromise. Each side has retreated to the fringes in a

desperate attempt to appeal to voters. Distressingly, it seems to be working, for the right-wing parties at least. Authoritarians are coming into power everywhere, appealing to the fear large parts of the population feel towards anyone different from themselves, at home or abroad. Much like your character in *Fable III* becomes an all-powerful monarch to protect Albion from the threat of an invasion from demons from a foreign land.'

ROUSSEAU, PAINE AND *A TALE IN THE DESERT*

The 1750 book *The Social Contract* by the Genevan *philosophe* Jean-Jacques Rousseau (1712–78) continued to develop Locke's concept. Rousseau's concept of the state of nature was much more solitary and less aggressive than Hobbes, with people living in small family units, with the natural freedom of operating entirely under your own will. He argued that in a larger society we lose that freedom, as unequal property and power quickly arises, and we become obsessed with reputation and possessions.

The way we regain freedom is through his social contract – where we become citizens, better versions of ourselves, with an equal say in the creation of making and administering the laws. By obeying laws we've made ourselves, we're obeying ourselves – a conception something like Socrates' concept in *The Crito*. This 'general will' through the rule of law maintains equality, but also is intended to protect minorities – because this isn't just a commitment to sticking to the law, but also a commitment to the good of all.

'As long as several men assembled together consider themselves as a single body, they have only one will which is directed towards their common preservation and general wellbeing. Then, all the animating forces of the state are vigorous and simple, and its principles are clear and luminous; it has no incompatible or conflicting interests; the common good makes itself so manifestly evident that only common sense is needed to discern it.'*

* Rousseau, *Of the Social Contract*, Book IV, Chapter 1, paragraphs 1 and 2.

Meanwhile, Rousseau's friend, the Scottish philosopher David Hume (1711–1776), very gently pointed out that the idea of a social contract involving the consent of the ruled, while an utterly delightful concept, had never actually existed anywhere. As he said:

> 'My intention here is not to exclude the consent of the people from being one just foundation of government where it has place. It is surely the best and most sacred of any. I only contend that it has very seldom had place in any degree and never almost in its full extent. And that therefore some other foundation of government must also be admitted.'*

Hume also argued that the concept makes no sense anyway. To have a social contract to start a society, you're putting the cart before the horse – after all, to make the contract you need to be able to make a promise, but that's already a social notion. Convention is deeper than contract; ordinary notions of life have to precede political society and promising is social currency. Hobbes said we need a leviathan to enforce, but Hume thinks we're capable of making these institutions ourselves. Indeed, as we discussed in the previous chapter, Hume felt generally that a utilitarian solution was most likely to produce peace and prosperity.

Despite those criticisms, Rousseau's idea of the general will influenced the French Revolution. Gradually, a consensus emerged that rule of the people was the optimum, legitimate form of government. And Hobbes', Locke's and Rousseau's ideas about the justifications for government – and the need for defences against the depredations of despots–influenced other philosophers like the Baron de Montesquieu, Alexis de Tocqueville and Thomas Paine, who in turn influenced the writing of the American Constitution, which enshrined those rights and duties.

The separation of powers
The core concept of this was the separation of powers – that certain institutions should constrain and balance each other. It's an idea,

* David Hume, *Of The Original Contract* (1758).

again, from ancient Athens, mentioned by Aristotle in his *Politics*, but revived by John Locke and refined by Charles-Louis de Secondat, Baron de La Brède et de Montesquieu (1689–1755) – commonly just called 'Montesquieu'. He was the first advocate of the classic three-part system of government eventually enshrined by the writers of the US constitution. This was the concept there were three institutions of government – the executive, the parliament and the judiciary – that had to be kept independent in order to prevent the state being captured by particular factions.

Of course, these aren't the only institutions that might be useful – merely the formalised ones. Twentieth-century political scientists experimented with ideas for others, though were mostly unable to try them out – but they were able to experiment a little with Japan's and Germany's post-war constitutions.

Only one commercial game has made serious efforts to experiment with political institutions like this. *A Tale in the Desert* (Pluribus Games, 2003) is a massively multiplayer online role-playing game set in Egypt, which has somehow continued to operate despite being very old and quite ugly. Unlike many MMOs, it ends roughly every eighteen months and restarts with a mostly clean slate. It's an economy and society simulator, with a player's main activities focused on personal and group challenges called 'Tests'.

A Tale in the Desert is notable for its use of social institutions to encourage players to improve the game. In the game, players can write, introduce and pass laws, and make new feature requests to the developers through in-game petitions.

The fifty-six tests often involve tests of trust or cooperation with other players. For example, the Marriage test has players giving each other reciprocal access to each other's accounts and in-game goods – meaning players should choose their spouse carefully, or risk losing access to everything they've built up in the game. Another test, that of the Demi-Pharoah, has the player seek to be elected to a position of power amongst their peers, enabling the player to ban seven other players from the game permanently. Another test involves the formation of a bureaucracy. Yet another, that of Festivals, requires one hundred players to act in unison within one hour.

Should a player complete all seven tests in a given discipline, they can organise the building of a monument to that discipline – and if they can find 127 disciples to celebrate it, they can change the challenges for the next run of the game. Essentially, this makes the game a huge exercise in collaboration – much like the modern democratic project. And (much like the modern democratic project) the split between Hobbes' view of people as fundamentally bestial and Locke's view of them as fundamentally cooperative are core disagreements that any institutions or governmental organisations – the communitarianism of ATITD or the constrained executives of modern democracies – struggle to deal with.

DEMOCRACY AND *DEMOCRACY*

Democracy, in this modern sense, is simply the current end point of the social contract – extending that contract to as much of the population as we can currently stomach and constraining our ruling government with the best institutions we can muster.

Yet, depending on who you listen to, modern democracy is either in crisis, or healthier than it's been for generations. At the time of writing (in late 2016), in that bastion of democracy, both of the last two Presidents of the United States have been vilified for their ethical positions: one has been damned for being a socialist and an élitist; the other for being sexist, racist and boorish.

The game series *Democracy* is a great model of the political systems in a generic Western country. Its creator Cliff Harris is clear that he's tried to avoid bias. He was just trying to create a game that he thought people were missing, rather than communicate a message:

> 'I had to try very hard in that game to have nothing in it that overtly gives away a kind of bias. So, you know, you win achievements for, like, eradicating poverty, but then you also win achievements for having, like, really negative things. When you get an achievement unlocked, such as Banana Republic for example, it's important that it's not saying to the player, "Excellent." It's just saying, "A particular set of

circumstances that is perhaps slightly unusual has arisen. How do you feel about it?"

'Ultimately there was, you know, a gap in the market for a game that says, "Politics is interesting, huh?", and that's it, without, kind of, saying, "And aren't poor people evil?" or, you know, "We should shoot the rich", or whatever. *Democracy* has no opinion, theoretically.'

The game of Democracy

Playing Harris' *Democracy 3*, you can see why democracy is such a constrained system to work under. The game is built from something like a neural network, which tracks the effect of every system change on any other. As you change funding for certain policies, or cancel or introduce other ones, you can see feedback patterns growing or shrinking other aspects of society. Every tweak you make unbalances the system, upsetting some group of voters. The act of running a society with a balanced budget generally inherently upsets some people in favour of others. In an autocracy, that doesn't matter so much, as long as you've a sufficiently strong military to prevent revolution – but in a democracy, unpopular behaviour can have you kicked out of office in short order, so you need to keep a rough majority of the population happy. Says Harris:

'There are endless complaints about *Democracy 3* and its assassinations, but whenever you look at what people are doing when they moan about assassinations it's just . . . nuts! You think, you know, "You try that, man. That is literally Obama, like, walking in and on day one saying, 'Right, send out the gun retrieval teams,' you know? It's like, "Yes, there would be chaos in the same way that if we just shut down all of our NHS hospitals and started charging at the door, that would lead to a lot of grief." So it's not that the population in *Democracy 3* is completely passive, and of course there are strikes in there too, but I think the game works best if you play it as a serious observer of politics thinking, "How do I navigate this?", rather than as a gamer thinking, "How can I break stuff?", because obviously you can break stuff really quickly, and real

politicians can break stuff incredibly quickly, but there's generally enough advisers around them to tell them, "Don't do this
stupid shit." '

The game also emphasises how necessarily short-sighted modern
democracies have to be. Whereas an autocracy or oligarchy like
China can make long-term goals that it has a fair idea its current
leaders will be in place to see, a democratically elected government
has two challenges. First, that it only has a short term, that it might
not get re-elected and that its policies may be rescinded by the next
administration. Second, that if the policies aren't rescinded, the next
government might receive the credit for them.

> 'The actual process of elections are a pain in the arse when
> you are actually in power, because you don't get to choose
> when they come, and you can definitely never put them off. So
> they always come in the middle of that situation where you've
> had to break something before you can fix it. When you're
> putting everything back together there's this fear that, you
> know, you'll get booted out and then the next guy takes all the
> credit. Any problem that can't be fixed in one term is at the
> bottom of the list because you might not get the credit for it.'

The dual incentives for an elected government – to get re-elected and
to run the country in the best interests of all the people in the long
term – rarely work together. Harris says, 'You get the results that you
incentivise, in politics and in economics. It's the designer of the
system to blame, often, more than the player, I think.' That's true of
games and of politics.

And the incentives in Democracy – both game and political
system – are to win. Which it's easier to do without strong philosophies. 'People who don't "get" the game complain that it's too easy,
because they say "I can do this and then I'll win, and I know it, and
so I'm bored now," which is completely missing the point. The game
never says that the point is to get re-elected, you know. It's just like,
"Here's politics. This is how we're representing it. Here's a user
interface. Bosh." People naturally want to win, and I think the

trouble with gamers is that normally the point of a game is to win, and there are no repercussions.' That makes Harris think that his next game needs to bring the consequences of your actions home more clearly.

Indeed, it seems that we're returning to Machiavelli again. Given the complexity of the political landscape, the politicians best equipped to deal with it have to specialise in managing all these competing strands – and ideology is baggage, as Harris recognises when talking about UK politics.

> 'We settled down into having people like Blair and Cameron, who are very much managers, not really with a crusade. You know, they make the speeches, but you can tell in their actions that it is like they are playing a game, like they're muddling through and don't want to upset anyone too much. Thatcher was quite happy to crush unions and really upset the left in order to achieve what she wanted to achieve, and we don't get that now. We get focus-group politics.'

The elective tyranny

And this is just the business of running a government, let alone getting elected. Harris doesn't even attempt to model that in *Democracy*, though he's published a second game series called *Political Animals* (Squeaky Wheel, 2016) that deals with a more realistic electoral process. That sort of game throws up even more problems with democracy, given how it shows that many people in most representative democracies have no say whatsoever in the electoral process; especially in somewhere as gerrymandered as the United States.

'How do you win an election?' asks Harris. 'Well, that depends massively on the process, and most people are unaware of the fact that the process in their country is different to everyone else's.' Harris is right that electoral systems – how the ballots are aggregated – have a huge effect on outcomes. Duverger's law of electoral systems states that plurality-rule elections (such as first past the post, in operation in the United Kingdom) structured within single-member districts tend to favour a two-party system, and that the double ballot majority system (France) and proportional representation (Israel) tend to favour multipartism. We can see that clearly with the Trump–Clinton election, where the otherwise-functionless electoral college system took the victory from Clinton who had won the popular vote.

In the UK, with its first-past-the-post system, more than half the constituencies are considered 'safe' – that is, they have nearly always voted for one political party. In those constituencies, it seems senseless to turn out to vote. In most others, voting for anyone other than one of the two leading candidates is wasting your vote. And, ultimately, voting for a smaller party candidate anywhere in the country is pointless, as they will never be involved in government so never get to have any effect on the law-making process, given the death of the House of Commons as a place of productive debate. Says Harris:

> 'People will fight furiously for their right to vote, and if you just go up to someone and say, "Yeah, we're not letting you vote this time" they go ballistic, but when you point out to them, "You can vote all you like. You're in a safe Labour seat or Tory seat. It's fucking irrelevant, mate" they're not really aware of that ... Those people live in a dictatorship, and we never even talk about that, and I think, "How?"'

Little wonder that so many games present such a cynical view of politics. As *BioShock 2*'s (2K Marin, 2010) writer Jordan Thomas says:

> 'What the *BioShock* series seems to say is that philosophies, when they come under the pressure of being implemented, fail; that every state is a philosophy that's being implemented. It might not be a coherent one, and lots of the time it's more of a pragmatic one, just doing what works, doing what the majority of the population will not rise up and revolt about. There's obviously all the constraints of political institutions, and electoral systems and political systems and all this stuff which provide extra framework.

'An ideal philosophy trying to get implemented in that context faces a lot of challenges, as socialism has faced in every country in the world, and as pragmatism in America or conservatism in the UK hasn't faced, because those aren't, strictly speaking, philosophies. They're more kind of "behave in a way that seems good to you at the time".'

As Thomas points out, 'If you need the involvement of a voting body of any kind, you end up having to compromise whatever high-level ideal you're selling to answer that question of, "What's in it for me?" It has to be a good mix of both. Which is why most conversations about philosophy only really show their teeth in thought experiments, where you can remove all other influences, which is sort of their tragedy, and also their interest. They're really, really great for the brain, in the abstract, but apply them to concrete scenarios, you go wait a minute. Who's this guy? What's his situation? Does he have time to think this way, this kind of stuff?'

DEMOCRACY IN CRISIS

Constance Steinkuehler was President Obama's advisor on video games; her official job title was Senior Policy Analyst – Games. As part of the Science and Technology Policy team, she spent twenty minutes with him every single day, briefing him on the issues that arose in her sector. She also was an advocacy voice, inside government, arguing that video games aren't inherently evil.

She feels she's changed that perception.

'Among Congress, and the Vice President's office and the President's office, there was a lot of ambivalence around games. I think there still is to some extent but I think that a good couple years of service has really changed their tune to where games are a medium for expression and a medium that can be an intervention.'

Given her affiliation, it's unsurprising that she saw the election of Donald Trump as an unparalleled disaster. The week after his electoral victory, we asked her if she thought democracy was in crisis.

> 'Oh, God. Is this really the time to ask me? Yes, I think it's in crisis. I think that liberal democracy is in crisis. I will also say that . . . You know the old adage in politics, "Never let a crisis go to waste"? I haven't lost my optimism. I feel like it's a major setback, or maybe it's a wake-up call of some sort, I'm not sure. I do feel that there's a certain spoiled complacency that happens when you have eight years of a president who has a sane agenda. You forget that it could be different.'

You'd think that she might have anti-democratic impulses, given that reaction. When asked if she thought that any other form of government could ever be as legitimate as a democracy, she says, 'I am not a political philosopher and I'm not a politician, so I can only answer that as a citizen. I would say that I doubt anyone else's capacity to rule me in my best interest better than I can rule myself, but in order to do that I have to be free from pressure and constraint. Then I have to actually have access to facts and information.'

That latter comment is crucial, and it parallels what Harris said at the start of this discussion: 'I believe in democracy with an engaged, educated and informed electorate – but, of course, that's where it all goes tits up.' In a democracy, the population need access to accurate data to make their decisions. Yet recent election campaigns in the West have been much like the 1930s, where populist anti-establishment politicians rose to power on incoherent promises that were against business-as-usual and capitalised on a general distrust of any authority and the data presented by any authority. 'I don't think over the long haul of history things are going down rather than up in terms of freedom for individuals and individual civil and human rights,' says Steinkuehler, 'but I do think that we've become complacent, especially in the face of how complex certain problems and issues are. A lot of the hardest problems right now that are the most in crisis, like the environment, aren't problems that you can solve one nation at a time.'

Yet turning individual desires into global action is . . . hard. 'You have this problem, like the linkage between an individual casting a vote in their best interest, from that small moment, all the way up to trying to solve a global problem like environmental climate change. Those links and connexions are really opaque, so people lose any sense of the import of what they do. I don't think the fact that we've eroded community and society on a very local level has helped at all.'

Despite that, Steinkuehler is optimistic about the electorate's motives.

'I feel like what looks like apathy, a good half of it gets explained by the nature of people feeling incredibly overwhelmed by the demands on their time. All of us are doing anything we can to get through a day and pay bills. We're at maximum capacity. Democracy requires a certain amount of time to read long-form journalism, to read the newspaper every day. Who does that?

'It's not that we're ignorant, it's not that we mistake Twitter for the *New York Times*. With Twitter we can at least read it on the thirty-second walk to the car. If you wanted to be the king, if you wanted to take a democracy and turn it into nothing but a despotism, the first thing you'd do is distract everyone and fragment their time this way. Everyone's too busy just living.'

Harris' simulation – and democracy generally – is predicated on people recognising changes to the political situation accurately. But what if some people don't trust publicly available government data, or scientific reports, or the news? What if their social media bubbles and fake news mean they never see that data? What if the short-termist nature of the political system is consistently making their situation worse off? What if they just feel hard done by the political system and want to express their Lockean right to revolt, albeit through the electoral system, but the electoral system stymies that? Can democracy work under such a situation?

Constance still has hope. That democracy will recover and that people will get involved once again. And curiously, she draws it from play.

'I will say this, and I got this from games and I got this from working in politics, but all it takes is maybe once for you to have the experience of working with a group of people to change something. It only takes that experience once for you to realise how powerful a group of people can be.

'I got that experience from running a huge guild in a Korean PvP game. The experience that you could have an idea and you can mobilise people and you can actually change how things work. I think that that experience, once you have it, makes it impossible to be cynical about your capacity or your obligation to participate.'

Again, the co-operation presented by certain games can be a force for good.

POSSIBLE FUTURES AND *EVE ONLINE*

But games don't just reflect reality – they let us model what possible futures we might live through, if certain variables have shifted. *A Tale in the Desert* lets us see what humanity might be like with more varied public institutions. The *Deus Ex* series (Ion Storm, 2000–03; Eidos Montréal, 2011–) has let us see what the world might look like if cybernetics generate a new privileged/weakened social class (in this case, the cybernetically augmented).

A good prediction of what a future political system might look like can be gleaned by looking at *Eve Online* (CCP Games, 2003). *Eve* is a massively multiplayer online game with a few unusual twists. It's set in a science-fiction universe, with an extremely hands-off government and large player-run corporations. It's a post-scarcity universe, where players can just survive without doing anything. This means they set their own goals, whether that's exploring wormholes, gathering the resources and blueprints to build better ships, or seizing a large part of the galaxy and running it as their private fiefdom.

Second, it operates on a single server for almost the entire world.*
This means everyone from Moscow to Des Moines to Johannesburg
is playing together, making for a strange melting pot of cultures. The
game encourages players to join the player-run corporations from
the start and the corporations actively recruit, meaning players soon
find themselves embroiled in whatever the corporation is doing.
Most of the time, corporations are trying to build up their arsenals,
defend their territory and acquire new territory. Mostly, that means
war. When it draws in more than one of the alliances of mega-corpor-
ations, it means player-driven war and destruction never seen in any
other game.

Unlike many games, however, *Eve* is really not wonderful as a
'social science Petri dish'. It's too complex; we simply can't track the
variables that easily from the outside. Much of its complexity comes
from the continuity of its existence. Like *A Tale in the Desert*, during
its fourteen years *Eve* has accrued institutions; unlike *A Tale in the
Desert*, many of its institutions have risen organically, without the
developer's intention, though often with its complicity.

That's because *Eve*'s political system is probably best described as
a weak constitutional monarchy. Theoretically, the ultimate power in
the game resides with the developer, CCP. They literally have the
capability to change anything in the world. Over time they've substantially expanded the range of actions in the universe, so players can
now build titanic carrier spaceships or space stations to secure star
systems for themselves. They've also established something like a
central bank, run by a team of economists, to regulate the market
and ensure that the supply of goods is kept up.

However, the community has been so vocal and active about its
rights in the game and its opinions on game changes that CCP has
increasingly let them take the lead. Indeed, to get a clearer, more

---

* Uniquely, China has its own server, run by a local Chinese publisher,
which isolates it from the rest of the world. This is a normal part of game
distribution in China, given the government's close regulation of all foreign
media and the commercial difficulties non-native companies face; for
example, it was only in late 2015 that it finally allowed foreign game consoles
into the country.

coherent idea of how the player base actually feels, CCP established an in-game representative democracy, the Council of Stellar Management. As the white paper establishing it says:

> 'The purpose of the CSM is to represent society interests to CCP. This requires active engagement with the player community to master EVE issue awareness, understanding, and evaluation in the context of the greatest good for the greater player base.'*

The council is comprised of game players voted for by their peers. Every account that's more than sixty days old has a vote. However, like any representative democracy, players have found incentives to bind themselves together for mutual advantage. For example, alliances and corporations tend to vote *en bloc* for their particular candidates. This has made them less representative of the general player base's feelings and more captured by particular special interest groups.

Diary of a space tyrant

And, like a traditional democratic party system, the group or party leaders aren't necessarily the actual representatives. The most famous of those group leaders is Alexander Gianturco, known more usually by his in-game character's name, The Mittani. He headed up the Goonswarm Federation, arguably the game's longest-lasting, most dominant faction (though he's no longer involved in the CSM himself). Before becoming a full-time space tyrant, he was a corporate lawyer. He says:

> 'When I began playing *Eve* in late 2005, I considered myself a Libertarian in the American political system; an ideological capitalist with a copy of Nozick's *Anarchy, State, and Utopia*. *Eve* crushed any notions of the success of pure capitalism from me and from the rest of our directorate after we attempted to implement Free Trade Zones in our territories at the time.

* http://cdn1.eveonline.com/community/csm/CSM-WHITEPAPER.pdf

After this I became extremely skeptical of ideology and certainty of any kind; I had been an ideologue and *Eve* taught me to focus only upon what can be tested and verified. *Eve* similarly taught me to be skeptical of anarchist notions; while Chomsky and Herman's *Manufacturing Consent* is part of our diplomatic team's reading list, New Eden has demonstrated that humans actively seek out and desire hierarchical structures and authority.'

From his perspective, the democratic systems put in place by the developer, CCP, are just a sham. 'Outsiders overestimate the impact of the CSM as some kind of representative democracy "running" *Eve*, which makes sense as it was heavily promoted by CCP in this way. It is not, and that's from the perspective of someone who received more votes than anyone in the history of the CSM during his election cycles.' Gianturco argues that CCP and the CSM themselves have almost no power in this political set-up.

'The core misunderstanding of *Eve* is that it is, in fact, a radical democracy. Players "vote" by choosing to join player organizations. Unlike in the real world there is nothing preventing a person from uprooting themselves and moving to the other side of the world – no borders, no scarcity-gated resources such as food and shelter, and no coercive barriers (capital, checkpoints, geography) to impair this macro-scale sorting behavior.'

This is the opposite of Pope's *Papers Please*, but isn't an implausible future – already in the real world the rich are used to this level of inter-state freedom.

The despot's return

What's notable is the kind of states this has created: autocracies, like the benevolent despots of the seventeenth century, as Gianturco explains:

'This is what makes *Eve* scary to those with quaint notions about human behaviour. In an environment where anyone can choose to join and follow groups – to choose their government, as it were – the player base of *Eve Online* over-whelmingly eschews voting-based democracies or councils and opts to join explicit autocracies that feature strong redis-tributive social programs. In *Eve*, these social programs are "ship replacement programs", mentoring systems, commod-ity buy-back programs, and the like.'

These states are autocratic, socialist and nationalist – but not expli-citly totalitarian, like fascist states. States like this are rare today – both Singapore and China share some, but not all, of their characteristics.

Autocracies haven't been the only forms of corporation set up in Eve – just the most successful, given the populace's free ability to change corporation at any time. Gianturco continues:

'*Eve Online* is both the testbed and graveyard of a number of political philosophies. In the absence of an externally imposed rule of law, player behavior in *Eve Online* allows us to see how humanity behaves in a post-scarcity environment. Practicality rules over principle, because any political philosophy or theory which cannot aid the survival of a community is discarded, or the community adhering to a philosophy that lacks utility or predictive power is exterminated by competing groups.'

People obviously have duties in *Eve*'s corporations – to obey their superior's diktats. But do they have concomitant rights? 'Rights?' scoffs Gianturco. 'There are no rights in *Eve*. Rights exist locally in the real world only where there is a monopoly on coercive force through the government to enforce the rule of law and said rights; like with international law, beyond one society's borders rights are at best a polite suggestion. There's no discourse about "rights" in *Eve*, either. In more than a decade of playing this game, that's the first time anyone has asked a question about rights.'

Gianturco draws on his wide reading of political philosophy to explain what he thinks this means, for *Eve* and for the fluid future of politics. 'You could argue that these autocracies are not autocracies because the players have "voted" by choosing to join them, and the autocracies cannot prevent their members from leaving should they fail to live up to their social contracts with their members; this is the path which sees agonistic democrats like Chantal Mouffe attempting to rehabilitate Carl Schmitt.' Both of these political philosophers criticised liberal, deliberative democracy. Indeed, this system in *Eve* seems closer to the factional patronage systems of the ancient Roman Empire, but with an ease of movement that's unlike any other modern human institution – and hence its implications for a putative future with increased popular freedom of movement.

> 'Take *Escape from Freedom, Manufacturing Consent, Rules for Radicals* and *The Crisis of Parliamentary Democracy*, mash them together, that's *Eve* – how humans behave when they can choose to follow anyone they wish in an environment with no rule of law. But it's not actually *Eve* – it's people as they wish to be, and that should scare the hell out of everyone. *Eve* is the abyss. I invite your readers and any academics with sterile notions of how humanity behaves to take a spin in the sandbox, it will sear any naiveté from their theories – here's looking at you, game theorists and traditional economists.'

IT'S ABOUT POLITICS IN GAMES

This has been a rush through the backbone of political philosophy as found in games. But there's so much more out there to talk about. The *Saints Row* (Volition 2006–) games' satire of corporate capitalism. *Tropico*'s (PopTop Software, 2001) comedic portrayal of kleptocracy. The *Metal Gear* series' (Konami and Kojima Productions, 1987–2016) focus on nuclear imperialism. *Divinity: Dragon Commander*'s (Larian Studios, 2013) unexpectedly nuanced display of factional politics. *Call of Duty* (Infinity Ward, Treyarch and Sledgehammer Games, 2003–) and *Battlefield*'s (EA DICE and Visceral Games, 2002–) glorification of war and death. *BioShock Infinite*'s commentary on American exceptionalism. The stereotyping of minorities in almost every major game franchise. *Civilization*'s (MicroProse, Activision and Firaxis Games, 1991–2016) almost Marxist view of history as endlessly progressive.

Strangely, given this absolute wealth of material, a recent movement from a small but loud subset of the game-playing audience wants to exclude discussions of politics and morality from video games and the surrounding conversations. Its proponents feel that game developers keep inserting ethical or political themes into games that don't need them. From the games media they demand 'objective' journalism, which seems to mean journalism that doesn't raise moral issues with games. To some of these players, games are just sources of fun that shouldn't involve politics.

We hope we've shown you that political philosophy isn't optional: that almost no setting (save for the extremely anodyne or purely mathematical) lacks political themes or is morally neutral; that games are enriched by political and ethical quandaries; that political discussions arise from the simple interactions of people, whatever the setting, with all the prejudices each of us has grown up with; that what to one person is an objective, neutral viewpoint always involves inequalities or prejudices against one group or another. In short: there isn't an objective setting, and to call for one is to ignore the rights of minorities and the oppressed.

And, as the journalist Keza MacDonald has pointed out,

'People who complain about not wanting politics in their games are probably not genocidal racist maniacs, but they probably are boring . . . It's indicative of a fear of being challenged and of a desire to impose your own worldview. Without politics, *BioShock* is pretty much just an underwater shooter. *Papers Please* is just a paperwork simulator . . . political themes often greatly enrich a story and sometimes give it thought-provoking real-world context that gives it an intellectual life and vibrancy outside the confines of the game (or book, or painting) itself. I suspect, ultimately, that a lot of the feeling behind "keep politics out of games" is really "keep politics that I don't agree with out of games".'*

* http://www.kotaku.co.uk/2015/03/23/why-everyone-should-want-politics-in-their-video-games

From our perspective, games give us great reasons to understand why our institutions are the way that they are, and perspective on possible political structures and the legitimacy of those that do exist. *Rust* shows us how grim a society without laws is, and how prone to failure and exploitation. *Fable 3* and *Crusader Kings* show how difficult it is to run a state, at any scale, with any form of government. *Democracy 3* shows us that we still have fundamental issues representing people's views in government, given the array of local and global political constraints. And *Eve Online* gives us an alternately terrifying and thrilling vision into what the future of politics may look like.

Limbo, positively purgatorial.

....

Maria: Wow, I feel light as a feather after that mushroom.

Luisa: Maria, watch out, you're going to land on that– Oh.

Maria: Ach, did I land on someone?

Luisa: It's a turtle. He doesn't seem hurt.

Maria: Oh, good!

Luisa: But when you landed on him, he ricocheted off like a bullet and hit about ten more mushrooms.

Maria: Oh, god.

Luisa: They're all dead. This is basically a crime scene now.

Maria: But, wait, they're not people. They're mushrooms and turtles. We eat them. I ate one earlier!

Luisa: This all comes from my letting you play video games all night long.

Maria: Now, wait a minute. I didn't mean to hurt these mushrooms. If they're even capable of feeling pain. And I certainly didn't learn to hurt them from playing video games!

Luisa: I guess jumping on turtles to kill mushrooms is slightly unlikely, even for video games. But you wouldn't be so reckless and violent if you hadn't sat up all night playing that one about killing sweet people. What was it?

Maria: *Candy Crush.* And it's not about– Wait, have you even played a game?

Luisa: Well . . . no. But I've read about them in the *Mushroom Kingdom Inquirer.*

Maria: When we get home, I'll show you some. Some, I admit, do involve killing thousands of people in bloody, cruel ways. But then, some don't.

Luisa: It's a deal! Just don't get me addicted.

Maria: So, uh . . . what are we going to do with all these mushrooms?

Luisa: Risotto?

CHAPTER TEN

Death, killing and coping:
Spec Ops, To the Moon

....

'. . . if the character doesn't hold a gun, designers don't even know what to do.'

David Cage (designer of *Heavy Rain*)*

'You know, you come from nothing, you're going back to nothing. What have you lost? Nothing!'

Crucified Man, *The Life of Brian* (1979)†

At first, it seems like an uplifting moment. Sgt Paul Jackson and his squad are in Basra, Iraq. It's 2011. They're part of 1st Force Recon, an enormous US military force, tracking down Khaled Al-Asad, an ultranationalist who has taken over a large swathe of the Middle East. Jackson has already fought extensively in the campaign, at first infiltrating the country, then engaging in all-out war with the ultranationalist forces. And now he's about to decapitate the revolution by capturing or killing Al-Asad.

Today, this storyline from *Call of Duty 4: Modern Warfare* (Infinity Ward, 2007) seems awkwardly prescient about the ISIS conflict, which makes the next part chilling. 1st Force Recon determines that Al-Asad is in the capital city, so the entire army pivots and starts flying that way in their helicopters. Yet, while you're rescuing a crashed pilot, everything changes. A radio report from a Navy Seal advance party states that Al-Asad isn't in the city, but he's generously

---

* http:/www.theverge.com/2013/2/6/3960630/david-cage-video-game-industry-grow-up-already

† Jones, Terry, Graham Chapman, John Cleese, Terry Gilliam, Eric Idle and Michael Palin. Monty Python's *Life of Brian* (Paragon Entertainment, 1999).

left a nuclear bomb there. As your squad attempt to flee the city in their transport helicopter, they are caught in the blast wave from the nuke. The screen fades out.

When it fades back in, you're still playing as Jackson. He wakes near the cockpit of his crashed helicopter and must crawl agonisingly from the wreckage. As he does, he sees the bodies of his squadmates and the pilot you rescued, and hears the crackling of the radio, as US high command orders a retreat. Falling from the back of the plane, he hurts himself falling onto what sounds like a broken leg. But, where normally in the *Call of Duty* games (Infinity Ward, Treyarch and Sledgehammer Games, 2003–), a short period of rest heals all ills, here Jackson crawls a little further, sees the devastation that the blast has wreaked – including an immense mushroom cloud – and collapses. And dies. A map of the region flashes up, notifying you that he was killed in action.

Later in the series you find that thirty thousand American soldiers died in the explosion and it's the motivation for much that happens in the next *Modern Warfare* game (Infinity Ward, 2009). But for the player it's significant because few games – and very few mainstream ones – have your protagonist dying, in your hands, permanently, for no good reason. Everything you did in the first half of the game – everything – was to no purpose. Everyone in the US army is dead. The villain – who cares little for civilian life – is victorious, even if he'll soon die. The rest of *Modern Warfare 2* and the whole of *Modern Warfare 3* (Infinity Ward and Sledgehammer Games, 2011) have you tracking down those responsible for revenge. The whole thing is covered up. You lost.

MURDER-SIMULATORS R US

If there's one thing that games should be authoritative on, it's death. Games are murder-simulators *par excellence*. Death in games is often taken as an easy design choice – and killing is often a core mechanic. It's widely recognised that 'To kill' is the most common verb in games, and the unique language of games reflects that: gib, frag, iron sights, DoT, strafe, gank, no scope, spawn, camping . . . they're all about murder.

Often a game is designed to fit a genre or an audience, and most genres are violent at core. The first-person shooter, the third-person shooter, the action-adventure, the RPG, the strategy game, the platformer, MMOs . . . only adventure games as a genre don't have death as their core mechanic (presumably because they have access to every other verb under the sun).

But the vast majority of games deal with death, albeit without much seriousness. The *Call of Duty* series has been as guilty of that as any other shooting game series. Players have been mostly immortal, able to weather a storm of bullets that would kill an average man. They magically heal when in cover, and if they do die they come back to life moments later, while their enemies have no such luck. Even here in *Modern Warfare 2*, in what's arguably the series' darkest moment, the game doesn't end for the player – you get to take control of another person and take your revenge. It's a fundamentally unbalanced view of warfare – and an unrealistic one of death.

Cartoon deaths in realistic games

Despite that, *Call of Duty* is a relatively realistic game. Like in the movies, most video-game deaths are too often cartoon deaths. Often, to squeeze the game into the common morality of a PG rating, there's death but with no blood, no consequences.

And death is rarely presented faithfully in games. There's often a simple collapse animation before the player gets to restart – perhaps a fade to red, to represent blood presumably covering your eyes. But you rarely get to see the real-world consequences. And you almost always get to live again.*

Gunshots in games are usually an instant kill on a shot to the head or a multi-shot kill elsewhere – knife wounds are almost always instantly fatal. There's often no effect on the capabilities of the victim until the final blow. In most games, an injured person can run, shoot and perform perfectly until the actual moment of death.

---

* We say 'almost' because certain exceptional games have been planned to give you a single play experience, commensurate with a single life. They almost entirely have been non-commercial (like *You Only Live Once*, discussed later). Though commercial games are occasionally announced with the same set-up, we've not known one to be released.

Yet the common gun in real life is more often non-fatal than otherwise. America's Center for Disease Control and Prevention said that, across the USA, there were 73,505 non-fatal firearm injuries in 2013 compared with 11,208 homicides and 21,175 suicides. And that's presumably only the reported non-trivial injuries.*

And a death from a wound isn't as reliable as games would have you believe. In real life, the shock of a gunshot is often enough to disable a victim. And once shot, death is neither guaranteed nor quick. It can take weeks to die from a gunshot, given the complexities of an injury – brain trauma and blood loss is a fast way to die, but infection can be very slow and painful.

Death and the forbidden planet

RimWorld has a more realistic view of death than most shooting games. In this management roguelike simulation, you take control of a handful of survivors on a randomly generated hostile planet. Theoretically, the aim is to survive long enough to build a spaceship and get off-planet, but few players last that long – most of the time you're scrabbling to survive, as disasters run amok and resources run out.

Similarly, the *UFO: Enemy Unknown* games (originally Mythos Games and MicroProse Software, 1994) – known today as XCOM, following the Firaxis reboot – feature characters you can name, customise and watch grow, shortly before they die. And the *Fire Emblem* games (Intelligent Systems, 1990–2017) allow your characters to form relationships with their mortal squadmates. Here, death means something.

In *RimWorld* (Ludeon Studios, 2013), death can come slowly or quickly. Like in its inspiration *Dwarf Fortress* (Tarn Adams, 2006), injuries from this hostile world can range from bruises and grazes to gunshot wounds and gorings. People can hover between life and death for weeks. If infection sets in, it can gradually run out of control, become untreatable and lead to a slow painful death – unless you can find some medicine and someone medically skilled enough to amputate the appropriate part. Often, if your colony runs out of

* http://www.vox.com/2016/6/15/11934246/gun-violence-america-questions

medicine, the best thing you can do is to wait and see if someone recovers – and, if not, prepare to euthanise them with the crude tools at your disposal. It's a brutally realistic vision of frontier death.

DODGING DEATH

Fable II (Lionhead Studios, 2008) dealt with the problem by going the opposite way – by never letting the player die at all, but scarring them instead. Mark Llabres Hill wrote the game and remembers the decision.

> 'It was probably to do with reducing player frustration over losing progress and having to replay sections, by making the game as accessible as possible. *Fable* was never about punishing players, which is why a lot of casual players were drawn to it and so many hardcore players hated it. Part of the thinking was that for many players scarring would actually be the strongest possible motive to do well in combat, since they would have invested a lot in the appearance of their Hero. But combat was so easy, I'm not sure how many actually got those scars.'

Going further, in some casual games, death has literally no effect. *Spider-Man: Friend or Foe* (Activision, 2007) was an action-adventure beat-'em-up with insanely easy difficulty, on-the-spot respawning and infinite lives. Dying in this game had almost no consequences beyond the player's character disappearing and reappearing in the same spot. Indeed, it had almost no challenge – you could just leave the game running and your AI buddy would defeat the enemies for you. Why make something so meaningful so inconsequential?

Monkey Island (LucasArts, 1990) even satirised the death-addiction of its contemporary adventure games. Titles like *King's Quest* (Sierra Entertainment, 1980–2016) and *Space Quest* (Sierra Entertainment, 1986–95) would lazily kill the player for every single incorrect decision. *Quest for Glory* (Sierra Entertainment, 1989–98) even killed you if you tried to use a lockpick on yourself, by explaining that you'd inserted it into your nose and given yourself a cerebral haemorrhage.

Monkey Island instead kept the player alive, no matter how badly they'd failed. For example, the one time you can fall off a cliff, the game showed a 'game over' screen . . . before bouncing you back onto the cliff edge, as your character said, laconically, 'Rubber tree.' Another time, you're tied to an idol and thrown off a pier, only for your character to reveal he can hold his breath for ten minutes, giving you more than enough time to solve the very simple puzzle. (If you're determined enough to wait the full ten minutes, he will however finally die.)

Endless torment

Many traditional games, like the *Sonic* (Sega, 1991–) and *Mario* (Nintendo, 1981–) series, give you extra lives. *Planescape: Torment* (Black Isle Studios, 1999) went the other way – by making individual deaths seem insignificant, but then emphasising gradually, as the story went on, quite how significant they were. Your lead character, the Nameless One, is unique amongst the Planes in that he can't die – or rather, he doesn't stay dead. However, each time he dies and returns, his memory fades so that, like the protagonist of *Memento*, he begins each time as almost a new person.

By the time we encounter him – The Nameless One – in the game, the amnesia effect seems to have faded and he's finally capable of retaining his memories. Death thus becomes a mechanic he can play with – solving death-trap puzzles created by his previous incarnations, for example, by dying repeatedly, or letting himself be killed to spy on the conversations of his killers.

However, it turns out that the Nameless One's deaths weren't insignificant. Later he discovers that his first long-forgotten incarnation had been a powerful sorcerer who'd performed a deed so infamous that he'd been damned for eternity to the lowest pits of hell, if he should die. In his desperation to buy the time to redeem himself, he'd had his mortality stripped away – but this trick had unexpected results when he died and self-resurrected soon after. For every death he'd suffered thereafter, another person somewhere else had died and been raised as a murderous, undead shadow, which pursued him hungrily. And those friends who'd travelled with him had been the most likely to die. Without hope of redemption or avoiding his fate, *Torment* becomes a game about dying in the right way.

Though *Torment* did involve combat, it also broke the chain between violence and in-game rewards. Advancing as a character is almost entirely done through self-revelation and conversation. Most items in the game are useless for combat – there are almost no weapons that look like weapons. And the combat almost feels deliberately bad (though it's always dangerous to interpret design failures as intentional).

Roguelikes and a more final death

But even these games don't feature real death. We have extra lives or respawns, or we restart the level. Indeed, normal death – permanent death – was so rare in video games that players coined a new word for it: **permadeath**, also known in many games as 'Iron Man' mode. For a long time, permadeath was restricted to the arena of the obscure genre known as 'roguelikes', named after the genre-originator, *Rogue*.

Rogue was originally developed around 1980 by Michael Toy and Glenn Wichman as a freely distributed game for Unix mainframe computers.* In roguelikes players create a character, then control it through a randomly generated dungeon, fending off an array of roaming monsters. It's a *Dungeons & Dragons* (Gary Gygax and Dave Arneson, 1974) perspective on the gaming world. It took thirty years for this genre to become a part of commercial games, with *Spelunky* (Mossmouth, 2008) kicking off the roguelike's entry into mainstream gaming, followed by *The Binding of Isaac* (Edmund McMillen, 2011), *FTL: Faster Than Light* (Subset Games, 2012) and *Rogue: Legacy* (Cellar Door Games, 2013).

Even so, modern roguelike games tend to give the player some inherited capabilities between lives. Achieving certain things in a game tends to unlock new abilities or in-game items for later runs, or even shortcuts to harder levels. So, in *Spelunky*, progressing deeply enough unlocks shortcuts – even after the character who

---

* Given its ancient origins, *Rogue* used 'ASCII' art to display its world and creatures, where keyboard characters are used to represent everything – so an 'ape' might be represented by the character '@' and a snake by an '$'. For players unfamiliar with this style of art it appears that your computer has crashed very badly.

unlocked them dies and you start anew – and completing certain achievements unlocks new characters to play as. In *Rogue: Legacy*, players can unlock new character classes and inherit characteristics from their predecessors. In *FTL*, new starship layouts can be unlocked. Killing and death are still your tools of progression.

Death in shooting games is something simple – but games like *RimWorld* remind us that death is a complex thing. Is someone dead when their vital processes start to fail or when they fail completely? Do we consider someone with total brain stem death to be alive (the courts do)? Would we consider a mindless body to be alive, if some science-fiction world like *The Swapper* (Facepalm Games, 2013) had allowed it to be transferred away (see Chapter 5)? What about a human being in a persistent vegetative state or a coma, such as Zoë Castillo in *Dreamfall: The Longest Journey* (Funcom, 2006)?

Do we consider someone whose vital signs have stopped to be alive, even if we can resurrect them? The protagonist in *Fallout 4* (Bethesda, 2015) has been in suspended animation – with no signs of life – for two centuries when they're awakened, and could have stayed like that without ever being resurrected. Yet her Vault III compatriots all had their cryonic units destroyed or powered down – so when would we have said they died? When they were first frozen, and their bodily functions stopped? Or when the hope of resurrection disappeared?

THE RISING TIDE OF FADING VIOLENCE

All this discussion of killing is terrifyingly misplaced and unrepresentative. Almost all deaths in video games are violent. Yet in the real world, violence is no longer the pre-eminent cause of death. In the second half of the twentieth century, as Yuval Noah Harari pointed out in his book *Homo Deus*, deaths from violence faded away:

'In most areas, war became rarer than ever. Whereas in ancient agricultural societies, human violence caused about 15 per cent of all deaths, during the twentieth century violence caused only 5 per cent of deaths, and in the early twenty-first century it is responsible for about 1 per cent of global mortality. In 2012 about 56 million people died throughout the world; 620,000 of them died due to human violence (war killed 120,000 people, and crime killed another 500,000). In contrast, 800,000 committed suicide and 1.5 million died of diabetes. Sugar is now more dangerous than gunpowder.'

Harari goes on to show that in 2010, obesity killed three million people. The WHO statistics also show that in 2001 malnutrition killed 3,800,000 people, smoking tobacco killed 5,400,000 people and hypertension killed 7,800,000 people. While terrorism, which dominates the news networks and hardcore video games . . .? A total of 7697 people in 2012. That's less than the eight thousand people who die from smoking in Wisconsin. Texting while driving is much more likely to kill you than terrorism.

That relative decline in real world violence as a cause of death is intriguing given that video games are often *blamed* for all sorts of violence. Walt Williams, the writer of the military shooter *Spec Ops: The Line* (Yager Development, 2012)*, expressed disquiet over the use of violence and death in his 2013 GDC† talk.

'When you're using an action as a tool, it's easy to disassociate from what that action is. When you play a shooter, that action is killing a person. When you sit down to play a shooter, you're essentially signing up to kill hundreds if not thousands of people over the course of the game.‡

'We're an industry full of very intelligent, often aggressive people, and we know that the blanket use of violence is wrong. It's getting harder and harder for us to play these games and to look at them critically and say, "This is okay. This makes sense." Especially as we get older, especially as we play more of them.'

I will admit personally,' Williams concluded, 'I would like to see less violent games out there, not because I think that they're bad or

* See Chapter 7.
† Game Developers Conference.
‡ http://www.theverge.com/2013/3/28/4157502/death-is-dead-how-modern-video-game-designers-killed-danger

wrong, but because I think that creatively, they're too easy. I think we're better than that . . . Is there something else that we can do? Is there something else that we can make?'

These violent games are seen by some people as a highly corrupting influence, especially on impressionable young minds. Hillary Clinton, as a New York senator in 2005, said, 'We need to treat violent video games the way we treat tobacco, alcohol, and pornography.'* She continued that this was 'backed up by 40 years of research telling us that violent media is bad for children'. Similarly, Donald Trump tweeted in 2012: 'Video game violence & glorification must be stopped—it is creating monsters!'† Both have since shifted their positions, but they're not unusual beliefs.

Virtual violence begetting real world violence seems intuitive. But it's worth noting that while that seems to be common sense, psychology is not about verifying or debunking common sense; common sense is not useful in science, psychology or philosophy because many of the things it tells us are simplifications or plain wrong, such as the sun going around a flat, immobile earth.

Surely if games were creating violence we should see that effect in the world? As Oddworld Inhabitants founder Lorne Lanning said to us, 'We have the statistical data. As violence in games rose, violent crime amongst youths dropped. You can't have both. If it's a toxic food, and people are getting healthier, how can it be a toxic food?' Well, some people have argued that even if games aren't increasing general violence, they might be creating individual incidents – such as the massacres at Sandy Hook, Columbine and Utøya, which were all carried out by 'gamers'.

Schwarzenegger's victims
In 2005, the state of California, backed by its then-governor and one-time action-movie star Arnold Schwarzenegger, passed a bill that was planned to restrict minors' access to video games. It claimed

* http://www.forbes.com/sites/insertcoin/2016/02/05/can-we-forgive-hillary-clinton-for-her-past-war-on-video-games/#58f1ff7998d6
† http://www.dailydot.com/layer8/donald-trump-hillary-clinton-video-games-violence/

that video games increase aggression, cause neurological damage and more. The state's lawyers pointed to a huge corpus of peer-reviewed scientific evidence backing up this claim. Given the mainstream rhetoric about violent video games, the pile of evidence and the conservatism of the court, that seemed reasonable.

Here's an excerpt from the Supreme Court of America's 2011 judgement:

'The State's evidence is not compelling. California relies primarily on the research of Dr Craig Anderson and a few other research psychologists whose studies purport to show a connection between exposure to violent video games and harmful effects on children. These studies have been rejected by every court to consider them, and with good reason: They do not prove that violent video games cause minors to act aggressively (which would at least be a beginning).

'Instead, nearly all of the research is based on correlation, not evidence of causation, and most of the studies suffer from significant, admitted flaws in methodology. They show at best some correlation between exposure to violent entertainment and minuscule real-world effects, such as children's feeling more aggressive or making louder noises in the few minutes after playing a violent game than after playing a nonviolent game.'

The judges went on in a similar vein for many pages, repeatedly damning the psychological evidence presented, before rejecting the bill 7:2 – an unusually strong majority. They cited the Brothers Grimm, *Looney Tunes* and *The Divine Comedy* as other equally violent media, all of which have freedom of speech protection under the First Amendment. 'Like the protected books, plays, and movies that preceded them, video games communicate ideas – and even social messages – through many familiar literary devices (such as characters, dialogue, plot, and music) and through features distinctive to the medium (such as the player's interaction with the virtual world). That suffices to confer First Amendment protection.'

Lorne Lanning thinks the judges were right:

'The statistics are there, violence is going down. It is glorifying that way of living, but so did *The Godfather* and *Goodfellas* and some of our favourite novelists. *Looney Tunes* was incredibly violent. *Grand Theft Auto* is not the content that I would make, but I'm going to buy it and play it and know it's going to be absurdly good fun. If you're not causing harm and you're employing lots of people, and people enjoy your product, more power to you, really. And if I wouldn't do the content, that's kind of irrelevant.'

Presumed guilt and the mob psychologists

Chris Ferguson, Psychology & Communication Professor at The University of Texas, explained to us how the American psychological community could have got this so wrong.

'Prior to the Columbine massacre, video-game research was pretty calm, and most scholars acknowledged the research was inconsistent. Then after Columbine a group of scholars started to make more and more extreme statements. Eventually that invited a lot of scrutiny about those claims, and ultimately, harsh criticisms.

'I think some of those scholars stepped so far out onto the plank that it's just difficult to retreat to more moderate language without losing face. A few have taken funding from anti-media advocacy groups too, but I think the main issue has to do mainly with personal egos, and a rigid ideology that has grown up about media violence generally over the past few decades and then was rigidly applied to video games in the 2000s post-Columbine.'

Indeed, the moral panic seemed similar to those in America around comic books, *Dungeons & Dragons* and video nasties in the 1950s, 1970s and 1980s. 'I use the example of comic books in the 1950s, where psychiatrists and congress together made extreme claims about the "harm" of such media,' says Ferguson. 'Ironically, you're seeing much the same pattern now. It's not so much that the hypothesis is bad, or that you couldn't even make an honest argument for negative effects. It's that so often the arguments are dishonest, simply ignoring evidence against the speaker's personal views.'

To prove that games cause violence, after all, you must show more than exposure to violent media correlates with aggression. You have to show that exposure correlates with violence, and that there's a causative link. It's a hard link to prove. So far the science, as evaluated by the courts and independent observers, has shown that there is at most a mild short-term correlation between gaming and aggression, with Dr Ferguson arguing that even this small correlation is down to statistical anomalies.

In 2010, the impartial Australian government carried out a meta-review that found that there was evidence that video games have short-term effects on aggression, though that evidence has been very badly presented, with many methodological flaws. This effect size is comparable, as Dr Anderson begrudgingly admitted in another court case, to other violent media – such as when children watch a *Bugs Bunny* cartoon or play *Sonic the Hedgehog*. The sole qualitative difference between games and music, books and films is (as we've discussed in Chapter 6) its fundamental interactivity. Is that any worse than my imagining a grisly death in a Stephen King book or seeing someone get dissected in a torture-porn film like *Saw*? The statistics don't seem to show that.

And even if violent video games do increase aggression, it has yet to be shown that this happens in more than the short term, in a way that's of a significant degree and that isn't caused by other underlying factors. Indeed, Ferguson's 2012 research paper found that 'depression, antisocial personality traits, exposure to family violence and peer influences were the best predictors of aggression-related outcomes'; violent video games didn't get a look-in. And a longer-term paper of his from 2014 showed that there had once been a correlation between US media violence and homicide rates – but that it had stopped in the 1950s.

Indeed, Constance Steinkuehler, President Obama's advisor on video games, reports that this is accepted at the highest levels of government – or at least it was in her relatively enlightened times.

'When Sandy Hook and other things happened, violence in video games, I was the person that dealt with those issues and had to stand on principle and research. Gave them research to squelch it and say "Look, you can go after this because it's political but don't go after this thinking that it's reality. There's no data to support this claim. If you want to do that, that's great, but it's a political move and you're on the wrong side of history." The truth will out. It may take a while, but the truth will out.'

SENSE AND DESENSIBILITY

Of course, just because there isn't a correlation with video games and violence doesn't mean we haven't been affected by it. In line with the studies we quoted, *Spec Ops'* Williams didn't think that video-game violence spreads to the real world – but he did think it had other effects. 'I don't believe that violent games make violent people, and I don't believe that violent games desensitize us to violence. I do, however, believe that violent games desensitize us to violence in games . . .'* Williams' intuitions were backed up by an April 2016 study that shows that a player's moral response to unjustified in-game acts of violence decreases as experience with the game increases.† 'The more enemies you kill, the more it feels like it's padded out,' says Williams. 'For an industry that in the past couple years has been striving to create more emotional connectedness between the game and the user, it's interesting how we've allowed killing to stay so mundane.'

Oddworld's Lanning agrees.

'The one that I'm not sure about is desensitisation. It's not something the government wants to stop. It makes people more willing to support wars, go to wars, police the wars. It's part of our programming. *Full Metal Jacket,* to the extreme. What I do think is harmful is when we get into modern war gaming, which is

* http://www.theverge.com/2013/3/28/4157502/death-is-dead-how-modern-video-game-designers-killed-danger
† https://www.sciencedaily.com/releases/2016/04/160408163742.htm

taking contemporary conflicts and glorifying those under false pretenses, not showing the tragedies of war, turning it into an entertainment sport. I think it's very offensive to people who are risking their lives out there [in war zones]. It's harmful because it's perpetuating ongoing lies that are harming people on the planet. I don't think it's making people into killers – though it is making people a better shot – and the evidence shows that it isn't causing them to go out and shoot more people.'

Lanning's contacts in the military are similarly dismayed, especially at the command levels. They want their troops to engage with the local culture, not sit around playing on their Xbox. 'If I had a problem with violence in video games, it's because it's supporting and popularising a larger problem and popularising it in this heroic way. Just talk to the guys coming back – it's not heroic. That's why the suicide rate is so high. And we're not talking about that. But we're popularising it. And that's very distasteful.'

In fact Lanning sees it all as a distraction, perhaps deliberate, from real-world atrocities.

'Remember the line about *Mortal Kombat* [Midway Games, 1992]? We thought the world was going to end because you were pulling out spines. But it was great fun! The problem was the news every night telling us we were murdering people in foreign climes for reasons that were totally unjustifiable. So when video games and violence were attacked, we could only stand up and say, "Oh, the irony. Really?" '

This apparent trivialisation of death and killing is disappointing because death is so important in life. Things that are alive are normally ascribed huge importance – things that we deem conscious even more so. Whether we say death is the end of the organic dying process (see Chapter 5), the cessation of consciousness (see Chapter 4), the end of rational thought, the last moment of hope or the start of the decline – the emotional strength of the event of a death is huge, whether it's a person or an animal. That moment is more powerful, morally and narratively, than almost anything else.

Thankfully, not all games just revel in the violence as *Doom* (id Software, 1993), *Wolfenstein* 3D (id Software, 1992) and their entire bloody creed do – some games have dealt with it in ways that are smart, both emotionally and philosophically.

THE HARM THESIS

Whatever we eventually agree constitutes death, games take as given the mainstream concept that dying is harmful to the individual concerned. That's what's known as the **harm thesis**. The assumption is here that more life is always good – that no one would choose to die when there's more living to be done – and hence death is harmful to that individual, and that they are justified in fearing it. It seems obvious, but philosophy is all about investigating the obvious to check we're right.

If we accept this thesis, then we consider self-sacrificing people or people without a fear of death to be insane or otherworldly. For example, Wynne in *Dragon Age: Origins* (BioWare, 2009) has already died once by the time you meet her, and is living on time borrowed from a benevolent spirit, but is perfectly happy with dying again – because she has few regrets about her life. 'I will not lie motionless in a bed with coverlets up to my chin, waiting for death to claim me,' she says. Similarly, the undertaker Membrillo in *Grim Fandango* has a certain fatalism: 'The moral of every story is the same: We may have years, we may have hours, but sooner or later, we push up flowers.'* And Grave Warden Agdayne in *Dark Souls II* (FromSoftware, 2014) says, 'Death is equitable. Accepting. Eventually, we all shall enter her embrace.'

A more complex and less-accepted idea is the posthumous harm thesis – that events after our death can harm us. This isn't because we can become zombies or vampires, but because things that matter to us can happen after we're dead. Unlike the previous harm thesis, this one doesn't seem intuitively true when we stop to think about it – but people still behave as if it is. For example, life insurance policies, where we act to keep our nearest and dearest well cared for

---

* *Grim Fandango*, LucasArts (LucasArts, 1998)

after we're gone – even though their wealth or poverty at that point can have no effect on our mouldering corpses.

Harm, disarmed

The ancient Greek philosopher Epicurus (see Chapter 8) rejected both these concepts.

> 'Accustom yourself to believing that death is nothing to us, for good and evil imply the capacity for sensation, and death is the privation of all sentience; therefore, a correct understanding that death is nothing to us makes the mortality of life enjoyable, not by adding to life a limitless time, but by taking away the yearning after immortality. For life has no terrors for him who has thoroughly understood that there are no terrors for him in ceasing to live.'

For him, Wynne's stance is perfectly rational – why worry about something that can't hurt you, and that you can't stop?

> 'Foolish, therefore, is the man who says that he fears death, not because it will pain when it comes, but because it pains in the prospect. Whatever causes no annoyance when it is present causes only a groundless pain in the expectation. Death, therefore, the most awful of evils, is nothing to us, seeing that, when we are, death is not come, and when death is come, we are not. It is nothing, then, either to the living or to the dead, for with the living it is not and the dead exist no longer.'

That is to say, when we're dead, nothing can affect us – and when we're alive, death hasn't affected us yet. To be harmed by death, on this reading, there must be a subject, a harm and a time. But they do not coincide. When we die, we cease to exist. Forever after, we are beyond harm. Obviously, if you believe in any of the major real world or in-game religions, you may have other views – but they are too varied to be discussed coherently here.

Socrates seems to agree with Epicurus, and in Plato's *Apology* he goes even further, by saying death is to be desired – though he was already condemned to death when he said this, so there could be a certain amount of rationalisation going on.

> 'Either death is a state of nothingness and utter unconsciousness, or, as men say, there is a change and migration of the soul from this world to another. Now if you suppose that there is no consciousness, but a sleep like the sleep of him who is undisturbed even by the sight of dreams, death will be an unspeakable gain.
>
> 'For if a person were to select the night in which his sleep was undisturbed even by dreams, and were to compare with this the other days and nights of his life, and then were to tell us how many days and nights he had passed in the course of his life better and more pleasantly than this one, I think that any man, I will not say a private man, but even the Great King*, will not find many such days or nights, when compared with the others. Now if death is like this, I say that to die is gain; for eternity is then only a single night.'

Later utilitarians† could answer Epicurus and Socrates simply – by stating that if we sum the utility of a life, to judge its happiness, surely more life has a greater chance of potential happiness. This, of course, assumes that on average life is more happy than not, so it's worth living more. Statistically, this is probably true – for example, a 2014 study showed that 77 per cent of people in the developed world claimed to be happy.‡ Dying early means we miss out on some utility, so death is harmful in that sense, to the greater project of utilitarianism.

But of course, we miss out on all sorts of things in our lives – I've not been genetically modified to fly or win the lottery or be born a genius. And every choice I make has me missing out on another possible route to greater happiness. Has the absence of these events that never happened 'harmed' me? This argument makes it sound

* A reference to the King of Persia, Artaxerxes II, at the time.
† See Chapter 8.
‡ ttps://www.theguardian.com/politics/2014/jul/16/most-people-developed-world-happy-ipsos-mori-poll

like the general maximisation of happiness is taking precedence over the actual feelings of the individuals.

There's also a question of timing. When exactly am I being hurt by my death? Not before my death. Not after my death. And during the process of dying, the dying is hurting me and the anticipation of my future loss, but the loss itself cannot hurt. Can my life as a whole really be 'worse' without any part of it being worse? If not, how can it be said to have harmed me, outside of time?

And, thinking particularly of those posthumous events, how could they harm me while I'm living? Causation doesn't travel backwards in time. We do have interests in things that occur in the future – but those interests are indeterminate in our lifetime, so how could we be harmed by them?

Furthermore, Epicurus's formulation – that death doesn't matter, because nothing after it can affect us – seems to be ignoring the moment of death. As we discussed earlier, it's not necessarily a moment, given how long it can be drawn out. Think of the Drell Assassin Thane Krios in the *Mass Effect* series (BioWare, 2007–12), who admits to having a fatal disease when you first meet him, but takes six months in the process of dying ... before succumbing to a very different fate. And, despite what Epicurus says, anticipation of our fate can also hurt us now, when we think of its effect on others dear to us.

DEATH AND OTHERS

After all, the dead person isn't the only victim of a death. Really, it doesn't matter so much if your death doesn't harm you – because it harms everyone around you. Every person shot is a mother's child. In *RimWorld*, like in real life, friends, family and co-workers all suffer when someone dies – they regularly grieve at their loved one's grave and will suffer sadness for weeks afterwards, to the degree of falling into psychotic breaks or dazed funks.*

---

* Of course, sometimes someone's death has a positive effect on other people – for example, when Albert Einstein travels back in time to kill Hitler in *Command & Conquer: Red Alert*. But that's less philosophically interesting.

To the Moon (Freebird Games, 2011) is a beautiful pixel game about coping, or failing to cope, with death. The plot is a strangely plausible blend of *Memento*, *Inception* and *Eternal Sunshine of the Spotless Mind*. Two scientists arrive at the bedside of a dying man, looking to use their memory-altering technology to give him one last happy memory before he passes away, to fulfil his one long-held desire. But his profound sense of loss relating to his dead wife and brother prevents that, meaning they have to dive deeper and deeper into his memories to find out why. Without spoiling too much, many years before a single incident had pushed his life onto a sad path. By rebuilding his memories from that point, the scientists are able to give him a happy death. But he has been profoundly harmed by the deaths in his life.

Similarly, *Brothers – A Tale of Two Sons* (Starbreeze Studios, 2013) is a two-character adventure game, tracking two young sons attempting to cope with the death of their mother and save their father, who's dying from a mysterious illness. The game starts with the youngest boy mourning one family member, and ends with him mourning another; throughout the tale, death is a constant theme, from a suicidal villager to a mortally wounded griffin and an entire valley of dead giants. The two boys, in particular, gamble their lives at every turn in their attempt to find a cure for their father's disease.

For us, the sun sets only once

The free Flash game *You Only Live Once* (Raitendo, 2009) was an affectionate parody of the tendency of video games to trivialise victims. You play a man rescuing his kidnapped girlfriend from a monster, Sir Giant Pink Lizard. It's a short, simple platformer, where you must defeat the lizard after making your way through his minion-infested castle.

You're more likely to make a mistake, though, as the game is tough. As soon as you take one hit or fall down one pit, the game ends and you're shown a cutscene with the real-world consequences of your actions. Your 'girlfriend' sees you die and calls an ambulance. The ambulance crew bemoan the pointlessness of your death. A TV news channel runs a story on it, accompanied by a warning from the police not to take the law into your own hands.

Either Sir Giant Pink Lizard or a minion is arrested by the police, either for murder or for health and safety violations. And it finishes on a candlelit memorial made by your friends at the spot where you died.

In the unlikely event you defeated the lizard, a policeman turns up and arrests you for murder. If you click continue, you're treated to two ambulance workers standing by the lizard's corpse. Click again, you have to attend the lizard's funeral, hear his eulogies, see his minions crying at his graveside and watch grass and flowers grow on the grave.

Whoever died, you can't replay the game – any attempt to do so just shows you your grave. And we, as people interested in ideas, can see that this is a pleasant conceit. However, the game creator received much abuse from players annoyed that, yes, they only lived once and that they couldn't replay the game. 'This game sucks,' said 'Vaeth' in a comment on the game's page. 'What game has multiple cutscenes for your death depending on how you die and doesn't let you play it ever again? Games are supposed to be enjoyed multiple times, not just once. That is why I give it a 1 star other than the fact that I can't give a 0 out of 5.' This person could do with a lesson in philosophy.

THE FUTURE OF DEATH

Some people, of course, don't care so much about philosophy. They don't accept the necessity of death and want to squeeze every last moment out of life, even if they spend those years of life on avoiding death. At the time of writing, the news has been filled with the antics of particular billionaires, who are understandably driving their resources to eliminating death – or at least staving it off for a while longer. The tech investor Peter Thiel revealed his interest in using the blood of the young to prolong his life; Oracle founder Larry Ellison has put $430 million towards fighting ageing; and Google has its Project Calico, which has committed hundreds of millions to the aim of 'curing death'.

Google's Chief Futurist, the author Ray Kurzweil, has long sought to extend his life, primarily through reduced calorific intake and taking more than a hundred (expensive) pills a day. 'I think people are kidding themselves when they say they are comfortable with death,' he's said. He has also said that he thinks by the year 2045 we'll be functionally immortal.

Yet even he thinks death is valuable.

> 'A great deal of our effort goes into avoiding [death]. We make extraordinary efforts to delay it, and often consider its intrusion a tragic event. Yet we'd find it hard to live without it. Death gives meaning to our lives. It gives importance and value to time. Time would become meaningless if there were too much of it.'*

Indeed, the German philosopher Martin Heidegger felt that the dread of death was necessary to grasp your freedom and the possibilities in your life – and hence to make authentic existence possible.

So is immortality to be desired or not? The English philosopher Bernard Williams argued that it was bad to live forever, even under the best of circumstances. Following Heidegger, he argued that boredom would set in, as your life-driving desires – for example, watching your children grow up or writing a book, say – are achieved or fade. 'It is not necessarily the prospect of pleasant times that create the motive against dying, but the existence of categorical desire, and categorical desire can drive through both the existence and the prospect of unpleasant times.' To keep wanting to stay alive, he thought you would have to replace your fundamental desires repeatedly, which he regards as abandonment of your identity – tantamount to death.†

The riches of immortal loss
Lost Odyssey (Mistwalker and Feelplus, 2007) provides an answer to Williams. This Japanese role-playing game is about immortals, and how they cope with the world. Like Williams, these immortals aren't

---

* *The Age of Spiritual Machines: When Computers Exceed Human Intelligence.*
† http://stoa.org.uk/topics/death/the-makropulos-case-reflections-on-the-tedium-of-immortality-bernard-williams.pdf

particularly spiritual beings and they don't believe in an afterlife. As their leader Kaim Argonar says, 'When people die, they just go away. If there's any place a soul would go, it's in your memories. People you remember are with you forever.'*

Over the course of a millennium, each of these immortals has lived many lives, with their memories fading over time. Still, each of them takes value in the lives they've led – particularly given that their children and partners are never immortal, so each one of them has seen their loved ones grow old and die. Who the immortals have been has changed repeatedly. Though over the course of the game they gradually regain their memories, they don't see their transformation as a loss. Whatever the questions of their continuity of identity (see Chapter 5), it's obvious that to all of us, transformation is not death – and preferable to it, to many people.

And they've seen many deaths too. One of the saddest scenes in the game has the immortals encouraging Kaim and Sarah's long-lost daughter, now their age and dying of an illness. She leaves behind her two mortal children, who Kaim and Sarah adopt and conduct through a long and moving funeral ritual – knowing full well that one day they will be mourning these children too.

In the unparalleled short story collection integrated into the game, 'A Thousand Years of Dreams' (Kiyoshi Shigematsu, 2006), the immortals see death again and again. Each of the stories deals with loss, from an immortal perspective. On one occasion Kaim sits by the deathbed of a young girl with a wasting disease, who was unable to travel, but to whom he has told tales of his journeys throughout her short life:

'He has been present at innumerable deaths, and his experience has taught him. Death takes away the power of speech first of all. Then ability to see. What remains alive to the very end, is the power to hear. Even though the person has lost consciousness, it is by no means unusual for the voices of the family to bring both smiles or tears.'

* *Lost Odyssey*, Mistwalker/Feelplus (Microsoft Game Studios, 2007)

Throughout Kaim's short stories, he presents a variety of methods of coping with death. What he never does is to treat each individual death as anything other than a tragedy – and for each death, he is ready, because from the viewpoint of eternity he knows that every person he meets will pre-decease him.

Like *Lost Odyssey*'s immortals, preparing for the death of others seems rational. Yet, unlike those immortals, we must also prepare for our own deaths – by abandoning those desires and projects that death might thwart, and by abandoning that dream of immortality. We must be cautious in this, because it can harm us too – by letting death limit our desires unduly. A simple aim then, might be to just take on goals we can achieve and eschew those projects that we can't complete within our lifetime. This is a message unlikely to be accepted by our immortality-hungry billionaires.

Our divided industry

To kill a single person is a monstrous thing. To witness a death is one of the hardest things to do. Yet many of the most popular games treat this killing and dying as the most trivial thing in the world. We find it desperately sad that this is the normal position of games. The broadening of the gaming market to the more casual experiences playable on a mobile phone, while infantilising in many ways, has at least moved gamers away from these unrealistic, hyper-violent games.

Despite their problems, games are also educative. They can show us how to grieve, what the value of life is, how to prepare for our death and that of our friends, and when killing is a mercy. Titles like *Brothers*, *To the Moon* and *Lost Odyssey* present death as a necessary concomitant of life. They show it cannot hurt us – but also show us how important it remains to treat each individual death as important, in the same way we treat each individual life as important – and to remember those left behind. That's an important message.

Final thoughts

....

Perhaps, in retrospect, we should have been less ambitious. After all, philosophy is about everything and games are about everything. Our remit, as it turned out, was to write about everything – squared. At least we can't complain about a lack of material.

Square as it is, we hope you've learned something from this brief foray into philosophy. Games have guided us through everything from 'I think therefore I am', through discussions of the good person and the good state, right up to questions about VR, transhumanism and AI. We've played with simulation theories in procedurally generated space, and seen dualist concepts on fire off the shoulder of Andrew Ryan. Even politics, red in tooth and claw, has had its inner workings eviscerated through the lights of *Eve Online* and *Democracy*.

Two studios particularly impressed us while working on the book. A hat-tip, first, to the creators of the *BioShock* series. The compromises of the medium and the commercial side of gaming may have made these mass-murder simulators – but the thought and craft put into their world-building and philosophy by Ken Levine, Jordan Thomas and others allowed them to explore nearly every core topic of philosophy without stepping away from being entertainment. It's sad that Irrational Games is no longer with us – but we're looking forward to what Thomas and Levine do with their future projects.

In terms of a successor studio to Irrational, we have high hopes for Frictional Games. No other game has so thoroughly explored a philosophical topic as *Soma*. Thomas Grip's team produced a masterpiece on what it means to be human, to be alive and to be a relevant moral actor – and which segued perfectly with the setting, game mechanics and story to produce a feeling of existential dread that we've not experienced anything like (except perhaps after reading Albert Camus' *L'Etranger* while eating bad seafood).

For our part, we've enjoyed our time on the book, but there are some topics we simply couldn't cram in. Our chapter on logic and video-game logic sadly fell by the wayside, crippled by the weakness of philosophical logic, which doesn't seem to have advanced very far from Aristotle and Frege. Our chapter on aesthetics – which would have finally, definitively answered the question 'are video games art?' – was too beautiful to survive. Our chapter on political philosophy swelled to such proportions that it could have easily been a book in itself. And, inevitably, we've neglected such things as the rich conceptual structures of Eastern philosophy, stuck as we are in our own points of view: Western and white. We hope that we've demonstrated how video games and philosophy can fit together, and have every confidence that more writers will explore this relationship as both academia and art develop. All said, there are a lot more than ten things games have to teach us.

APPENDIX I

Bibliography

....

—, 'Doom', *Edge Magazine* (April 1994)
—, 'You Can Discover More About a Person in an Hour of Play than in a Year of Conversation', *Quote Investigator* (30 July 2015), http://quoteinvestigator.com/2015/07/30/hour-play/
—, 'CSM White Paper' (CCP, 2008). Retrieved from http://cdn1.eveonline.com/community/csm/CSM-WHITEPAPER.pdf
—, 'Electoral Statistics for UK: 2015' (Office for National Statistics, 24 Feb 2016). Retrieved from https://www.ons.gov.uk/peoplepopulationand-community/elections/electoralregistration/bulletins/electoralstatistics-foruk/2015
—, 'Guardians of the Threshold', *Correctional Compass* (Florida Department of Corrections, 6 May 2003). Retrieved from http://web.archive.org/web/20061006124151/http://www.dc.state.fl.us/pub/compass/0305/2.html
—, 'Voting Turnout Statistics' (Statistics Brain, 2016). Retrieved from http://www.statisticbrain.com/voting-statistics/
—, *King James Bible* (1611)
—, 'Free Will', *In Our Time* (BBC Radio 4, 10 March 2011)
Abrahams, Marc, 'Experiments show we quickly adjust to seeing everything upside-down', the *Guardian* (12 November 2012), https://www.theguardian.com/education/2012/nov/12/improbable-research-seeing-upside-down
Addams, Shay, *The Official Book of Ultima* (Compute Publications, 1992)
Aristotle and Irwin, Terence, *Nichomachean Ethics* (Hackett Publishing, 1985)
Arouet, François-Marie AKA 'Voltaire', *Candide, ou l'Optimisme* (1759)
Badham, John, dir., *War Games*, screenplay by Lawrence Lasker and Walter F. Parkes, prod. Leonhard Goldberg, Rich Hashimoto, Harold K. Schneider, Bruce McNall (United Artists, Sherwood Productions, 1983)
Baggini, Julian, *Freedom Regained: The Possibility of Free Will* (Granta Books, 2015)
Baudelaire, Charles, 'Enivrez-Vous' (*Le Figaro* No. 937, 7 February 1864)
Bechara, Antoine, 'The role of emotion in decision-making: Evidence from neurological patients with orbitofrontal damage', *Brain and Cognition*, pp. 30–40 (Elsevier, June 2004)

Bentham, Jeremy and Bowring, John, *The Works of Jeremy Bentham, vol. 10 (Memoirs Part I and Correspondence)* (1843)

Bentham, Jeremy, 'Théorie des peines et des récompenses' collected in *The Rationale of Reward* (J. and H. L. Hunt, 1825)

Bentham, Jeremy, *A Fragment on Government* (1776)

Bentham, Jeremy, *An Introduction to the Principles of Morals and Legislation* (1789)

Block, Ned, 'Troubles with functionalism', *Minnesota Studies in the Philosophy of Science*, 9, pp. 261–325 (1978)

Bostrom, Nick, 'Are You Living in a Computer Simulation?', *Philosophical Quarterly*, 53:211, pp. 243–55 (2003)

Bradbury, Ray, *The Illustrated Man* (Doubleday & Company, 1951)

Brown, James Robert and Fehige, Yiftach, 'Thought Experiments', *Stanford Encyclopedia of Philosophy* (12 August 2014), https://plato.stanford.edu/entries/thought-experiment/

Campbell, Joseph, *The Hero with a Thousand Faces* (Pantheon Press, 1949)

Carroll, Lewis, *Alice's Adventures in Wonderland* (Macmillan, 1865)

Chalmers, David J., 'The Matrix as Metaphysics', *Philosophers Explore the Matrix*, p. 132 (2005).

Confucius, *Analects* (fifth to second centuries BC).

Conrad, Joseph, *Heart of Darkness* (*Blackwoods Magazine*, 1899)

Dawkins, Richard, 'What is your dangerous idea?', *Edge, 2006* (John Brockman, 2006)

Dennett, Daniel C. and Searle, John R., '"The Mystery of Consciousness": An Exchange', *The New York Review* (21 December 1995), http://www.nybooks.com/articles/1995/12/21/the-mystery-of-consciousness-an-exchange/

Descartes, René, *Meditations on First Philosophy*, 1641, translated by John Cottingham (Cambridge University Press, 1996)

Dow, Tony, dir., 'Heroes and Villains', *Only Fools and Horses*, written by John Sullivan, prod. Gareth Gwenlan (BBC, 1996)

Epicurus, translated by Robert Drew Hicks, *Stoic and Epicurean* (Longman, 1910)

Fiedler, Glenn, 'Floating Point Determinism' (Gaffer on Games, 8 April 2017). Retrieved from http://gafferongames.com/networking-for-game-programmers/floating-point-determinism/

Foot, Philippa, 'The Problem of Abortion and the Doctrine of Double Effect', *Oxford Review*, 5, pp. 5–15 (1967)

Freud, Sigmund, *Beyond the Pleasure Principle* (1920)

Gambini, Bert, 'Violent video games eventually lose their ability to produce guilt in gamers: Why is this happening?' (ScienceDaily, 8 April 2016). Retrieved from https://www.sciencedaily.com/releases/2016/04/160408163742.htm

Gay, John, 'Dissertation concerning the Fundamental Principle of Virtue or Morality' in King, William, *An Essay on the Origin of Evil* (1731)

Gettier, Edmund, 'Is Justified True Belief Knowledge?', *Analysis*, 23:6, pp 121–3 (1963)

Gibson, William, *Neuromancer* (Ace, 1984)

Goethe, Johann Wolfgang von, *The Sorrows of Young Werther* (1774)

Gray, Peter, 'Cognitive Benefits of Playing Video Games', *Psychology Today* (20 February 2015), https://www.psychologytoday.com/blog/freedom-learn/201502/cognitive-benefits-playing-video-games

Green, Melanie, 'Transportation Into Narrative Worlds: The Role of Prior Knowledge and Perceived Realism', *Discourse Processes*, 38:2, pp 247–66 (2004)

Gygax, Gary and Arneson, Dave, *Dungeons & Dragons* (1974)

Hall, Granville Stanley, *Adolescence: Its Psychology and Its Relations to Physiology, Anthropology, Sociology, Sex, Crime, Religion and Education* (D. Appleton, 1904)

Harari, Yuval N., *Homo Deus: A Brief History of Tomorrow* (Vintage, 2016)

Harwood, A. C., *C. S. Lewis at the Breakfast Table, and Other Reminiscences* (Macmillan, 1979)

Hawking, Stephen, *Black Holes and Baby Universes and Other Essays* (Bantam Dell Publishing Group, 1993)

Hayasaki, Erika, 'In a Perpetual Present', *Wired* (April 2016)

Hillcoat, John, dir., *The Road*, screenplay by Joe Penhall, prod. Nick Wechsler, Steve Schwartz and Paula Mae Schwartz (2929 Productions; Dimension Films, 2009)

Hobbes, Thomas, *Leviathan* (1651)

Hofstadter, Douglas, *Gödel, Escher, Bach: An Eternal Golden Braid* (Basic Books, 1979)

Hume, David, *An Enquiry Concerning the Principles of Morals* (1751)

Hume, David, *Essays and Treatises on Several Subjects* (1758)

Huxley, Aldous, *Brave New World* (Chatto & Windus, 1932)

Jackson, Frank, 'Epiphenomenal Qualia', *The Philosophical Quarterly*, 32:127, pp. 127–36 (1982)

Jackson, Steve and Livingstone, Ian, *The Warlock of Firetop Mountain* (Puffin Books, 1982)

Jacobs, David, *Dallas* (Warner Bros. Television, 1978)

Jones, Terry, dir., *Monty Python's Life of Brian*, written by Terry Jones, Graham Chapman, John Cleese, Terry Gilliam, Eric Idle and Michael Palin (HandMade Films, 1979)

Kant, Immanuel, *Critique of Pure Reason* (1781)

Kant, Immanuel, *Groundwork of the Metaphysic of Morals* (1785)

Kant, Immanuel, *Metaphysics of Morals* (1797)

Kurzweil, Ray, *The Age of Spiritual Machines: When Computers Exceed Human Intelligence* (Penguin Putnam, 2000)

Laplace, Pierre Simon, *A Philosophical Essay on Probabilities* (1814)

Lewis, David, 'Mad Pain and Martian Pain', *Philosophical Papers: Volume I* (Oxford University Press, 1983)

Lingard, Richard, *A Letter of Advice to a Young Gentleman Leaving the University Concerning His Behaviour and Conversation in the World* (Benjamin Tooke, 1670)

Locke, John, *Two Treatises of Government* (1689)

Lokhorst, Gert-Jan, 'Descartes and the Pineal Gland', *Stanford Encyclopedia of Philosophy* (18 September 2013), https://plato.stanford.edu/entries/pineal-gland/

Lumière, Auguste and Lumière, Louis, *L'arrivée d'un train en gare de La Ciotat* (Société Lumière, 1896)

Lynn, Jonathan, dir., *Clue*, screenplay by Jonathan Lynn and John Landis, prod. Debra Hill (PolyGram Filmed Entertainment; Paramount Pictures, 1985)

MacDonald, Keza, 'Why Everyone Should Want Politics in Their Video Games' (Kotaku, 23 Mar 2015). Retrieved from http://www.kotaku.co.uk/2015/03/23/why-everyone-should-want-politics-in-their-video-games

Machiavelli, Niccolò, *The Prince* (1513)

McCarthy, Cormac, *The Road* (Alfred A. Knopf, 2006)

Mill, John Stuart, *On Liberty* (1859)

Mill, John Stuart, *The Subjection of Women* (1869)

Mill, John Stuart, *Utilitarianism* (1863)

Mohler, Corey, Existential Comics (2013–).

Nolan, Christopher, dir., *Inception*, written by Christopher Nolan, prod. Emma Thomas and Christopher Nolan (Warner Bros. Pictures, 2010)

Norman, Andy, 'How to Play the Reason-Giving Game' (15 September 2007), https://www.academia.edu/4269933/How_to_Play_the_Reason-Giving_Game

Nozick, Robert, *Anarchy, State, and Utopia* (Basic Books, 1974)

O'Neill, Patrick Howell, 'Trump and Clinton are both wrong about video game violence' (The Daily Dot, May 26 2016). Retrieved from http://www.daily-dot.com/layer8/donald-trump-hillary-clinton-video-games-violence/

Parfit, Derek, *Reasons and Persons* (Oxford University Press, 1984)

Patil, Indrajeet et al, 'Affective basis of judgment-behavior discrepancy in virtual experiences of moral dilemmas', *Social Neuroscience*, 9:1, pp 94–107 (2014)

Pearce, David, 'Is Humanity Accelerating Towards ... Apocalypse? Or Utopia?' (2012). Retrieved from https://ieet.org/index.php/IEET2/more/pearce20120621

Plato translated by Jowett, Benjamin, *Crito* (1900)

Plato translated by Jowett, Benjamin, *The Apology* (1900)

Plato translated by Jowett, Benjamin, *The Dialogues of Plato* (1871)

Plato translated by Jowett, Benjamin, *The Republic* (1894)

Plunkett, Luke, 'Ronnie O'Sullivan Falls Over Playing VR Pool', Kotaku (13 October 2016), http://www.kotaku.co.uk/2016/10/13/ronnie-osullivan-%20falls-over-%20playing-vr-%20opool

Plutarch, *Life of Theseus* (first century AD)

Pronin, E., Wegner, D. M., McCarthy, K., and Rodriguez, S., 'Everyday magical powers: the role of apparent mental causation in the overestimation of personal influence', *Journal of Personality and Social Psychology*, 91:2, pp 218–31 (2006)

Putnam, Hilary, 'Mind, Language, and Reality', *Philosophical Papers: Volume 2* (Cambridge University Press, 1979)

Putnam, Hilary, 'What Wiki Doesn't Know About Me', Sardonic Comment (30 October 2014), http://putnamphil.blogspot.co.uk/2014/10/what-wiki-doesnt-know-about-me-in-1976.html

Rand, Ayn, *Atlas Shrugged* (Random House, 1957)

Rand, Ayn, *The Fountainhead* (1943)

Rawls, John, *A Theory of Justice* (Belknap Press, 1971)

Reid, Thomas, *Essays on the Intellectual Powers of Man* (Dublin: Printed for L. White, 1785)

Rice-Oxley, Mark, '77% in developed world are happy but wish life was simpler, says poll', the *Guardian* (16 July 2014). Retrieved from https://www.theguardian.com/politics/2014/jul/16/most-people-developed-world-happy-ipsos-mori-poll

Robertson, Adi, 'Death is dead: how modern video game designers killed danger' (The Verge, 23 March 2013). Retrieved from http://www.theverge.com/2013/3/28/4157502/death-is-dead-how-modern-video-game-designers-killed-danger

Roser, Max, 'Democracy' (OurWorldInData.org, 2016). Retrieved from https://ourworldindata.org/democracy/

Rosseau, Jean-Jacques, *The Social Contract* (1750)

Rowling, J. K., *Harry Potter* series (Bloomsbury Publishing)

Ryan, Kevin, 'The Butterfly Effect', (Gamasutra, 31 March 2015). Retrieved from http://www.gamasutra.com/blogs/KevinRyan/20150331/239636/The_Butterfly_Effect.php

Ryle, Gilbert, *The Concept of Mind* (University of Chicago Press, 2002)

Schulzke, Marcus, 'Simulating Philosophy: Interpreting Video Games as Executable Thought Experiments', *Philosophy & Technology*, 27, pp. 251–65 (2014)

Schwartz, Steven, *The Seven Deadly Sins* (Gramercy, 2000)

Searle, John R., 'Minds, brains, and programs', *Behavioral and Brain Sciences*, 3:3, pp. 417–57 (1980)

Shigematsu, Kiyoshi, and Rubin, Jay, *He Who Journeys Eternity: Lost Odyssey: A Thousand Years of Dreams* (2006)

Stratton, G. M., 'Vision without inversion of the retinal image', *Psychological Review*, 4:5, pp. 463–81 (1897)

Stuart, Keith, 'David Cage on grief, game design and Beyond: Two Souls', the *Guardian* (4 July 2012), https://www.theguardian.com/technology/gamesblog/2012/jul/04/david-cage-beyond-preview

Tassi, Paul, 'Can We Forgive Hillary Clinton For Her Past War On Video Games?', (*Forbes*, 5 February 2016). Retrieved from http://www.forbes.com/sites/insertcoin/2016/02/05/can-we-forgive-hillary-clinton-for-her-past-war-on-video-games/#58f1ff7998d6

Tolkien, J. R. R., *The Lord of the Rings* (George Allen & Unwin, 1954–5)

Turing, A. M., 'Computing Machinery and Intelligence', *Mind*, 49, pp. 433–60 (1950)

Verbinski, Gore, dir., *Pirates of the Caribbean: The Curse of the Black Pearl*, screenplay by Ted Elliott and Terry Rossio, prod. Jerry Bruckheimer (Walt Disney Pictures, Jerry Bruckheimer Films; Buena Vista Pictures Distribution, 2003)

Wachowski, Lana and Wachowski, Lilly, dir., *The Matrix*, written by the Wachowskis, prod. Joel Silver (Warner Bros., 1999)

Walsh, E., Long, C., and Haggard, P., 'Voluntary control of a phantom limb', *Neuropsychologia*, 75, pp. 341–8 (2015)

Washington, George, 'To the Bishops, Clergy, and Laity of the Protestant Episcopal church in the States of New York, New Jersey, Pennsylvania, Delaware, Maryland, Virginia, and North Carolina, in general Convention assembled' in *The Life of George Washington, Commander-in -chief of the American Armies, and First President of the United States* (Jared Sparks, 1839)

Webber, Jordan Erica, 'The Witness: how Jonathan Blow rejected game design rules to make a masterpiece', the *Guardian* (9 February 2016), https://www.theguardian.com/technology/2016/feb/09/the-witness-how-jonathan-blow-rejected-game-design-rules-to-make-a-masterpiece.

Weir, Peter, dir., *The Truman Show*, written by Andrew Niccol, prod. Scott Rudin, Andrew Niccol, Edward S. Feldman and Adam Schroeder (Scott Rudin Productions; Paramount Pictures, 1998)

Welsh, Oliver, 'Irrational's Ken Levine: To Infinite and beyond' (2010). Retrieved from http://www.eurogamer.net/articles/2010-08-12-irrationals-ken-levine-interview

Williams, Bernard, *Problems of the Self* (Cambridge University Press, 1973)

Bibliography (games)

2K Boston and 2K Australia, *BioShock* (2K Games, 2007)

2K Marin, *BioShock 2* (2K Games, 2010)

3909 LLC, *Papers, Please: A Dystopian Document Thriller* (3909 LLC, 2013)

A.I. Design, *Rogue* (Epyx, 1980)

AlphaDream, *Mario & Luigi: Bowser's Inside Story* (Nintendo, 2009)

AlphaDream, *Mario & Luigi: Dream Team* (Nintendo, 2013)

Amccus, *Harvest Moon* (Pack-In-Video, 1996)

Arkane Studios, *Dishonored* (Bethesda Softworks, 2012)

Atlus, *Persona 3* (Atlus, 2006)

Atlus, *Shin Megami Tensei II* (Atlus, 1994)

Bethesda, *The Elder Scrolls series* (Bethesda, 1994–2011)

Bethesda Game Studios, *Fallout 3* (Bethesda Softworks, 2008)

Bethesda Game Studios, *Fallout 4* (Bethesda Softworks, 2015)

Bethesda Game Studios, *The Elder Scrolls IV: Oblivion* (Bethesda Softworks, 2006)

Bethesda Game Studios, *The Elder Scrolls V: Skyrim* (Bethesda Softworks, 2011)

Bethesda Softworks, *The Elder Scrolls: Arena* (Bethesda Softworks, 1994)

Big Blue Box Studios & Lionhead Studies, *Fable* (Microsoft Game Studios, 2004)

BioWare, *Baldur's Gate* (Interplay Entertainment, 1998)

BioWare, *Baldur's Gate II: Shadows of Amn* (Black Isle Studios, 2000)

BioWare, *Dragon Age II* (Electronic Arts, 2011)

BioWare, *Dragon Age: Inquisition* (Electronic Arts, 2014)

BioWare, *Dragon Age: Origins* (Electronic Arts, 2009)

BioWare, *Mass Effect* (Electronic Arts, 2007)

BioWare, *Mass Effect 2* (Electronic Arts, 2010)

BioWare, *Mass Effect 2: Arrival* (Electronic Arts, 2011)

BioWare, *Mass Effect 3* (Electronic Arts, 2012)

BioWare, *Mass Effect: Andromeda* (Electronic Arts, 2017)

BioWare, *Neverwinter Nights* (Atari, 2002)

BioWare, *Star Wars: Knights of the Old Republic* (LucasArts, 2003)

Black Isle Studios, *Planescape: Torment* (Interplay Entertainment, 1999)

Blizzard Entertainment, *Warcraft III: Reign of Chaos* (Blizzard Entertainment, 2002)

Blizzard Entertainment, *World of Warcraft* (Blizzard Entertainment, 2004)

Bohemia Interactive, *ARMA 2* (Bohemia Interactive, 2009)

Bohemia Interactive, *DayZ* (Bohemia Interactive, 2013)

Brenda Romero, *Train* (Brenda Romero, 2009)

Bulkhead Interactive, *The Turing Test* (Square Enix, 2016)

Bungie, *Destiny* (Activision, 2014)

Capcom, *Ghost Trick: Phantom Detective* (Capcom, 2010)

Capcom, *Phoenix Wright: Ace Attorney* (Capcom, 2001)

Capcom, *Phoenix Wright: Ace Attorney – Justice for All* (Capcom, 2002)

Capcom, *The Magical Quest Starring Mickey Mouse* (Capcom, 1992)

CCP Games, *Eve Online* (CCP Games, 2003)

CD Projekt RED, *The Witcher* (CD Projekt and Atari, 2007)

CD Projekt RED, *The Witcher 3: Wild Hunt* (CD Projekt RED, 2015)

Cellar Door Games, *Rogue: Legacy* (Cellar Door Games, 2013)

ConcernedApe, *Stardew Valley* (Chucklefish Games, 2016)

Connor Fallon and Valeria Reznitskaya, *Socrates Jones: Pro Philosopher* (Connor Fallon and Valeria Reznitskaya, 2013)

Core design, *Tomb Raider* (Eidos Interactive, 1996)

Croteam, *The Talos Principle* (Devolver Digital, 2014)

Crows Crows Crows, *Dr. Langeskov, The Tiger, and the Terribly Cursed Emerald: A Whirlwind Heist* (Crows Crows Crows, 2015)

Destructive Creations, *Hatred* (Destructive Creations, 2015)

Dontnod Entertainment, *Remember Me* (Capcom, 2013)

Double Fine Productions, *Psychonauts* (Majesco, 2005)

EA DICE, *Battlefield* series (Electronic Arts, 2002–16)

Edmund McMillen and Florian Himsl, *The Binding of Isaac* (Edmund McMillen, 2011)

Eidos Montréal, *Deus Ex: Human Revolution* (Square Enix, 2011)

Eidos Montréal, *Deus Ex: Mankind Divided* (Square Enix, 2016)

Endnight Games, *The Forest* (Endnight Games, 2014 early access)

Eul, Steve Freak, and IceFrog, *DOTA* (Warcraft III: Reign of Chaos mod, 2002)

Facepalm Games, *The Swapper* (Facepalm Games, 2013)

Facepunch Studios, *Garry's Mod* (Valve Corporation, 2006)

Facepunch Studios, *Rust* (Facepunch Studios, 2013 early access)

Firaxis Games, *Alpha Centauri* (Electronic Arts, 1999)

Firaxis Games, *XCOM 2* (2K Games, 2016)

Firaxis Games, *XCOM: Enemy Known* (2K Games, 2012)

Freebird Games, *To the Moon* (Freebird Games, 2011)

Frictional Games, *Soma* (Frictional Games, 2015)

FromSoftware, *Bloodborne* (Sony Computer Entertainment, 2015)

FromSoftware, *Dark Souls* (Bandai Namco, 2011)

FromSoftware, *Dark Souls II* (Bandai Namco, 2014)

FromSoftware, *Demon's Souls* (Sony Computer Entertainment, 2009)

Funcom, *Dreamfall: The Longest Journey* (Aspyr, 2006)

Galactic Cafe, *The Stanley Parable* (Galactic Cafe, 2013)

Game Freak, *Pokémon Green/Red/Blue* (Nintendo, 1996)

Gary Gygax and Dave Arneson, *Dungeons & Dragons* (Tactical Studies Rules, Inc., 1974)

GSC Game World, *S.T.A.L.K.E.R.: Shadow of Chernobyl* (THQ, 2007)

Harry Giles and Joey Jones, *The Chinese Room* (Harry Giles and Joey Jones, 2007)

Hello Games, *No Man's Sky* (Hello Games, 2016)

Hide&Seek, *Castle, Forest, Island, Sea* (The Open University, 2013)

id Software, *Doom* (GT Interactive, 1993)

id Software, *Wolfenstein 3D* (Apogee Software, 1992)

Infinity Ward, *Call of Duty* (Activision, 2003)

Infinity Ward, *Call of Duty 4: Modern Warfare* (Activision, 2007)

Infinity Ward, *Call of Duty: Modern Warfare 2* (Activision, 2009)

Infinity Ward and Sledgehammer Games, *Call of Duty: Modern Warfare 3* (Activision, 2011)

Infinity Ward, Treyarch and Sledgehammer Games, *Call of Duty* series (Activision, 2003–16)

Intelligent Systems and Nintendo, *Fire Emblem Awakening* (Nintendo, 2012)

Intelligent Systems and Nintendo SPD, *Fire Emblem* series (Nintendo, 1990–2017)

Interplay Entertainment, *Fallout* (Interplay Entertainment, 1997)

Ion Storm, *Deus Ex* (Eidos Interactive, 2000)

Ion Storm Austin, *Thief: Deadly Shadows* (Eidos Interactive, 2004)

Irrational Games, *BioShock Infinite* (2K Games, 2013)

Irrational Games and Looking Glass Studios, *System Shock 2* (Electronic Arts, 1999)

Kevin Ryan, *The Incredible Machine* (Dynamix, 1993)

Konami, *Metal Gear Solid* (Konami, 1998)

Konami and Kojima Productions, *Metal Gear* series (Konami, 1987–2016)

Larian Studios, *Divinity: Dragon Commander* (Larian Studios, 2013)

Lionhead Studios, *Fable II* (Microsoft Game Studios, 2008)

Lionhead Studios, *Fable III* (Microsoft Game Studios, 2010)

Looking Glass Technologies, *Ultima Underworld II: Labyrinth of Worlds* (Origin Systems, 1993)

LucasArts, *Star Wars: The Force Unleashed II* (LucasArts, 2010)

Lucasfilm Games, *The Secret of Monkey Island* (Lucasfilm Games, 1990)

Ludeon Studios, *RimWorld* (Ludeon Studios, 2016 early access)

Maxis, *SimCity* (Maxis, 1989)

Maxis, *SimCity* (Electronic Arts, 2013)

Maxis, *SimCity 2000* (Maxis, 1994)

Maxis, *The Sims* (Electronic Arts, 2000)

MercurySteam and Kojima Productions, *Castlevania: Lords of Shadow* (Konami, 2010)

Midway, *Mortal Kombat* (Midway, 1992)

Mistwalker and Feelplus, *Lost Odyssey* (Microsoft Game Studios, 2007)

Mojang, *Minecraft* (Mojang, 2011)

Mossmouth, LLC, *Spelunky* (Mossmouth, LLC, 2008)

MPS Labs, Microprose, *Firaxis Games, Civilization* series (Microprose, Infogrames, 2K Games, 1991–2016)

Mythos Games and MicroProse Software, *UFO: Enemy Unknown* (MicroProse, 1994)

Namco, *Tekken* (Namco, 1994)

Naughty Dog, *The Last of Us* (Sony Computer Entertainment, 2013)

Naughty Dog, *Uncharted: Drake's Fortune* (Sony Interactive Entertainment, 2007)

NetherRealm Studios, *Mortal Kombat* (Warner Bros. Interactive Entertainment, 2011)

Neverland Co., *Rune Factory: Tides of Destiny* (Marvelous Entertainment, 2011)

Next Level Games, *Spider-Man: Friend or Foe* (Activision, 2007)

Nintendo, *Animal Crossing* (Nintendo, 2001)

Nintendo, *Mario* series (Nintendo, 1981–2017)

Nintendo, *Super Mario Bros. 2* (Nintendo, 1988)

Nintendo, *Super Mario Galaxy* (Nintendo, 2007)

Nintendo, *The Legend of Zelda* (Nintendo, 1986)

Nintendo, *The Legend of Zelda: Link's Awakening* (Nintendo, 1993)

Nintendo, *The Legend of Zelda: Spirit Tracks* (Nintendo, 2009)

Number None, *Inc., Braid* (Microsoft Game Studios, 2008)

Obsidian Entertainment, *Fallout: New Vegas* (Bethesda Softworks, 2010)

Origin Systems, *Ultima* (California Pacific Computer Company, 1981)

Origin Systems, *Ultima III: Exodus* (Origin Systems, 1983)

Origin Systems, *Ultima IV: Quest of the Avatar* (Origin Systems, 1985)

Origin Systems, *Ultima IX: Ascension* (Electronic Arts, 1999)

Origin Systems, *Ultima V: Warriors of Destiny* (Origin Systems, 1988)

Origin Systems, *Ultima VI: The False Prophet* (Origin Systems, 1990)

Origin Systems, *Ultima VII Part Two: Serpent Isle* (Origin Systems, 1993)

Origin Systems, *Ultima VII: The Black Gate* (Origin Systems, 1992)

Origin Systems, *Ultima VIII: Pagan* (Origin Systems, 1994)

Paradox Development Studio, *Crusader Kings* (Paradox Interactive, 2004)

Paradox Development Studio, *Crusader Kings II* (Paradox Interactive, 2012)

Paradox Development Studio, *Europa Universalis IV* (Paradox Interactive, 2013)

Paradox Development Studio, *Europa Universalis: Rome* (Paradox Interactive, 2008)

Pippin Barr, *Trolley Problem* (Pippin Barr, 2011)

PlatinumGames, *Bayonetta* (Sega, 2009)

Pluribus Games, *A Tale in the Desert* (Pluribus Games, 2003)

PopTop Software, *Tropico* (Gathering of Developers, 2001)

Portalarium, *Shroud of the Avatar: Forsaken Virtues* (Portalarium, 2014 early access)

Positech Games, *Democracy* (Positech Games, 2005)

Positech Games, *Democracy 3* (Positech Games, 2013)

Presto Studios, *Myst III: Exile* (Ubisoft, 2001)

Quantic Dream, *Beyond: Two Souls* (Sony Computer Entertainment, 2013)

Quantic Dream, *Detroit: Become Human* (Sony Interactive Entertainment, in development)

Quantic Dream, *Heavy Rain* (Sony Computer Entertainment, 2010)

Quantic Dream, *Omikron: The Nomad Soul* (Eidos Interactive, 1999)

Question, *The Magic Circle* (Question, 2015)

Raitendo, *You Only Live Once* (Raitendo, 2009)

Relic Entertainment, *Homeworld 2* (Sierra, 2003)

Remedy Entertainment, *Max Payne* (Gathering of Developers and Rockstar Games, 2001)

Riot Games, *League of Legends* (Riot Games, 2009)

Rockstar North, *Grand Theft Auto* series (Rockstar Games, 1997–2013)

Rockstar North, *Grand Theft Auto V* (Rockstar Games, 2013)

Rovio Entertainment, *Angry Birds* (Chillingo, 2009)

Running With Scissors, *Postal* (Ripcord Games, 1997)

Sega, *Virtua Cop* (Sega, 1994)

Sega and others, *Sonic the Hedgehog* (Sega, 1991–2016)

Sierra, *Quest for Glory* (Sierra, 1989–98)

Sierra, *Space Quest* series (Sierra, 1986–95)

Sierra and The Odd Gentlemen, *King's Quest* series (Sierra, 1980–2016)

Sierra On-Line, *King's Quest* (IBM, 1984)

Sony Computer Entertainment Santa Monica Studio, *God of War* (Sony Computer Entertainment, 2005)

Spotkin, *Contraption Maker* (Spotkin, 2014)

Squad, *Kerbal Space Program* (Squad, 2015)

Square, *Chrono Cross* (Square, 1999)

Square, *Final Fantasy VII* (Square, 1997)

Squeaky Wheel, *Political Animals* (Positech Games, 2016)

Starbreeze Studios, *Brothers: A Tale of Two Sons* (505 Games, 2013)

Studio Wildcard, *Ark: Survival Evolved* (Studio Wildcard, 2015 early access)

Subset Games, *FTL: Faster Than Light* (Subset Games, 2012)

Taito, *Operation Wolf* (Taito, 1987)

Tarn and Zach Adams, *Dwarf Fortress* (Bay 12 Games, 2006)

Telltale Games, *The Walking Dead* (Telltale Games, 2012)

The Chinese Room, *Everybody's Gone to the Rapture* (Sony Computer Entertainment, 2015)

The Fullbright Company, *Gone Home* (The Fullbright Company, 2013)

The Fun Pimps, *7 Days to Die* (The Fun Pimps, 2013 early access)

Thekla, Inc., *The Witness* (Thekla, Inc., 2016)

Tom Jubert, *Ir/rational Redux* (Tom Jubert, 2012)

Treyarch, *Call of Duty: Black Ops* (Activision, 2010)

Triangular Pixels, *Unseen Diplomacy* (Triangular Pixels, 2016)

Troika Games, *Arcanum: Of Steamworks and Magick Obscura* (Sierra, 2001)

Ubisoft, *Assassin's Creed* (Ubisoft, 2007)

Ubisoft, *Assassin's Creed* series (Ubisoft, 2007–16)

Ubisoft Montreal, *Myst IV: Revelation* (Ubisoft, 2004)

Ubisoft Montreal, *Tom Clancy's Splinter Cell: Conviction* (Ubisoft, 2010)

Ubisoft San Francisco, *South Park: The Fractured but Whole* (Ubisoft, in development)

Untame, *Mushroom 11* (Untame, 2015)

Ustwo, *Monument Valley* (Ustwo, 2014)

Valve Corporation, *Counter-Strike* (Valve Corporation, 2000)

Valve Corporation, *Half-Life 2* (Valve Corporation, 2004)

Valve Corporation, *Portal* (Valve Corporation, 2007)

Valve Corporation, *Portal 2* (Valve Corporation, 2011)

Valve Corporation, *Team Fortress 2* (Valve Corporation, 2007)

Visceral Games, *Dante's Inferno* (Electronic Arts, 2010)

Volition, *Saints Row IV* (Deep Silver, 2013)

Volition, *Saints Row* series (THQ, Deep Silver, 2006–15)

Wadjet Eye Games, *The Blackwell Legacy* (Wadjet Eye Games, 2006)

Westwood Studios, *Command & Conquer: Red Alert* (Virgin Interactive, 1996)

Wube Software, *Factorio* (Wube Software, 2012)

Yager Development, *Spec Ops: The Line* (2K Games, 2012)

ZeniMax Online Studios, *The Elder Scrolls Online* (Bethesda Softworks, 2014)

List of games by chapter

....

1 VIDEO GAMES AS THOUGHT EXPERIMENTS

Mass Effect 3 (BioWare, 2012)
Soma (Frictional Games, 2015)
The Chinese Room (Joey Jones & Harry Giles, 2007)
Train (Brenada Romero, 2009)
The Walking Dead (Telltale Games, 2012–)
The Swapper (Facepalm Games, 2013)
The Talos Principle (Croteam, 2014)
BioShock (2K Games, 2007)
Dungeons & Dragons (Gary Gygax and Dave Arneson, 1974)
Ir/rational Redux (Tom Jubert, 2012)
Castle, Forest, Island, Sea (Hide & Seek, 2013)
Socrates Jones: Pro Philosopher (Tom Jubert, 2013)
Ace Attorney (Capcom, 2001–)
Planescape: Torment (BlackIsle 1999)
Skyrim (Bethesda, 2011)
Trolley Problem (Pippin Barr, 2011)

2 KNOWLEDGE AND SCEPTICISM

The Legend of Zelda series (Nintendo, 1986–)
Phoenix Wright: Ace Attorney – Justice for All (Capcom, 2002)
League of Legends (Riot Games, 2009)
Ghost Trick: Phantom Detective (Capcom, 2010)
Sid Meier's Alpha Centauri (Firaxis Games, 1999)
Monument Valley (Ustwo Games, 2014)
Fallout 3 (Bethesda, 2008)
Fallout 4 (Bethesda, 2015)
World of Warcraft (Blizzard Entertainment, 2004)
Max Payne (Remedy Entertainment, 2001)
Call of Duty: Black Ops (Treyarch, 2010)
Spec Ops: The Line (Yager Development, 2012)
Angry Birds (Rovio, 2009)
The Magical Quest Starring Mickey Mouse (Capcom, 1992)

Super Mario Bros. 2 (Nintendo, 1988)
Mario & Luigi Dream Team (AlphaDream, 2013)
The Legend of Zelda: Link's Awakening (Nintendo, 1993)
Heavy Rain (Quantic Dream, 2010)
Bloodborne (FromSoftware, 2015)
Saints Row IV (Volition, 2013)
Assassin's Creed series (Ubisoft, 2007–)
SimCity 2000 (Maxis, 1994)
No Man's Sky (Hello Games, 2016)
Destiny (Bungie, 2014)

3 VIRTUAL REALITY: A REAL REALITY?

Unseen Diplomacy (Triangular Pixels, 2016)
Monument Valley (Ustwo Games, 2014)
Fallout 3 (Bethesda, 2008)
Saints Row IV (Volition, 2013)
Soma (Frictional Games, 2015)

4 PHILOSOPHY OF MIND

Dungeons & Dragons (Gary Gygax and Dave Arneson, 1974)
Baldur's Gate (BioWare, 1998)
Neverwinter Nights (BioWare, 2002)
Star Wars: Knights of the Old Republic (Bioware, 2003)
Dwarf Fortress (Tarn Adams, 2006)
Fallout series (Interplay, 1997–2001; Bethesda, 2008–)
The Swapper (Facepalm Games, 2013)
Psychonauts (Double Fire productions, 2005)
The Talos Principle (Croteam, 2014)
The Legend of Zelda: Spirit Tracks (Nintendo, 2009)
Soma (Frictional Games, 2015)
Beyond: Two Souls (Quantic Dream, 2013)
The Sims (Maxis and The Sims Studio, 2000–)
Blackwell series (Wadjet Eye Games, 2006–14)
Ghost Trick: Phantom Detective (Capcom, 2010)
Omikron: The Nomad Soul (Quantic Dream, 2000)
Chrono Cross (Square, 1999)
Fire Emblem Awakening (Intelligent Systems and Nintendo SPD, 2012)
Demon's Souls (FromSoftware, 2009)
Dark Souls (FromSoftware, 2011–16)
Dante's Inferno (Visceral Games, 2010)

The Elder Scrolls series (Bethesda, 1994–2011)
The Elder Scrolls Online (ZeniMax, 2014)
Baldur's Gate 2 (BioWare, 2000)
Persona 3 (Atlus, 2006)
Rune Factory: Tides of Destiny (Neverland Co., 2011)
Spelunky (Mossmouth, 2008)
The Turing Test (Bulkhead Interactive, 2016)
Star Wars: The Force Unleashed II (LucasArts, 2010)
Mass Effect series (BioWare, 2007–)
Detroit: Become Human (Quantic Dream, upcoming)
Fallout 4 (Bethesda, 2015)
Minecraft (Mojang, 2011)

5 PERSONAL IDENTITY AND SURVIVAL

BioShock Infinite (Irrational Games, 2013)
The Swapper (Facepalm Games, 2013)
Mushroom 11 (Untame, 2015)
Remember Me (Dontnod Entertainment, 2013)
Mass Effect 2 (BioWare, 2010)
Mass Effect 3 (BioWare, 2012)
The Witcher 3 (CD Projekt RED, 2015)
Final Fantasy VII (Square, 1997)
Mother 3 (Brownie Brown and HAL Laboratory, 2006)
Star Wars: Knights of the Old Republic (BioWare, 2003)
Soma (Frictional Games, 2015)

6 ON FREE WILL: THE UNIQUENESS OF GAMES

The Last of Us (Naughty Dog, 2013)
Dwarf Fortress (Tarn Adams, 2006)
Spelunky (Mossmouth, 2008)
The Elder Scrolls series (Bethesda, 1994–2011)
Assassin's Creed series (Ubisoft, 2007–)
Deus Ex: Mankind Divided (Eidos Montréal, 2016)
Monkey Island (LucasArts, 1990)
Deus Ex: Human Revolution (Eidos Montréal, 2011)
The Stanley Parable (Galactic Cafe, 2013)
Shin Megami Tensei II (Atlus, 1994)
Bayonetta (PlatinumGames, 2009)
The Incredible Machine (Kevin Ryan, 1993)
Contraption Maker (Kevin Ryan, 2014)

Kerbal Space Program (Squad, 2015)
BioShock Infinite (Irrational Games, 2013)
The Turing Test (Bulkhead Interactive, 2016)
Mario & Luigi: Bowser's Inside Story (AlphaDream, 2009)
The Swapper (Facepalm Games, 2013)
Portal 2 (Valve Corporation, 2011)

7 THE CALL OF DUTY AND *ULTIMA*'S VIRTUES

Spec Ops: The Line (Yager Development, 2012)
The Elder Scrolls IV: Oblivion (Bethesda, 2006)
The Elder Scrolls V: Skyrim (Bethesda, 2011)
Metal Gear series (Konami and Kojima Productions, 1987–2016)
Star Wars: Knights of the Old Republic (BioWare, 2003)
BioShock Infinite (Irrational Games, 2013)
Dragon Age II (BioWare, 2011)
Mass Effect trilogy (BioWare, 2007–12)
God of War series (Sony Santa Monica, 2005–15)
Planescape: Torment (Black Isle Studios, 1999)
Dishonored (Arkane Studios, 2012)
Operation Wolf (Taito, 1987)
Virtua Cop (Sega, 1994)
Mortal Kombat 9 (NetherRealm Studios, 2011)
Ultima series (originally Origin Systems, 1981–)
Fallout series (Interplay, 1997-2001; Bethesda, 2008–)
S.T.A.L.K.E.R. (GSC Game World, 2007–9)

8 ON UTILITARIANISM: BIOWARE'S BADDIES

Mass Effect 2: Arrival (BioWare, 2011)
Harvest Moon (Amccus, 1996)
Animal Crossing (Nintendo, 2001)
Stardew Valley (ConcernedApe, 2016)
Mass Effect trilogy (BioWare, 2007–12)
Dragon Age: Origins (BioWare, 2009)
Fallout 3 (Bethesda, 2008)
System Shock 2 (Irrational Games and Looking Glass Studios, 1999)
Fallout (Interplay Entertainment, 1997)
Fallout: New Vegas (Obsidian Entertainment, 2010)
Arcanum: Of Steamworks and Magick Obscura (Troika Games, 2001)
Portal (Valve Corporation, 2007)
BioShock 2 (2K Marin, 2010)

BioShock (2K Boston and 2K Australia, 2007)
BioShock Infinite (Irrational Games, 2013)
Phoenix Wright: Ace Attorney (Capcom, 2001)
Dragon Age: Inquisition (BioWare, 2014)
Call of Duty series (Infinity Ward, Treyarch and Sledgehammer Games, 2003–)
Papers, Please (3909 LLC, 2013)
Super Mario Galaxy (Nintendo, 2007)
Gone Home (The Fullbright Company, 2013)

9 ON POLITICS: FROM AUTOCRACY TO DEMOCRACY (AND BACK AGAIN)

Papers, Please (3909 LLC, 2013)
SimCity (Maxis, 1989)
Democracy (Positech Games, 2005)
Crusader Kings II (Paradox Development Studio, 2012)
Europa Universalis IV (Paradox Development Studio, 2013)
Europa Universalis: Rome (Paradox Development Studio, 2008)
Call of Duty: Modern Warfare (Infinity Ward, 2009)
BioShock Infinite (Irrational Games, 2013)
Arma 2 (Bohemia Interactive, 2009)
DayZ (Bohemia Interactive, 2013)
Ark: Survival Evolved (Studio Wildcard, early access)
7 Days to Die (The Fun Pimps, early access)
The Forest (Endnight Games Ltd, early access)
Rust (Facepunch Studios, early access)
Harvest Moon (Amccus, 1996)
Stardew Valley (ConcernedApe, 2016)
Fable III (Lionhead Studios, 2010)
Fable II (Lionhead Studios, 2008)
Fable (Big Blue Box Studios, 2004)
A Tale in the Desert (Pluribus Games, 2003)
Political Animals (Squeaky Wheel, 2016)
BioShock 2 (2K Marin, 2010)
Deus Ex series (Ion Storm, 2000–3; Eidos Montréal, 2011)
Eve Online (CCP Games, 2003)
Saints Row series (Volition 2006–)
Tropico (PopTop Software, 2001)
Metal Gear series (Konami and Kojima Productions, 1987–2016)
Divinity: Dragon Commander (Larian Studios, 2013)
Call of Duty series (Infinity Ward, Treyarch and Sledgehammer Games, 2003–)
Battlefield series (EA DICE and Visceral Games, 2002–)
RimWorld (Ludeon Studios, 2013)

Civilization series (MicroProse, Activision, and Firaxis Games, 1991–2016)

10 DEATH, KILLING AND COPING: *SPEC OPS, TO THE MOON*

Call of Duty 4: Modern Warfare (Infinity Ward, 2007)
Call of Duty series (Infinity Ward, Treyarch and Sledgehammer Games, 2003–)
Call of Duty: Modern Warfare 2 (Infinity Ward, 2009)
Call of Duty: Modern Warfare 3 (Infinity Ward and Sledgehammer Games, 2011)
Fable II (Lionhead Studios, 2008)
Spider-Man: Friend or Foe (Activision, 2007)
Monkey Island (LucasArts, 1990)
King's Quest series (Sierra Entertainment, 1980–2015)
Space Quest series (Sierra Entertainment, 1986–96)
Quest for Glory (Sierra Entertainment, 1989–98)
Sonic series (Sega, 1991–)
Mario series (Nintendo, 1981–)
Planescape: Torment (Black Isle Studios, 1999)
Dungeons & Dragons (Gary Gygax and Dave Arneson, 1974)
Spelunky (Mossmouth, 2008)
The Binding of Isaac (Edmund McMillen, 2011)
FTL: Faster Than Light (Subset Games, 2012)
Rogue Legacy (Cellar Door Games, 2013)
Spec Ops: The Line (Yager Development, 2012)
Oddworld series (Oddworld Inhabitants, 1997–2016)
Mortal Kombat (Midway Games, 1992)
Doom (id Software, 1993)
Castle Wolfenstein (Muse Software, 1981)
UFO: Enemy Unknown (Mythos Games and MicroProse Software, 1994)
Fire Emblem (Intelligent Systems, 1990–2015)
RimWorld (Ludeon Studios, 2013)
Dwarf Fortress (Tarn Adams, 2006)
The Swapper (Facepalm Games, 2013)
Dreamfall: The Longest Journey (Funcom, 2006)
Fallout 4 (Bethesda, 2015)
Dragon Age: Origins (BioWare, 2009)
Grim Fandango (LucasArts and DoubleFire, 1998)
Dark Souls II (FromSoftware, 2014)
Mass Effect trilogy (BioWare, 2007–12)
To the Moon (Freebird Games, 2011)
You Only Live Once (Raitendo, 2009)
Lost Odyssey (Mistwalker and Feelplus, 2007)

Philosophers and philosophies by chapter

....

1 VIDEO GAMES AS THOUGHT EXPERIMENTS

Philippa Foot
The trolley problem
Thought experiment
Ship of Theseus
Frank Jackson
The knowledge argument (Mary the colour scientist)
James Robert Brown
Marcus Schulzke
Propositional logic
Euthyphro
Immanuel Kant
Categorical imperative
Ad hominem

2 KNOWLEDGE AND SCEPTICISM

The tripartite (JTB) analysis of knowledge
Guy Longworth (interviewed)
Gettier counter-examples
Edmund Gettier
Illusion
Hallucination
René Descartes
Cogito ergo sum (I think, therefore I am)
Argument from dreaming
Malicious demon/super-scientist
The Matrix
The simulation argument
Nick Bostrom
Functionalism

3 Virtual reality: a real reality?

Illusion
Hallucination
David Chalmers (interviewed)
Fiction
Virtual fictionalism
Virtual digitalism
The Matrix
Mirrors
Cognitive penetration of perception
Cognitive orientation
The experience machine

4 Philosophy of mind

Monism
Dualism
Substance dualism (Cartesian dualism)
Identity theory
Functionalism
Soul
René Descartes
Lucy O'Brien (interviewed)
Cogito ergo sum (I think, therefore I am)
The law of the indiscernibility of identicals
Afterlife
Gilbert Ryle
Category mistake
The ghost in the machine
Type identity theory
Token identity theory
Daniel Dennett
John Searle
David Chalmers
David Lewis
Hilary Putnam
Multiple realisability of mental states
Artificial intelligence
The Turing test (Alan Turing)
Ned Block
China Brain

The Chinese Room
John Searle
Qualia

5 PERSONAL IDENTITY AND SURVIVAL

MWI (many-worlds interpretation of quantum mechanics)
Numerical identity
Qualitative identity
Katherine Hawley (interviewed)
Indiscernibility of identicals
Identity of indiscernibles
Leibniz's law
Cogito ergo sum
Persistence question
Physical continuity
Ship of Theseus/Trigger's Broom
Memory criterion
John Locke
Thomas Reid
Brave officer
Transitivity of identity
Derek Parfit
Psychological connectedness
Psychological continuity

6 ON FREE WILL: THE UNIQUENESS OF GAMES

Free will
Liberty
Determinism
Causality
Compatibilism
Fatalism
Sigmund Freud
Robyn Waller
Julian Baggini
Pierre Simon Laplace
Chaos theory
Quantum indeterminacy
Simon Blackburn
Benjamin Libet

9 On politics: from autocracy to democracy (and back again)

10 Death, killing and coping: *Spec Ops, To the Moon*

The posthumous harm thesis
Epicurus
Plato/Socrates
The apology
Ray Kurzweil
Bernard Williams
Martin Heidegger

Index